THE PERFECT PITCH

THE BIOGRAPHY OF ROGER OWENS, THE FAMOUS PEANUT MAN AT DODGER STADIUM

DANIEL S. GREEN

www.rogerowenspeanutman.com

Llumina Press

Requests for permission to make copies of any part of this work should be mailed to Permissions Department, Llumina Press, PO Box 772246, Coral Springs, FL 33077-2246

ISBN: 1-932560-29-7
Printed in the United States of America

Library of Congress Cataloging-in-Publication Data

Green, Daniel S.
  The perfect pitch : the biography of Roger Owens, the famous peanut man at Dodger Stadium / Daniel S. Green.
     p. cm.
  ISBN 1-932560-29-7 (pbk. : alk. paper) -- ISBN 1-932560-30-0 (hardcover : alk. paper)
  1. Los Angeles Dodgers (Baseball team) 2. Owens, Roger, 1943- 3. Dodger Stadium (Los Angeles, Calif.)--Employees--Biography. I. Title.
GV875.L6G74 2004
796.357'64'0979494--dc22
                                                          2003021850

This book is dedicated to my Mom & Dad, Ruth & Bob, for being the most supportive, loving, wise, and unselfish parents that anyone could ever be so blessed to have.

I love you both.

-Daniel S. Green

In Loving Memory

Mary Nicoleta Owens
December 6, 1914 – June 12, 2003

Ross Wheeler Owens, Jr.
June 26, 1910 – June 22, 1984

If you love your job, you'll never have to work another day in your life.

-Author Unknown

Roger proves that everyone in America can achieve success. Determination, work ethic and will power have triumphed for Roger. His example proves prosperity is within reach if you will commit.

-K•Swiss Athletic Footwear

Table of Contents

F

Foreword

They call me the Dodger Peanut Man.

My name is Roger Owens, and I'm known internationally as the Peanut Man. Those who already know of me might think it silly of me to introduce myself, especially when so many people have become more than fans. In fact, they have become friends, welcoming me into their homes. I have dedicated my entire adult life to working for peanuts and making a difference in people's lives in a positive and unique way. I am a peanut vendor and entertainer who sells peanuts at all home games for the Los Angeles Dodgers. After 45 years on the job, I have made the lost art of "pitching peanuts in the stands" a real science. Overhand, underhand, behind the back, and under the leg throws have become my trademark, and they have helped build a full-time, peanut-pitching career. As a goodwill ambassador, I have showcased my talent throughout the United States as well as in other various parts of the world.

I guess you could say I'm happy working for peanuts. People are my bag and Dodger Stadium is my home away from home. Dodger Stadium is a place I always enjoy being at, and I consider it a privilege to have a job where I can meet so many wonderful people. It's a big part of my life. The ballpark is a happy place, and it brings out the best in everyone. I look forward to each game, because each game is never the same. Dodger Stadium has changed my life through the years and has helped me to be more successful. I have learned to become self-made through my own efforts, to communicate, and to appreciate others, no matter what color or background. My life is more meaningful by just being a role model to young kids and being the best I can be. It has been said before, but I'll say it again. I'm definitely *nut* your average role model.

Through the years, many people have been fascinated with my work and the way I do my job. Pitching peanuts has become a game within a game. People have said, "It's cool!" So many people have asked about how and why I got started, about my family background, and where I came from. They also asked what was the secret to my success and how I became so famous. Many times, they told me that someone should write a book about my life story.

Well, here it is.

It's a success story that, really, could happen only in America. My fame didn't happen overnight. It took hard work. Success is something you don't just stumble over and discover. You must work at it, and you must expect more from yourself. You never fail until you stop trying. Take pride in whatever you do. You don't always have to come in first to be a winner. Just be yourself, be honest, and be proud. As one who is used to running up and down the steps while selling peanuts at the stadium, I always knew how important one's footing was. One thing in life that would definitely make you fall is the use of drugs. Losers use drugs, not winners.

I'm the oldest of nine children, and I came from a poor family, struggling to make ends meet in Los Angeles. My mother was taken away from us, and so we were sent to live in foster homes. Many years later, I faced my greatest challenge. It was something that I survived, and as a result, the event gave me a second chance in life. From then on, life had more meaning. It had more purpose. We were a family that believed, and still do believe, in God and miracles.

Giving 1000 percent and staying out of "low gear" early in life has helped shape my character. I have always had an infectious zest for life and genuine love for people. After building confidence in my own abilities, I was able to go on each day.

What a thrill it was to work so many special events, such as the Olympics, the World Series, and the Rose Bowl, just to name a few. I have found personal happiness selling peanuts, working at my day job as a shipping company salesman, and meeting a charming young woman at the stadium and then having a romantic relationship and marriage. I can only say that these things have changed my life forever.

If you want to do something well, you must be dedicated and willing to sacrifice. And remember, people might doubt what you say, but they will always believe what you do. People who fail sometimes don't realize that the simple answer to everyday achievement is to keep fighting. It's strange, but health, happiness, and success depends upon the fighting spirit of each person. Life doesn't just happen to us. We make it happen! Work hard, and watch good things happen.

I have heard that competition doesn't create character—it exposes it. My dad once told me that there are two kinds of people—those who do the work, and those who take the credit. He told me to try to be in the first group, because there's always less competition there.

There's one poem that I have enjoyed and would like to share.
It reads:

Watch
Watch your thoughts…they become words.
Watch your words…they become actions.
Watch your actions…they become habits.
Watch your habits…they become character.
Watch your character…it becomes your destiny.

The following is the true, life story of Roger Owens, the Famous Peanut Man at Dodger Stadium. It is dedicated to my father, Ross, and my mother, Mary, to my six sisters and two brothers, to Sharon, my best friend, sweetheart, and fiance as well as to the special family of close friends whose love and friendship will always be treasured. Take a journey like no other, and experience the happy and sad moments in the incredible story of a legendary peanut man.

"Two Bagger"

-by Hugo A. Jimenez, 10/09/1993,
Given to Roger in 1999

"Peanuts" was the call,
that excited the crowd.
"Gimme a bag,"
a man yelled out loud.
But, this was too easy.
He was three rows away.
"Hold on just one minute,"
fans heard Roger say.
He walked ten rows higher,
and turned with a smile.
He threw over his shoulder,
to the screaming man's child.
The boy, in amazement,
Said, "Dad, that was great.
He should be a pitcher,
Throwing over home plate."
A Dodger tradition,
a man with such style.
Astonished the young,
And made grown men smile.
Some people sell peanuts,
but that's just not Roger.
'Cause you're more than a player,
when you are a Dodger.
He is part of the family,
Loved by all the fans.
Enhances each ballgame.
The crowd gives him a hand.

𝓒 1

Fortunate Son

In through the large, open doors of the hospital entrance, the cold, morning wind flowed. The air was charged with the scents of carnations and tulips planted outside, and as it drifted indoors, it contrasted with the frozen, sterile odor of the place. A tall, jovial mail clerk paused his routine to join the group of people standing at the receptionist's desk and listening to the radio. The front entrance seemed to be the only quiet place, as they stood transfixed by the President's words. Some stared at their shoes in silence, and others looked at the ceiling, but all were dependent on the assurance found in Roosevelt's voice. Nevertheless, the hospital was busy, and it seemed as though the warmth in the receptionist's smile was reflected on the faces of every doctor and nurse. The red roses on every desk gave it away.

It was Valentine's Day, 1943.

The mail clerk's attention was now fixed on delivering the mail. His duty carried him to every area of the hospital. As he walked down the clean hallways, he noticed reprinted masterpieces from Monet and contemplated the many techniques of an artist's paintbrush. An artist himself, the mail clerk sighed at the thought of ever visiting the Louvre in Paris. However, the colors of his thoughts were smudged like turpentine on oil paint as audible cries of newborns carried through the hallways. With his curiosity getting the best of him, he decided to stop outside at least one delivery room and listen to the excitement within.

"Heyyy! Praise God for our son!" shouted the young, boisterous, Welsh father.

"Congratulations, Mrs. Owens," said the doctor to the young Italian mother, sitting up with a pillow behind her and enjoying a moment of serenity.

Just over a year before, these two people met in a church service, where many still mourned the previous month's devastation at Pearl

7

Harbor. It was 31 year-old Ross Wheeler Owens, Jr. who literally kicked the feet of a 27 year-old registered nurse named Mary Nicoleta DiRisio. Her feet were resting under the pew on which he had been sitting in front of her. He turned around to apologize and was immediately captivated. From there, "pardon me" became "I do" nearly three months later. They were married on March 6, 1942. Mary, who was charmed with how much a gentleman her husband was and with his caring and loving ways, was soon expecting a child. On February 14, 1943 they had their first son, Roger Daniel Owens.

Roger Owens, who received his middle name from Mary's immigrant father Daniel, was taken home that day from the hospital in Glendale, California, to their small home in Eagle Rock. As they pulled into the driveway, a boy hopped along the sidewalk in front of their house, dragging a stick across the picket fence, which badly needed a paint job. With the words of a song stuck in his head thanks to his grandmother, the boy sang "Jeepers, creepers, where'd ya get those peepers" over and over again in his best Louis Armstrong voice. Ross noticed the boy and waved to him, while the kid went merrily along. Ross, glowing with pride, opened the screen door for his wife and new baby and then followed them inside.

Roger's father, Ross, only four years earlier had left Tulsa, Oklahoma at the age of 28. He had already graduated with an A.A. Degree from a community college in Wichita, Kansas. He arrived in California, and by the time Roger was born he had found employment as a shipping clerk at a pickle factory. On the side, Ross was an ordained Baptist minister, whose goals included reaching out through missionary work and helping unify various church denominations throughout the Los Angeles area. Mary had left behind her small town life in Homesville, Pennsylvania and worked as a nurse in New York. After some time, she moved to California to find work and to enjoy the great weather. Now Mary worked less and stayed at home to take care of their newborn. Within a few months, Ross and Mary learned they were on their way to having their second child. It was another curly towhead, but this time a little girl named Ruth Josephine Owens, born on July 9, 1944, barely a month after D-Day.

It was the end of summer, 1945, and World War II was over. After the war, Ross witnessed to people how America might have helped win a war, but it was not "off the hook" in God's eyes. There was still much work to be done to improve the country's condition. True or not, America would survive. Many Americans sought higher levels of opportunity and prosperity. The people of America had faced the barren, dimly lit back alleys of the Great Depression and had lived through a hard-fought, four-year war. Americans embraced a sense of normality and looked once again to the simpler things in life to carry them through the workday. The country rolled up its sleeves and began a new era of working hard and playing hard. But Americans also needed lazily spent weekends with barbecues and picnics to find sanity, entertaining friends and family with stories of baseball games and baseball legends of bygone eras. Whether people lived near the choppy, wind-blown seas of the vast Atlantic, along the banks of the massive, winding Mississippi, or near the glittering waters of the awesome Pacific, every American found something to relate to, but nothing held the country together like baseball.

Every town had its heroes.

Williams. Spahn. "Lefty" Grove. Greenberg.

Feller. Musial. DiMaggio. Snider.

Every store had customers who were convinced their team would win the World Series. But New York had the privilege of having three teams, the Dodgers, Giants, and Yankees. Rivalries between the teams only proved that while wars fought over the future of humanity might have ended, wars for pennants and championship rings were always being waged. Veterans of World War II, the true heroes who helped preserve the country and its way of life, could now find comfort in watching baseball games. In family picnics all across the nation, it was possible to find at least one young man, back from the fighting lines, sitting peacefully with his young family on the cool grass and recalling one U.S.O. show in particular. While reminiscing about how Bob Hope brought out a stunning Greta Garbo to show the uniformed boys what they were "fighting for," the young man opened his eyes and smiled as he affectionately ran his fingers over his father's old ball cap, its once royal blue now faded and its stitches of the white letter "B" now unraveled. The young veteran knew immediately that all the soldiers fought for more than Garbo. They fought for a free way of life.

They fought for baseball.

While this sentiment was shared among people day after day, every street corner soon filled with neighborhood kids eager to grab their mother's broom handle and a beat-up baseball to set up a game of "stick ball." While some of the kids sat on their front porches thinking of their beloved Brooklyn Dodgers, other kids daydreamed about how their mighty Yankees could easily beat the bunch of Brooklyn bums from across town.

Little Roger, with blonde, curly locks and glistening blue eyes, was a growing boy still unaware of the desperation his father faced in providing for a family, which was soon to include a set of fraternal twins, a girl named Priscilla Louise and a boy named Philip Appleman, and by 1948, another sister named Esther Anne Owens. As Roger sat down to eat breakfast one morning, his mother looked at Ross.

"We're always running out of food. I can't buy milk fast enough, because the kids are drinking it up as soon as I buy it," Mary said.

The steadfastness of Ross' faith in God was evident in his response, even though the stress should have brought beads of sweat rolling down his balding head. He calmly said, "I know, Mary. For my part, I can drive a milk truck, and for the Lord's part, He will provide." Little Roger didn't quite comprehend the determination of such a faith, but he did know that Mom and Dad were praying that they would get through tough times. After all, they were starting to receive food and clothing from several people at church.

Roger always found time to play with his younger sister Ruthie. Even Ross' mother Emeline, who lived in Los Angeles, would love to visit just to watch the little ones. On many occasions, Mary dressed them up and took pictures. With a teddy bear in tow, or dressed in little sailor outfits, they could get away with anything. Roger was proud to have a little sister like Ruthie, with her sky-blue eyes and hair that was slowly turning from blonde to brown. They also adored their younger siblings. But growing up during the end of the 1940's and into the early 1950's meant increasing distress because the Owens family was barely getting by.

They moved to a small house on 2130 Palm Avenue in National City, near San Diego, California. The house was built next to a large dry canyon. Staring out of the bedroom window, six year-old Roger watched the cotton clouds, their edges glowing in the mid-day sky. He rested his hands on the windowsill and noticed how pleasing the warmth from the sun felt on his hands. Standing there, he saw how fat the cumulus clouds were, yet how empty they must be to touch. Suddenly, he heard his stomach grumble. Lately, it was a sound that everyone in the Owens family had heard. The creaking of wooden floors and the crying of babies throughout the night proved to be stressful. But nothing could compare to the frustration of having empty stomachs and empty cupboards, and when Mary's stomach growls interrupted her own prayers, she wept uncontrollably.

Some days, Roger noticed how his mom wore the same tattered house clothes for days in a row. He wanted to believe things would get better. He saw Ruthie playing with her dolls, but that did little to reassure him. After a while, they began to get adjusted to their new place. Things stayed the same with the Owens family, but within a year, Mary was expecting another child.

The time had passed, and finally Mary was ready.

She was going to have her next child, so they gathered all that they needed, and Ross' old Ford took off like a steam engine locomotive, slow at first, then full speed. They arrived at the hospital and, although this was familiar for Mary, she was nervous. Finally, after several hours of agonizing labor, she gave birth to a daughter. Already decided, Ross and Mary announced the baby's name, Pauline Elizabeth. While they smiled, the doctor suddenly noticed the baby wasn't responding well.

"Mrs. Owens, we need to help the baby. Just sit tight for me okay?" the doctor said resolutely, but with an underlying uneasiness.

They ran some tests, but time was running out, and the baby began to show signs of losing its first and only battle. The doctors did all they could, but after several hours they could do no more.

Little Pauline died in the delivery room.

Ross held his wife's hand firmly.

As tears gathered, overfilled, and slid down the contours of their saddened faces, they remained still. Beads of Mary's perspiration formed on her forehead and then slid down the sides of her eyebrows. As they mingled with her tears, they glided down both sides of her face. Then, one by one, they dropped from her chin onto one of the petals of her flower-print hospital gown. Ross sat forward in his chair holding Mary's hand, and he quickly went into prayer before God. Ross and Mary sat there for nearly an hour, while Mary's soreness from delivering the baby was overshadowed by the aching of her spirit.

To them, Pauline was a flower whose blossom would be seen not in the sight of men but of angels.

Despite this, Mary would always acknowledge Pauline as one of her children.

For many days, Mary walked around the house quietly. She didn't eat much, and if not for her children, she would have secluded herself within the four walls of her bedroom.

After some time had passed, the grief had run its course, and suddenly all the problems rushed back, like waves forming on the horizon and crashing thunderously on the shore. The family's situation wasn't improving. Ross' efforts to earn more money were hopelessly inadequate with five children to clothe and feed. His door-to-door campaign, which raised money for his missionary labor, was just not enough to bring financial stability.

Another year had passed, and Ross continued to work with the church as well as to find additional work as a taxi driver, but as always it wasn't enough, and the stress was volcanic.

It had been unusually quiet lately between Roger's mom and dad. At dinner, the only sounds were the clanking of forks on plates and the whining of his younger siblings.

One night, the threads of silence were tearing, as soft voices could be heard from inside the bathroom. Ross was speaking in deep, easy dulcet tones, but Mary was crying.

"We're having another one, Ross," Mary said solemnly as she stared down at her light-blue slippers. Ross lifted up her chin and looked at his wife compassionately. He saw no glistening in her deep-set, brown eyes. He noticed how the stress had taken its toll on her brown, slightly curly hair, turning many strands of it gray. Ross also saw her lips, pouting in sadness just above her strongly defined jaw. Yet, with the admission that a baby was on the way, Ross' heart filled with joy that God would provide yet another child. However, he was keenly aware of just how stricken with anguish he and his wife were. By now, Ross was working several jobs to make ends meet for his family, which was about to include his sixth child. For nearly a decade Mary's existence had been focused on taking care of the children or dealing with pregnancy. The only stability she knew, with regard to money and food, was that there was no stability.

Finally the day came to have the baby. They were prepared for anything. This time, it was a healthy baby girl. They named her Elizabeth Anne, taking the middle name Elizabeth from Pauline's name. Ross and Mary rejoiced and enjoyed the moment.

"That's one more for heaven," said Ross jubilantly, as he did every time a child was born.

The doctors and nurses smiled.

After a few days the celebration came to an abrupt halt because of the many daunting challenges in their lives. It seemed as though their happiness was a candle's flame, flickering near an open window on a relentlessly windy day.

Mary was slowly losing hope. To add to her distress, in less than a year she was expecting yet *another* child.

One Saturday morning, she again bowed her head and told Ross the news.

As she told him, Ruthie, Philip, Priscilla, and Esther were playing with their toys. Roger, however, had the radio on, which was broadcasting a Saturday Dodger game. He listened with a grin the size of the outfield at Ebbets Field. He heard the crowd, roaring like a lion at the circus, tamed only by a Dodger victory. His mom and dad held each other, and again she cried uncontrollably and wailed loud. The sound was drowned by a 7th inning Dodger rally, Barber's plea for Robinson to be safe on a suicide squeeze, and the wild chanting of the Brooklyn crowd. He stared at his baseball pennants that were on the wall. Roger was happy.

During the next few days, Mary was busy with a few of her household routines, but she seemed solemn and demanded less of her kids, as though interaction was the biggest chore in her day.

"Dad, have you noticed how mom has been acting lately?" asked Roger.

"What do you mean, son?" replied Ross.

"Well, she said she was gonna take us to get ice cream. Then, she said that she never said that and wanted to sleep instead. Then today she stayed in her room all day. When she came out, I went up to her, but she walked right by me," he continued.

"I think she hasn't been getting enough rest. You can pray for her before you go to sleep, Roger," his dad responded.

The day had come again. As she had done seven times before, Mary brought another child into the world. With a change of clothes packed, Mary was physically prepared, but she wasn't emotionally ready to give birth. To say she was ready to bear another child would be to imply that there was contentment in her life. She was not content, especially with having no certainty of adequate provision for her children. She seemed more machine than woman, more programmed and less spirited.

The Owens family continued to suffer at the hands of poverty. Its grip held them tightly, slowly suffocating Mary's spirit. The newest arrival, Lois Marie, had been born months ago, but in her mind the labor pains still lingered. Growing inside her were thoughts of futility, sorrow, emotional stress, and desperation. Her thoughts gave birth to a hypnotic state of melancholy, and she considered ending her life. She held out for nearly a year, but when she realized one more baby was due, her very being was filled with despondency, as though receiving intravenous drips of depression. Drained of all hope, suicide was her only solution.

Living in National City, but dying within, Mary was merely an ember of the fire that once burned so brightly. Quiet yet intelligent, she exhibited such an anchored character that only dire situations such as these could shake her. Her inability to make a difference financially shattered her fortitude and burdened her heart.

She stared into nothingness.

Her eyes blinked. They opened to a frightening new dimension.

Mental breakdown.

Devoid of promise and purpose, she gave in to the voices that spoke to her. These same voices haunted her and held her down as they injected memories of her two twin brothers who had died as infants in the great flu epidemic of 1918, and of her beloved younger sister, Virginia, whose dress had caught fire from waving around sparklers on one July 4th, and whose life was extinguished before her very eyes. The voices also recalled a time when a menacing neighbor girl approached young Mary. She threw a small pebble at her, and it became lodged in Mary's right eye, leaving her partially blind. The voices taunted her about her present conditions, and she obeyed them. One day, she took a walk. One month pregnant, she strolled outside her house. She saw an oncoming car. Suddenly, the sounds of loud horns and the head-turning shriek of brakes became a concerto of catastrophe as Mary threw herself in front of the car. Fortunately, she survived.

One night, Mary made her way to the front door. She looked at the clock in the kitchen. It was 1:30 a.m. She closed the front door behind her and walked down to a nearby park and sat there. Holding her hands together, she looked down at the ground and other times stared up at the stars. After an hour, she sighed and walked back home.

"Mary? Where did you go?" Ross asked as he waited outside in front of the house.

"To the park," she replied.

"Why?" he added.

"I don't know," was all she could say. Ross put his coat on her, put his arm around her, and walked her back inside.

A week later, Mary put on a coat and walked out of the house, but this time it was 2:30 a.m. She walked to the park and sat there for an hour. She talked to herself, and then sat in silence. Again she looked at the ground, as if she were studying encrypted scratches in the cement, and then looked up into the navy blue heavens, full of flashing stars, some of them burning out thousands of light years away. She took a deep breath and then sighed, as though exhaling all of her spirit. She walked back home.

"Mary, where did you go?" Ross asked as he again waited outside for her.

"To the park," she answered.

"Why?" he added.

"I don't know," was all she could say. Again, Ross put his arm around her, walked her back inside, and tucked her into bed.

Less than a month later, in a moment uninterrupted by doorbells, phone calls, and crying babies, Mary walked into the bathroom and cut her wrists. She was found bleeding and was rushed to the hospital where she required stitches on both wrists.

These events were kept away from the kids, but Ross needed to address his children in a family meeting to pray for their mom.

One evening, Ross was in his room on his knees in prayer. He was thanking God again for an envelope he had found in their mailbox earlier that day. In the envelope there was $10 in cash. It had been left anonymously as a gift for the struggling family. After reviewing a few Bible verses, Ross stood up and went into the living room. Roger was doing chores in the kitchen when, suddenly, he heard his dad rounding up all the kids with his commanding voice. It was now 1953, and 10 year-old Roger was curious as to why his mom was taking a nap, missing the family prayer.

"Dad, shouldn't we go get mom so she can join us?" asked Roger.

"No Roger. She's resting."

To the older kids, it was clear that something was wrong even before Ross began to speak. Roger couldn't sit still. The only other time he got this nervous was when he was listening to his Dodgers over the radio, and the game was close. It was the ninth inning and they were down by two. The Duke of Flatbush, Duke Snider was at bat. He could win the game with one swing of the bat, since there were two Dodgers on base, Jackie Robinson on third jumping up and down in anticipation, and Pee Wee Reese on second. Roger sat closer to the radio, charmed as much by the noise from the Brooklyn crowd as the crack of Snider's bat as he swung mightily, sending the cowhide ball to its resting place over the wall in right-center field. But it was his dad's voice that brought him back away from Barber's play-by-play.

"Roger?" his dad boomed.

"Sorry, sir," Roger sheepishly answered.

"Roger, Ruthie, Priscilla, Philip, everyone listen up. Your mom isn't feeling well. I want all of you to pray for her right now okay?" he asked.

"Okay, Dad," said Roger and Ruthie harmoniously while the younger ones nodded their heads and stared with blank-eyed innocence.

They sat still and prayed quietly. Ross was on his knees praying beside them.

Roger tried not to look his dad directly in the eyes for more than a moment, but he often managed to catch a look at him when his dad wasn't aware. Sometimes, Roger saw his dad's steely blue eyes and, when they squinted in disapproval, they could snare the guilt out of him, like he had pulled a rug from under his feet. He continued to study his dad's face. Roger didn't know much about the purpose of one's life or the salvation that his dad believed in, but he did know that his dad's smile was enough to relax his soul.

$\mathcal{C}$ 2

Off to the Beattys

The next morning Ross got a phone call from Patton State Hospital in San Bernardino, California. He had called them previously to explain that his wife required medical attention for her mental condition. They told him that some hospital officials should be arriving soon to pick up Mary and bring her to the hospital. Elizabeth, age two, and Lois, age one, stood quietly as Ross was on the phone. After the phone call, Ross sat down on the sofa. Elizabeth and Lois carefully walked over to the couch, where he picked them up to sit next to him. He sat in silence but reminded himself of all the other things that needed his attention. He had to make several phone calls to the social workers, as well as fill out an application for financial relief through the county agency. He also thought of how he would deal with his kids living in foster homes and how they would deal with it too. Ross began to feel the pressure build within, and it made him start to sweat.

He paused.

Suddenly, he felt tears well up in his eyes. Wiping them as fast they appeared, he bowed his head, then got up and told his girls that he would be right back. He headed for the bathroom and, once inside, bowed his head in front of the sink.

He cried.

He began to talk softly as though to himself, but he was praying.

As he prayed, he admitted his weaknesses but asked for strength. He asked God to take care of his wife and to help him through all of this. He looked in the mirror and noticed how blood shot his eyes had already become. What had seemed like an eternity in the bathroom, in reality was only a few minutes. He wiped his face clean with running water and made his way back to the living room. His girls, both cute little brunettes with big brown eyes, looked at him cheerfully, kicking their legs in the air since they were too small to reach the floor. He smiled at them, and the tension in his stomach eased.

An hour had passed and Ross was drinking a glass of water as he heard a car outside. Mary had her things ready to go, and they escorted her out to the car. Ross walked with her and kissed her cheek before she got in. As they drove away, Ross felt weak and went inside to eat something and have more water.

He picked up the phone and called the social workers to see if they were ready to go to the school to pick up his kids. They said they were, and upon hearing their confirmation, Ross called the school and spoke with the principal to notify him that he would be there soon to take his kids out.

About a week earlier, Ross had personally visited one of the county-approved places for the girls to live. He had noticed it was not only a foster home, but was a ranch located in Alpine, California. He had picked up the phone, dialed, and had spoken with Mrs. Beatty. She and her husband lived on the ranch and took care of their animals. The Beattys previously lived in a smaller house, but moved to a larger ranch as their foster care grew. They had arranged a meeting, and Ross drove there.

On the way there, it was sweltering inside Ross' car. His tie and collar were both undone, and his gray fedora would have been soaked through had he not placed it on the seat next to him. The soft sound of displaced dirt on the road under his car was exchanged for louder, earthier sounds of grumbling gravel as he approached their country house.

As the mid-day weather heated up like an oven ready to bake oatmeal cookies, it brought warm, dry air, and the Beatty ranch appeared to be an oasis of hospitality. He grabbed his fedora and looked uncomfortably conservative in his gray tweed suit. Dipping his hat, he introduced himself. Mrs. Beatty, wearing a light-blue dress with white lace ruffles and an apron tied around her wide waist, welcomed Ross with a smile that warmed him beyond the 90 degrees outside.

They walked inside.

As if the ginger bread characters sewn on her apron weren't welcoming enough, she had a pitcher of home-brewed lemonade, sweating as it beckoned him. The sparkling ice cubes were dancing, diving, and circling as she picked it up and poured him a glass. If it weren't for the business at hand, Ross would have fallen asleep to the gentle humming of the round, metal fan in the kitchen as it sent refreshing cold air to his face. He noticed the bucket of ice placed in front of the fan to make the air cooler. Then Mr. Beatty walked up the wooden stairs of the back porch, stomped his heavy boots free of dirt, and opened the screen door. He leaned over and kissed his wife, and then he gave Ross a smile so wide that it covered up his eyes. He wiped his hands on his faded overalls, cleared his throat, and welcomed him like they were long lost friends.

"Hello Mr. Owens. I'm Harold Beatty. How are ya, sir?" he asked as they shook hands like aging, amiable heavyweights.

"Just fine, thank you. You can call me Ross," he replied.

"My wife, Edith, here makes a mean glass of lemonade, don't you think?" Mr. Beatty asked.

"Yeah she certainly does. I think I'll just let you describe how the ranch looks, and I'll sit here with the pitcher," he said as they shared a laugh together.

Mr. Beatty invited Ross to take a look around their house as well as the ranch outside. He strolled through the living room, holding his hat at his side, and followed the Beattys. They gave him a grand tour including all the bedrooms. The house had all the touches of a benevolent country home, with family photographs, hand-sewn coffee coasters with houses stitched into them, a Bible on the coffee table, lamps with doilies under them, wonderfully decorated rooms for young girls to stay, and the smell of dust and cinnamon everywhere.

They took Ross outside, and they went over to the animals. The heat had been long forgotten, but as they made their way to the horses, the heat seemed to be an overbearing intruder. Ross took a deep breath and turned slowly in a circle, capturing the panoramic moment in his mind. He turned around, patted the horses, and then followed the Beattys around the ranch until they decided that Ross had seen everything. Whether he had seen the entire ranch or not, he knew that he missed being indoors.

He looked at his watch and realized he had other errands to do. They watched him and politely gave him the opportunity to get back to his day's business.

"Thank you Ross for visiting us today," said Mrs. Beatty.

"It was my pleasure," he replied.

"Well, when you decide to bring your girls, we'll be here," said Mr. Beatty.

"Okay then," he added.

"Would you like more lemonade before you leave?" she asked him.

"I'd appreciate that very much," he replied. They walked back inside. He finished two full glasses and eyed the pitcher. He would have had two more, but he would have emptied it.

"Thank you both again. Take care and God bless," he said.

"You too, Ross. We'll wait to hear from you real soon," Mr. Beatty added.

Ross got back in his car, undid his collar and tie, and placed his fedora back on the seat next to him. They stood waving at their doorstep, and he waved back. He drove off, exhaled deeply, and felt relief.

He got back home and went straight for his bed. Exhausted from the drive and heat, he sat down on his bed and lay back with his arms over his head and the top of his hands on his brow. He stared at the ceiling and thought of the ranch. He remembered Mrs. Beatty and her brown hair, curled into a perm, and Mr. Beatty's slicked back silver hair and denim overalls. His thoughts, like the horses he had seen, galloped until they put him to sleep.

After an hour he woke up and washed his face. He felt refreshed and decided to make some phone calls to a social worker to find a place for his boys. After talking on the phone, he went outside to find if the car needed maintenance. He opened the hood and checked the oil level. A friendly neighbor lady walked over to him. Mary and the lady were friends, and she knew what had been going on lately with the family.

"Hello Ross. How are you doing today?" she asked kindly.

"Fine, thank you ma'am. How are you today, Tillie? How's John and your children?" he responded.

"Just fine. Just fine. Ohh they're just doing swell, thank you," she said while grinning the kind of smile that had as much gums as it did teeth. "So have you found a place for the girls yet, hmmm?" she continued.

"Not yet, but I visited one today that was promising," he said politely as he added motor oil to the car.

"Well if you can't find a home to take *all* those girls, I could surely help. If it would be helpful, I wouldn't mind adopting little Esther. With her short blonde hair, she's just cute as a --," she added.

"Adopt?" Ross answered abruptly. "My kids aren't up for adoption. I plan on keeping my family together." He lifted the hood high and let it shut. He wiped his hands on a towel, wiped the sweat off the top of his head and forehead with his handkerchief, excused himself, went inside, and shut the door.

After cooling down, he sat down on the edge of his bed and prayed.

A few days later, he called Mrs. Beatty to let her know of his decision to send his girls there to live.

"Hello, Edith?" asked Ross.

"Yes this is Edith," Mrs. Beatty responded.

"This is Ross Owens. I'm calling to let you know I'd like for my girls to stay with you at the ranch. I think it would be a good place for them to be right now. There will be three at first, but perhaps after six months, I'll bring the two little ones, Lois and Elizabeth," he said.

"Well good. We are planning to have other girls living here later on, but as you know there is plenty of room. When would you like to bring them?" she asked.

"Well, I'm working with a social worker on this, but I'm sure within two days. Is that okay with you?" he asked.

"That'll be just fine, Ross. We'll be here," she added. As soon as they hung up the phone, Mrs. Beatty began preparing a room for the three Owens girls to stay.

Now, Ross found himself sitting in the front seat of his car, Elizabeth and Lois in tow, trying hard to start the stubborn car so that he could get his kids out of class and take them to their new homes.

Ross was physically prepared to go, but he wasn't emotionally ready. To say he was ready to give his children over to new homes would be to imply there was contentment in his life. He was not content, especially with no certainty of the kind of life it would mean for his children.

He drove to the school and headed toward the office building. He asked for the principal. The man, who was older, lean and had a gray mustache, acknowledged Ross and promptly had a secretary fill out forms to summon Roger and Ruth out of class. She told her young student assistant to go to each class and deliver the summons to each teacher. The social worker was already there, waiting for almost twenty minutes. Ross noticed him and greeted him as everyone waited.

In class, Roger sat reading quietly along with the rest of the students. Ruth, in another class in an adjacent building, saw some of her classmates raise their hands in eagerness to answer a math question. They both watched as their teacher was handed a small piece of paper. They were told to report to the principal's office right away. In both classes, it was quiet enough to hear every "oooooh" from the other kids. Roger and Ruth were shocked that they would be asked to visit the dreaded principal's office.

While the teachers restored order, the brother and sister were off to the main office building. Roger got there first, and then Ruth walked in. They both were now slightly frightened at the sight of their dad. It didn't matter that he was an imposing figure at six feet who had the aura and look of a respected fire chief. It didn't matter to them what he did for a living either, whether he was out to stop spreading fires or, simply, was on fire for spreading the Gospel. At that moment, they just knew that their father was in the principal's office. Ross told Roger and Ruth the news and how they would be on their way to foster homes that same day. The two were puzzled at how quickly things could change, but nevertheless they trusted their dad's judgment.

That afternoon, all the kids that were in school, including seven year-old Priscilla, were taken back home and were allowed to pack what few clothes and toys they had into little boxes. Within minutes, the three girls were ready to go to the ranch, and the two boys were set to go with the social worker to their new foster home. Priscilla, with her brown hair and brown eyes, then sat on the bed, which she shared with her sisters, and began to think about the times she had in that house. She remembered when she fell out of a tree and broke her collarbone. To avoid a costly medical bill, she wasn't allowed a hospital visit but instead had to let it heal on its own, often keeping her up for hours at night. She recalled the "haunted house" that she and her brothers and sisters visited, and how her dad had to go catch chickens in the back yard and cut their heads off so they could have dinner. She also re-membered how she was recently baptized with her brother, Philip, in the small, storefront church where her dad was a pastor for a short time.

It had been only six hours earlier, at five o'clock in the morning, that Ross had awakened and walked into the rooms of his children. Roger, age ten, and Philip, age seven, were still asleep, as well as all the girls. Quietly, Ross walked over to their bedside and prayed over each one. He finished praying and then stood watching them, rolled up in their blankets.

He felt helpless.

In his thoughts, he imagined himself much more successful, per-haps something like his wealthy, younger brother and entertainer, Jack. He imagined a world with the kids running around in perfect content-ment, and in that world, he could have time to play catch with his boys, buy dresses and toys for his girls, provide wonderful things for his wife, have warm cooked meals every night, go to restaurants, or go hiking in the mountains. He even dreamed of one day being able to go to the Holy Land and be baptized in the Jordan River.

All these things he pictured as the things a family should be able to do. Even so, he was an honorable man. He knew that he served God and kept God's commands despite the lack of material wealth. He didn't feel disappointed in his role of father, whose measure of success, ultimately, was in depending on God and teaching his kids the ways of the Lord.

But sometimes he just wished he could do more.

He wanted to take all the blame, but he knew that if the word blame was used, it had the unmistakable tinge of failure, and as long as he served his God, nothing he did, as a faithful husband or father, would ever be seen as a failure. This, however, did not keep him from envisioning a life not of excess but at least of reasonable comfort.

By now the kids were standing quietly, waiting for their dad to help load the car. Then Ross walked into their rooms to see if they were ready. As he noticed their small, cardboard boxes, packed neatly with a few clothes, he was determined to one day bring his family back together again. Disheartened that he was sending his kids away to live somewhere else and unsure for how long, he began to feel the pressure all around him, as though he were the rag doll packed tightly between folded clothes, and locked in a small suitcase.

But it was time.

They collected all of their belongings, got in the car, and headed to Beatty's Ranch. Roger and Philip said their goodbyes and left with the social worker. It was easy as long as each other's car was in sight, but the moment the two cars took different streets, the moment the Owens kids could no longer see each other through the back windows was the moment that hurt. It was the beginning of their separation, and as incomprehensible as time and distance were to their young minds, so too was it perplexing that they should find themselves thrown into new lives, new environments, and new worlds.

Edith and Harold Beatty welcomed them as they drove up. It was 12:00 noon, and Mrs. Beatty already had lunch made for the carload of shy but hungry Owens girls. Ross promised to stay for only an hour, as he had to get back to his work. The girls, Ruth, Priscilla, and Esther, took an immediate liking to the place.

They ran around the ranch as if every dog, cat, horse, and donkey were waiting just for them. Ross went inside and talked with Edith and

Harold, while the girls examined the place like exuberant gumshoes looking for signs of life. The only thing that interested them more than the black and white Shetland ponies was their pink, blue, and white bedroom, decked out with blankets, mirrors, books, and vases full of magnolias, daisies, sunflowers, and tulips. The window was open, and the wind flung the curtain up and down, boasting an inviting, cool breeze that whirled throughout the bedroom.

They walked back to their dad, shy but smiling nonetheless, as if to say about the ranch, "We'll take it."

"Looks like they plan on staying," said Mrs. Beatty with a large grin.

"I believe so," said Ross.

Out the back door the girls went, off to retrieve their belongings from the car and to bring them to their room. Since lunch was waiting for them, they were allowed to eat before they unpacked, even though unpacking for them might have taken only minutes. Still, there would have been the time-consuming, inevitable matter of "who-gets-to-sleep-where" and "who-gets-what," so unpacking could wait.

Nonetheless, the Owens girls were apprehensive at being some-where completely new. The fact that Mrs. Beatty was as welcoming as chocolate chip cookies and teddy bear hugs certainly helped win their affection, so that within a day they were already calling her Aunt E. She served peanut butter and jelly sandwiches and fruit juice for lunch that first day, and that didn't exactly hurt the cause either.

After lunch, Ross said goodbye to the Beattys and to his girls. Ross found it hard to leave them there, but as usual it wasn't noticeable on the outside. As they waved from their porch, they disappeared into the distance from his rear view mirror. He strategically placed the little ones, Elizabeth and Lois, in the back seat so he could have the privacy he needed to let his streaming tears fall in peace.

Elizabeth and Lois were getting restless, since they weren't getting enough sleep. Ross was sure that they would be knocked out in no time with the warm temperature and the cool breeze coming through the car windows during the drive back home.

He was right.

The social worker and the two Owens boys had already made it to their new home. The middle-aged couple escorted the boys inside. It wasn't an impressive place, and neither were the people. But after all, not everyone could be like the Beattys.

Roger and Philip weren't exactly thrilled with their new home, but it had to do for now. They unpacked their things in their new bedroom, and the couple responded hospitably, which was out of their character but well timed under the watchful eye of the social worker. Finding it acceptable, the social worker said goodbye to the foster parents, shut the door, filled out paperwork in his car for a few minutes, and drove off. Suddenly Roger and Philip felt as though the only ones they had in the world were each other.

Roger and Philip looked around their room. They knew it needed some Dodger pennants on the wall. The boys did their best to make the best of things, but having someone other than their own parents tell them that it's late and it's time to clean up and go to bed just seemed to make the whole situation worse.

A week later, the boys began noticing how much beer and wine their new foster parents were drinking. To them, this was a foreign and moral intrusion on their living space. They were not accustomed to the presence of alcohol in their house. Every sip of wine and chug of beer seemed as threatening as thunder and lightning. They lived under a cloud of grief and felt the downpour of discomfort, and within a couple of months, they desperately wanted to call their dad.

Roger and Philip consoled each other in their room at night, often sharing all the things that they saw the couple do or say. One night, Roger and Philip were working on a jigsaw puzzle together. Roger couldn't help but think how he missed listening to *The Lone Ranger* on the radio every night after doing his homework. Somehow, he wished that the Lone Ranger would learn about their misery, and, while riding Silver, crash through the front door, splintering it into a million pieces, and rescue him and his little brother.

It had been just a few months, and the Lone Ranger finally arrived. It wasn't the masked man, dressed in sky blue, white hat, and red neck-erchief, guns drawn, and riding a gallant horse. It was a man they were much happier to see.

Dad.

Although dismayed at the circumstances, Ross knew he still had to find another place for his boys. He had talked with the social worker to find a place for Roger and Philip that would be as fun and exciting as Beatty's Ranch for girls. They did, or so it seemed.

$\mathcal{C}$ *3*

Ranch of Burden

Located in San Diego County, there was a foster home that was also a ranch. However, if Beatty's Ranch was a slice of fresh apple pie, then Naylor's Ranch for boys was a piece of stale burnt toast.

Roger and Philip could hardly contain themselves at the thought of living at a ranch like their sisters. They had heard nothing but good things from their dad about the girls' foster home.

They drove up to the place and everything seemed fine. However, when Ross drove away, the overweight, aging woman, with hair that formed long, crusty strings, saturated with oil and the dirt it attracted, walked up closely to Roger and Philip. She bent over, and her huge, domed back seemed to rise into the sky. She looked down at them. Her eyes squinted, and her face shifted to the left as she gave a menacing smirk. From behind her large frame, her tall intimidating son appeared, looking as battered by the elements as his mother, Mrs. Naylor, and looking as equally ready to take it out on an unsuspecting little foster boy. The stench she gave off was incredible. It was the kind of odor that could inspire a weather-beaten, embittered, old carnie to set up a carnival booth where the attendant didn't guess their weight, but rather how many weeks since their last shower. Then Mr. Naylor appeared. A small man, feeble and understandably henpecked, Mr. Naylor walked closer and smiled with approval as though the boys were the day's lunch. The boys took their eyes off him to look at Mrs. Naylor and her son.

The boys went to bed early that night, but in the morning, they were better off staying in bed having a nightmare than waking up.

"Okay all of you, get your worthless little butts up and out of bed. It's time to get to work," Mrs. Naylor yelled at the top of her lungs.

At 5 a.m., it was still dark outside. Roger, Philip, and the other three foster boys were groggy and moved slowly. Finally, they pushed their covers back. The Owens boys had not recovered from the reality of where they were. But that didn't last too long.

They reported to the kitchen for breakfast. They were each given small servings of oatmeal with milk but no sugar. They slopped up their oatmeal, pausing to watch open jawed as the woman inhaled her stack of syrup drenched pancakes, eggs, and warm, crispy bacon. She was hunched over wolfing down her breakfast, while her long, stringy hair moved up and down all over the syrup on her plate.

As soon as she finished her breakfast, she wanted the boys to be introduced to the ranch and start working. The boys began their death march outside to the large area behind the house. There were pens full of goats, chickens, sheep, turkeys, and they had dogs and guinea pigs too. Mrs. Naylor even had beehives for which she would have the honey collected. In reality, the Naylor family had a business, for which they manipulated the foster care system to provide them with needy foster kids or, as Mrs. Naylor saw it, cheap labor.

"Listen up all of you. There's plenty of work to be done this morning. You're not going to school until you do all of your chores. You got that?" she roared.

The boys murmured their agreement.

"You got that I said?" she yelled even louder.

"Yes ma'am!" they all yelled.

"And that means cleaning the pens and getting the chicken eggs and getting the honey from the beehives in the morning, and feeding the goats, sheep, turkeys, and my dogs in the evening when you get back from school," she continued.

The boys stood almost shoulder-to-shoulder as she barked her orders. Philip looked away from her and noticed her son, standing next to her.

"And if you don't complete any of your chores, my son has my every blessing to whip you with his belt," she said as she pointed to her 19 year-old son, standing there with a malicious grin on his face and gently slapping his folded belt against the palm of his hand. "I'll help you get started today only, and by tomorrow you better know everything. Oh yeah, I almost forgot. Your sack lunches will be waiting in the kitchen. Don't forget them, or my dogs will get to eat again," she continued and then gave out a long, raspy laugh.

The Owens boys couldn't believe the situation they were in. Standing in shock, they remained motionless until they saw the woman's son standing with a belt. They rushed off to the animal pens, while Mrs.

Naylor walked only a few steps behind them. She showed them everything that they needed to know, and before long it was already time to
catch the bus and go to school. They grabbed their lunches, went to the
front of the house, and saw the bus approaching. They stood on the side
of the road and boarded the school bus together. As the bus rolled toward town, the boys sat in silence until they were almost at school.

"We have to stay there from now on, Roger?" asked Philip solemnly.

"Yeah," Roger replied with a sigh. "We better not tell Dad, or
they'll find out we told. Did you see that belt?"

"Yeah," he answered. Then he paused. "I didn't get any sleep." He
then tapped Roger on the shoulder. "I'm scared," little Philip said.

"Me too," said Roger.

Both of them got off the bus and walked slowly. Their eyes barely
open and with stomachs already aching again in hunger, they said bye
to each other and then made their way to class.

At the end of the afternoon, they were back on the bus, heading
back to the ranch.

When they arrived, they were expected to do more work. Mrs. Naylor had them do some housework before they worked outside.

She grabbed a broom and walked over to Philip.

"Here, take this. I want you to sweep this here wood floor. Don't
you miss a spot. I want it so I could almost see my reflection," she
added.

"Who would wanna see your face anywhere?" he murmured quietly
as she walked away.

"Young man, are you talking back to me?" she said standing over
him, breathing in his face.

"No ma'am," he replied, nearly shaking.

He swept the floor busily but then slowed down to watch the other
boys as she ordered them to feed the animals. Just as Roger was about
to exit through the back, Mrs. Naylor walked quickly over to Philip.

"What do you think you are doing, sweeping until we fall asleep? We
don't have all night!" she yelled. "What's this? I told you not to miss a
spot." She then grabbed Philip by his ear and brought him to his knees,
pressing his face close to the floor. "Do you see this dirt?" she asked.

"Yes ma'am," he responded.

"Well sweep it up. Do you think we're living in a pen like animals?" she demanded, yanking his ear harder.

"No ma'am," he answered, his voice trembling. Tears began to form in his eyes in response to the burning pain around his ear.

She brought him back up by his ear. Then she walked toward the other boys, but they took off like bottle rockets to tend to their chores.

A week later, the Owens boys were up early and were off to do their morning chores. By the time the bus had arrived, they still had not finished with collecting the honey from the beehives. They looked at the bees and then at each other. Their eyes became wide in disbelief as the school bus engine roared and then squeaked loud as it stopped by the front of the house. The bus sat idling, but it rumbled as if calling the boys away from their wretched work. They didn't see Mrs. Naylor's son anywhere.

The boys worked faster, carelessly causing more of the honey, glowing yellow and amber as it reflected light from the early morning sun, to drip off the sides of the containers and slowly fall to the ground. Sweating and shaking, the boys left the containers and started for the door to go inside, get their lunches, and leave for school. Suddenly, Mrs. Naylor's son appeared from inside the house, and the boys nearly ran into him, sending a surge of adrenalin through them. Their reaction made them jump, as though they were jolted from a high voltage line. They stood shaking even more as the Naylor son cracked his folded belt against the side of his right leg and yelled, "Where do you think you're going?"

"Our bus is here, and we have to catch it so we can go to school," replied Roger, who was slightly out of breath.

"I don't care. You can go when you're both done," said the Naylor son.

The boys walked slowly back to the bees and finished their work for the morning. Roger and Philip grabbed their lunches and walked to the front. By now, not even the fumes from the school bus could be seen in the distance. Roger looked up at the sky, blue and cloudless, while Philip saw some rocks near his feet and kicked them.

"Looks like we'll walk," Roger said.

"Peanut butter sandwiches, stale bread, and goat's milk for lunch again," said Philip angrily as he inspected the paper sack.

They walked the three miles to school, as Philip took small bites of his sandwich.

The next day, they barely finished their chores on time and had to run hard to catch the bus, as it was about to take off. Once onboard,

Roger and Philip just sat quietly, catching their breath. Looking out of the windows, they saw rows of trees passing by, an eagle soaring high above, and the dirt that was stirring up as they went along. They looked through the back window and were relieved to see how the distance between them and the terrifying ranch increased with every second. Roger turned around and sat back in his seat. He closed his eyes and remembered the vast expanse of the open canyon near his old home, and how some of them would go looking for owls and rabbits. After their supper, some of the kids, including Roger, went to their neighbor's house to watch the *Roy Rogers Show* and *Hopalong Cassidy*. The sounds from the bus' engine seemed to stir Roger's thoughts even more as he recalled characters like Zorro, Rin Tin Tin, Superman, Lone Ranger, the Little Rascals, The Range Rider, and Lassie. Since he watched Lassie many times, Roger dreamt of having a dog of his own. His mind raced in preoccupation with the idea of someday owning a dog, or maybe even two dogs, and then having to decide what kind of dogs, and what would he name them, and what tricks would he teach them. The bus stopped. Roger and his brother got up and exited the bus. It was time for school.

When they got back home later that day, Roger and Philip entered the house and Mrs. Naylor quickly noticed.

"What took you so long?" she yelled as small bits of food flew out of her mouth.

"The bus was late," Roger replied.

"Well then you can be late for dinner. Go get to work," she demanded.

"Yes, ma'am," the boys answered, slightly louder than the growling noises their stomachs had been making.

At Beatty's Ranch, the Owens girls were ready for dinner. They had washed up and sat around the table ready to give thanks. Mrs. Beatty brought over a plate full of honey-baked ham. On the stove, she had a pot full of mashed potatoes from which she would serve. They had slices of bread, some peas and steamed carrots, and glasses full of cold water that they could wash it all down with. The girls were as slim as the posts near the horse stalls, so they ate every bit of their food.

After dinner, everyone sat on the porch, as the sun was slowly setting. Mr. Beatty, known as Uncle Harold to the girls, began smoking a cigar as usual. This time he looked at his cigar and unraveled the gold foil band that was around the cigar. He took it off and placed the band on Ruthie's finger, as though it were a ring. She smiled and stared at it.

Priscilla and Esther wanted a ring too, so the next time he smoked a cigar he told them he would give them the ring. Soon, all three had one.

The next day, after school, Ruthie and Esther went over to look at the horses.

The two black and white Shetland ponies, War Paint and Half Pint, and Becky the donkey were eager for their attention. The girls were petting them as Mrs. Beatty walked outside to bring them some lemonade. Mr. Beatty was already outside fixing the horse stall. He smiled as the horses nudged the girls' hands through the fence.

"Uncle Harold, can I ride War Paint today?" asked Ruthie.

"Sure you can. But first, what do you say about learning how to lasso rope?"

"Really?" she asked in amazement.

"Of course. You can tie this rope and use it to do trick roping. When you get really good, you can stand on Half Pint's back while lassoing yourself inside it. What do you think?" Mr. Beatty asked.

"Okay, I'll try it," said Ruthie.

By the end of the day, Ruthie, Esther, and Priscilla were all learning how to trick rope, but it was Ruthie who, after a few days, showed a real talent for it. Before long, she could trick-rope like she was born with a lasso in her hand.

At Naylor's Ranch, the boys continued to work hard, get very little sleep, and eat their usual small helpings of food each day. They were developing a work routine that paralleled that of farmers three times their age. The boys were filled with terror at the thought of telling their dad about their problems, only to have Mrs. Naylor find out. For all they knew, the ranch might as well have been on another planet, guarded from outside intruders with barbed wire, and large alien dogs that salivated as they barked ferociously, an armed troop of Naylor clones marching in circles, and a pressurized dome, which reached into the sky and covered the expanse of Naylor's property. Even Buck Rodgers wouldn't have been able to penetrate the dome.

The boys were becoming more depressed and frightened each passing day. They missed the bus more often due to their workload each morning, and they added hitchhiking to their list of ways of getting to class.

One day, as they sat on the floor reading books for their classes, they heard a familiar voice, and ran into the front room. Standing there was their dad, whose presence seemed odd and completely unfitting, as though two different dimensions crashed together, transporting him into the hostile environment in which they lived. He stood there, like a hero in all his warmth and glory. His aura filled the room and caused old Mrs. Naylor to recede into the kitchen, as if her all encompassing powers were no match for his. As they ran to him and greeted him with an embrace that could shame a grizzly bear, the boys showed desperation that belied their outward condition. Their grip held like steel clamps, shut tightly around a six feet tall piece of lumber.

Roger nearly let the truth roll off his tongue as Ross walked into their room. His blue eyes looked up at his dad, and stared long enough at him, as if his eyes were confessing all of the awful details. Ross hugged his boys and stayed a little longer, just to look around and see that they had food.

"Dad?" asked Roger, aware that he had now committed himself to telling him the truth. He had to think of something quick.

"Yes, Roger?" replied Ross, noticing Roger's worried expression.

"Uhhh, how's mom doing?" he asked, knowing it better be a good question to match his anxiety.

"Well, she's doing a little bit better. You have another baby brother. We named him Paul Immanuel. She had him at the hospital where she's being helped. Some other lady has been kind enough to take care of him for a while," he explained.

Roger and Philip were excited by the idea of having another brother, but their thoughts were soon fixed on their dad, as he was about to leave.

"Was there anything else, boys?" Ross asked, standing near the door.

"No, sir," Roger replied.

They walked their dad out to the car.

After they said goodbye, Ross drove off.

The boys walked back inside the house, kicking dirt all the way to the front door. They knew full well that they wanted to tell him about all the problems, but they just couldn't do it. Mrs. Naylor's husband was turning the radio stations like a madman, searching for something to listen to.

He turned to one station. A deep voice said, "And in the news today," but it was too late to hear the rest of it. The receiver was making the rounds in the hands of Mr. Naylor.

Next, they heard someone singing, "I looked through the window. I peeked through the blind, and asked him to tell me what was on his mind. He said, 'Money, honey! Money, honey! Money, honey if you wanna get along with me.'" He let out a shriek and turned it, but Roger and Philip smiled at each other as though they would have danced to the catchy rhythm under happier circumstances. Their smiles faded as quickly as they appeared.

Finally, Roger's eyes opened wide as he heard the sounds of a large crowd. It was a Dodger game! "Why don't you pick a station and leave it!" screamed Mrs. Naylor from the kitchen. The boys were standing there for at least five minutes before Mrs. Naylor noticed them.

"Don't you have work to do?" she said.

"Yes, ma'am," they replied.

"Then get to it," she said.

Roger and Philip went back into their room and did their homework. They were quiet for the next few days.

Several more months passed by.

Roger and Philip endured more of Mrs. Naylor's nagging and all of the work they had to do every day. There was no time for playing baseball, or collecting cards, or riding bikes, or looking for neighbor kids. It was work, work, work, sunrise to sunset, and they hated it. The lucky, old, late afternoon sun rolled around, high in the heavens all day, taunting them as sweat streamed down their faces. The same sun shone high above the cries and laughter of boys and girls having fun, miles and miles away. They were the chain gang of the Naylor ranch, the boot camp troops of the Naylor unit, the inmates of cellblock Naylor. But they did it, because they didn't stand a chance against Naylor's son.

Finally, the day came.

Ross drove out to the Naylor compound. The Owens boys caught wind of the exhaust from their dad's car. Their unsharpened instincts spoke to them, but they stood in uncertainty until they actually heard his voice. Then, they saw him standing at the front door, impeccably dressed in a dark suit and dark fedora.

The boys ran to him, holding on to him for life, as if Mrs. Naylor had them by the feet, pulling them away, laughing her raspy laugh.

They begged him to take them out to dinner. He agreed.

Ross treated his young boys to a local restaurant. They all sat down. Roger began to cry. Philip, seeing his older brother, began to whimper and cry. Ross was embarrassed but calm. A waitress walked over to the table.

"Is everything okay?" she asked with the warmest, calmest voice anyone could ever speak.

"Yeah. Could you please give us a few minutes?" Ross asked quietly, his voice stumbling with emotion.

"Yes sir. Take your time," she replied and then walked away.

"What's wrong, boys?" he asked.

"We want to leave the ranch, Dad," Roger answered, sniffling and doing the out of breath crying that requires a pause in between each word.

"Yeah, we can't take it anymore," chimed in Philip, with tears glistening under the restaurant lights.

The Owens boys began to describe every last detail about the ranch and Mrs. Naylor. Ross appeared calm, but inside he was fuming. He continued to listen.

"And they have a son that wanted to whip us with a belt, even if we looked at him wrong," Roger added, still overcome with emotion and tears.

"She even pulled my ear to the ground and said I was good for nothing," said Philip, who then cried louder realizing the harshness of what he just admitted.

"Alright boys. I'm going to call the social worker right away. That's no place for you to be. You'll be out of there. I promise," he said.

"Thanks Dad," they said, as they hushed somewhat.

Ross switched their mood back to their hunger by asking them what they wanted to eat. They knew things would be all right now.

𝒞 4

Moving and Mending

A fter two days had passed, Ross returned again to Naylor's Ranch. This time, the county social worker had informed the Naylors that Ross would be picking up his kids for good. Ultimately, the county worker and authorities showed up and shut down the ranch. The boys jumped up and down, and went on and on in their excitement about how happy they were to leave that place. The county already had another home in mind for the Owens boys. They knew the boys had already been through enough, so they sent them to live in the welcoming home of a deputy sheriff, his wife, and their son, who was close to Roger's age.

On their way to Sheriff Worthan's home, Ross and his boys talked about how their mom was doing in the hospital. He said that she was improving, but was not ready to return home.

Upon arriving at the new home, they were greeted in the driveway by Mrs. Worthan. She was out planting pink and yellow orchids in a flowerbed, which had sides made of light beige stucco. A young woman in her thirties, she was modern *and* down home, like peach cobbler served on artsy, urban dinner plates. She showed them around the place, as if the boys belonged there. Finally, she brought them to their bedroom where they began unpacking their things. As Ross walked around, Mrs. Worthan left the boys to themselves and noticed Ross looking at some pictures on the wall, holding his hat at his side.

"You sure do make a handsome family," Ross said.

"Well thank you, Mr. Owens. Would you like any soda, water, or any juice?" she asked.

"Sure, I'll take a Coke if you have any. If not, water sounds good too," he replied.

"Sure we have some cola. I'll pour some in a glass with ice for you," she added.

35

"Thank you very much," he said as she handed it to him. He took a sip, as if trying to make the refreshment last, savoring the cold, cola taste.

"Drink it all, if you're thirsty. You can have another bottle to go if you'd like," she said.

"Why thank you ma'am. I think this day God's grace has even extended to a cold bottle of pop," he said smiling.

She laughed as he finished the drink and began looking for the boys in their new bedroom. He found them looking out of a window, and told them he was ready to leave. Against their protesting, Ross assured them things would be much better and then made his way to the door. He was stopped in his tracks.

"I didn't think you were about to leave so soon, Mr. Owens. I called the station, and my husband should be here any moment. He'd like to meet you if that's alright with you," Mrs. Worthan said.

"Oh that's okay with me. Can I sit down for awhile?" Ross replied.

"Sure, make yourself comfortable," she answered.

Mr. Worthan arrived about ten minutes later, and greeted his wife with a kiss not more than a few steps from the door.

"Hello, Mr. Owens. I heard your boys have been through a bit of rough weather," said Mr. Worthan.

"Yes, sir, they have," said Ross.

Just then, their son walked inside, already done with school for the day.

"Hey Stanley, come here for a minute," asked Mr. Worthan. "I want you to meet Mr. Owens. His boys are going to live with us for awhile."

"Pleased to meet you, sir," said young Stanley.

"Same here young man," replied Ross.

"As we were saying, Mr. Owens, your boys should find it smooth sailing living here," said Mr. Worthan. Immediately, Stanley looked up at his dad and gave him a grimace that defied his father's self-complimentary assessment of their family. "Yeah, well it would be smooth sailing for you if you did your homework like you're told and took out the trash at least once a year," Mr. Worthan added, recognizing his son's sour face. Ross held back his laughter, as if he had a bad case of indigestion.

"Can I get you anything?" asked Mr. Worthan.

"No, I'm fine," responded Ross.

"Stanley, the other boys are in the guest bedroom. Go introduce yourself to them," his mom said.

The two fathers talked for nearly twenty minutes, but then both had to be on their way. Ross thanked them several times, said goodbye to his boys, and walked out to his car. He looked at the empty car seat to his right and imagined Mary sitting there.

He sighed.

After a moment, he prayed that he wouldn't let envy set in. He started the engine, revved it a bit, and drove off, feeling somewhat fortunate that the car started on the first try.

By now, Ross' little girls, Elizabeth and Lois, were ready to join their older sisters at Beatty's Ranch. Ross drove them out to the ranch, where Mrs. Beatty was expecting them. Adjustments were made to the girls' bedroom to include space for their two little sisters, or the "babies", as the Owens girls called them.

Life at Beatty's Ranch was like a rodeo heaven, a haven of hay in the middle of San Diego County. It would have been complete if only Roy Rogers and Dale Evans were the true owners of Half Pint and War Paint, and stopped by regularly to check on their beloved miniature horses.

All of the Owens girls were happily living at the ranch, and the Owens boys were finally finding out what is what like to live in a foster home where people cared.

After just a few days, Roger and Philip were feeling at home with the Worthan family. To Roger, the bathroom felt less like a strange room, with perfect decorations and neatly folded towels, and more like a place to take refuge, carelessly leaving splashes of water on the sink, as though in a hurry to keep up the pace of the others playing outside. Even the kitchen, as time went by, changed its reputation from hallowed ground to a place where he served himself.

Soon Mr. Worthan began planning trips for the "family." He talked of going to the mountains, ball games, and out to dinner.

Even movies.

Under the roof of Ross' house, as Roger already knew, movies were absolutely not allowed. Ross objected to their use of violence and depiction of all kinds of morally threatening content. This man of God, who had been considering publishing Christian newsletters for local churches and already had a local Christian radio program, *The Baptist Hour*, which ran for about six months, saw fit to take his kids to see only one movie, *The Ten Commandments* with Charlton Heston.

At the Worthan home, however, Roger and Philip were feeling like they belonged there. They didn't see their dad much, who was off visiting their mom every two weeks, working, and saving money to eventually bring the family together. Their mom was by now a stranger in a far away place, and all five of their sisters were content with their world. It was Mr. and Mrs. Worthan, Stanley, Roger, and Philip who made up this new band. It was not Roger's family, yet it was. Life with them was a train ride, ready to be boarded. But by the time the ride would end, Roger and Philip would not budge easily.

One day, Mr. Worthan shouted loud from the center of the living room that they were all off to the mountains. He announced they had only ten minutes to get ready or the "express train" was leaving without them. Roger, Philip, and Stanley shot off to their rooms and packed a suitcase with such enthusiasm that it seemed like they planned on being rewarded with an autographed baseball from the Dodgers.

They were all heading to the mountains. On the way there, Roger's attitude alternated between being contemplative and acting spirited. But Philip and Stanley made faces, as if challenging him to join in their silliness. They had the time of their lives, hiking, trying to follow small animals, eating, telling stories, and skipping stones on nearby lakes. Finally, the boys fell asleep on the trip back to the Worthan home.

Tall, and a forceful presence, with dark hair and moustache, Mr. Worthan commanded the respect of the Owens boys. They admired him for the authority he possessed with or without his badge and revolver, which he carried even when wearing civilian clothes. The boys were treated as sons, no better and no worse than Stanley. Roger noticed the way Mr. Worthan walked with confidence, and how he balanced engaging activities with strictness and order.

It was spring 1954, and Roger was eleven years old. One day, Roger saw that no one was around. He had seen it from a distance just the day before, but he was too ashamed to examine it closely. There it was in the kitchen, posted on the wall. It was a calendar, but not an ordinary calendar.

It was a Marilyn Monroe calendar.

Hanging there in plain view, it must have been a favorite of the Worthans, since Mrs. Worthan didn't object to it. They admired it and, like any other pre-teen boy, so did young Roger. But fearing he would be caught standing a little too close and staring a little too long, Roger hurried off to see what his brother and Stanley were up to.

Life with the Worthans was more than Roger and Philip could ever dream, since they had never known the comfortable completeness of a caring family. There was a television, and it captivated the boys every moment after homework was done, except for when it got late, and they were sent to bed so Mr. and Mrs. Worthan could watch anything they wanted, especially after midnight.

One evening after dinner, the Worthans treated all the boys to a movie. They stopped what they were doing, piled into the car, and drove to a nearby drive-in theater. With the Worthan couple up front and the three boys in back, everyone's attention was fixed on the enormity of the friendly gorilla that scaled the limited dimensions of the silver screen. They sat still, nearly inhaling the buttered popcorn and marveling at the realism of *Mighty Joe Young*. On the way home after the movie, the boys were making gorilla faces with their fingers and, because they were packed close together, they were griping at each other as though fighting for space like territorial apes. Many nights were like this for the Owens boys. Although they didn't always watch a movie, the Worthans did take the boys out to restaurants.

Roger grew increasingly aware of his ability to tease his younger brother. It was well within his power to do so, and perhaps because of the three-year age difference or because of occasional anxiety, he enjoyed making Philip's life somewhat unbearable. Philip responded with some complaints but not without recourse. He brought Stanley on his side, and they retaliated with verbal assaults against Roger's taunting. It was the kind of teamwork that proved a bit overbearing, so Roger backed down, even to the point of it backfiring. He began to feel as though Stanley and Philip were the close ones now. Somewhat disappointed, he still found that life there was much to his liking.

Between the television, the movies, the trips, the food, and of course, the Monroe calendar, the Owens boys had it made. They had never experienced anything like this before, but they still felt incomplete. They were a part of a wonderful family, but they knew they had many sisters out there somewhere. They weren't that close to their dad anymore, and had no real bond to speak of with their mother, but nonetheless they felt a duty to their real family. Even so, outside forces that governed the reality of their existence were still at work, and such forces kept them with the Worthans.

Nearly a year had passed since the boys first moved into the Worthan home. While sitting in front of the television one Saturday afternoon, Mr. Worthan began speaking to the Owens boys, who were scarfing down hot dogs and potato chips.

"You boys said that you have some sisters in foster homes. Is that right?" Mr. Worthan asked.

"Yes, sir. All five of them live on a ranch," Roger replied.

"What are their names?" he asked as he produced a piece of paper from his back pocket.

"Ruth, Priscilla, Esther, Elizabeth, and Lois," said Roger.

"Okay thanks," he responded, while taking a large gulp from his bottle of cola. Then Mr. Worthan got up, quietly walked into the bathroom, and then came out and made a phone call from his bedroom.

"I'll be back in a while. I'm going down to the station. Want anything from Foster's Freeze?" Mr. Worthan asked.

"Yeah, I wanna large scoop of vanilla ice cream on a cone," replied Roger.

"Me too," said Philip.

"Me three," said Stanley, as his dad took a mental note of the easy order and shut the front door behind him, not bothering to lock it since he knew his wife was there.

He returned several hours later, but the boys had already helped themselves to some frozen cherry Popsicles. He had their ice cream cones, and they were still hungry enough to finish those off as well.

"I went down to the station to look up where your sisters are living and, thanks to some clerks there, I found out which foster home they're at and how to get there," Mr. Worthan said.

Just as the news was delivered, Roger felt an enveloping surge of warmth shoot through him. He sat there, unaware that ice cream was melting and was dripping down onto the rolled up cuffs of his dark blue jeans. The possibility of seeing his sisters compelled his every thought to swirl around Mr. Worthan's words, like a toy train circling one miniature town over and over.

He jumped up and got ice cream on the carpet, and Stanley laughed. Stanley suddenly felt out of place since Philip didn't notice the ice cream mess, and didn't find reason to laugh. Stanley quickly sat down as Mr. Worthan gave him a stern look.

Roger and Philip looked at each other and then back at Mr. Worthan. Then they sat on the couch next to him.

"You boys want to go visit your sisters?" he asked.

"Yeah we sure do Mr. Worthan. When can we go?" Roger answered, still hiding his emotion somewhat.

"We'll go tomorrow. How does that sound?" he continued.

"Oh boy, that sounds good," Roger said.

"What do you think Philip?" Mr. Worthan said.

"I finally get to see my sisters again?" asked Philip.

"Yeah you finally get to see your sisters again," he responded, smiling.

Then the Owens boys jumped up and down making loud cheering noises, and Stanley sat there feeling happy for them. Mrs. Worthan was in the bedroom and came in to hear what all the noise was about. She found out why, and thought it was the sweetest thing for him to do. She whispered something into her husband's ear that made him smile devilishly.

Roger and Philip were thrilled that the next morning they were off to Beatty's Ranch. The Beattys had been called that evening, and Uncle Harold and Aunt E informed the girls that their brothers would be on their way the following day.

It was late Sunday afternoon, and the Beattys had already returned from the church service they usually took the girls to. The Worthans finally drove up to the ranch entrance. Mr. Beatty's large grin made everyone including Roger feel as though they already knew them. The boys got out of the car, and Roger looked around the huge expanse of the land. He looked up into the sky, seeing the bristled, scattered clouds slowly float like ships navigating a weightless, blue heaven. The high clouds made the sky appear to fade up into the very floor of outer space.

Roger was wistful.

They greeted some of the dogs first, playful from the sudden burst of human activity. Then they walked into the house. Everyone was in awe of such a well-kept country home, and how hospitable the Beattys were. They found themselves sitting on the edge of the comfortable sofas and listening to faint, yet high-pitched, voices that revealed some stirring from beyond the hallway. One face peeked out, and then some squeals were heard. Mrs. Worthan laughed. Mrs. Beatty stood up, as though quietly fed up with the girls' shyness.

"Come on girls. Your brothers are here," Mrs. Beatty calmly said, but loud enough.

The Owens girls ditched their usual long sleeve, plaid shirts and blue jeans for their clean, quite girly, dresses. Not out of preference did they want to wear them, but because they were told to. Despite their embarrassment, the girls walked into the living room, and the Beattys and the Worthans thought they looked like beautiful young ladies. Roger and Philip saw their sisters for the first time in over a year and a half. Ruth, nearing age eleven, Priscilla at eight, Esther, age six, and the only blonde of the group, and the "babies", Elizabeth and Lois, fast approaching four and three, were thrilled to see their brothers. Formality immediately turned into kid revelry. The girls were allowed to change into jeans and shirts so they could rough house with their brothers. Even the dogs barked with excitement, causing all the animals to kick up dust as though they too were invited to the party.

Roger and Philip were given a tour of the whole ranch. They found out that some of the girls had their own horses, and that they had learned how to lasso and do trick roping. The boys were a bit ashamed to tell them about their experience at the Naylor ranch, so they held off on admitting the details, but they did explain how they went to the mountains and did all kinds of neat things with the Worthans. Everyone had a story to tell, but everyone seemed to just get louder and louder so they could be heard. Finally, evening drew closer, and they were all called inside. After a couple more hours of playing indoors and watching television, the Beattys warned the girls it was getting late, and the Worthans knew it too. The Owens girls finally had to say goodbye to their brothers until the next time they could visit. Mr. Worthan promised the Owens kids that Roger and Philip would be back, and more often. They would even have the whole day together when they visited again. The Worthans drove off, and the Owens girls spent all their energy talking and being hyper until it put them to sleep, while the Owens boys, and Stanley too, fell asleep on the way home.

Mr. Worthan made good on his promise, and every three months, he took the boys to see their sisters. Each visit lasted the better part of the day, about eight hours, but to the kids time flew by, seeming more like eight minutes.

The year was 1955, and it had snuck up on the Owens boys like Stanley playing Cowboys and Indians. Roger and Philip had been with the Worthan family for nearly two years. They loved their home, but with each encounter with their sisters, they realized how hard it was to leave them. They cried and hugged, and then missed them during the months they were away. They felt like a family, and all they needed now was a good set of parents. The preacher and the nurse would more than do, if the kids were convincing enough.

Soon after, Ross made one of his infamously infrequent visits. Into his bedroom, Roger took his dad by the hand and sat him down.

"Dad, we've been visiting the girls at the ranch a few times already," Roger said.

"I know, Roger," Ross replied.

"Every time we go there, we realize how much we want to be a family again," Roger continued.

"But son, I can't take care of all of you without your mom's help. I don't have the money either," Ross responded.

"Yeah but Dad, we're getting older. We can help out with things. We really want to be a family, Dad," he pleaded.

"How are you going to help?" Ross asked.

"We would make a great team. We could do all kinds of things around the house. The girls could cook, wash, iron clothes, and do chores, and us boys could find part time work to get more money for you," Roger insisted.

Ross took a deep breath and looked hard into his son's blue eyes. It's true, if all three "babies" were counted, that they would total nine, the same number needed for a baseball team. But Ross, acting as a player/manager, doubted that they could pull off such a victory.

"I don't know, Roger. You all are still so young," he said. "I wouldn't have much time for you all. I couldn't expect the girls to do that much cooking and washing, on top of all their studying. I'm trying to get our family together, but I'm not sure now is the time, Roger," he added.

"But Dad, with everyone pitching in, we can make it," Roger said.

Ross paused.

Ross worked as a salesman in various jobs, but a sincere, heart-rendered plea from his young boy to bring the family back together was the best sales pitch he had ever heard.

In fact, it was the perfect pitch.

"Okay then. I'll ask the county for help finding a housekeeper. But all of you need to do your part. Is that understood?" Ross asked firmly.

"Yes, sir," he answered.

Ross excused himself into the Worthan bathroom next to the boys' bedroom. He closed the door.

He turned on the warm water to cover the sound of his weeping.

"Thank you, Lord," he said quietly and often, while tears poured down his face.

He composed himself and told the boys to please stay just a little bit longer at the Worthans while he returned home to find a house or apartment. He told the social worker, the Beattys, and the Worthans of his decision.

The day that the Owens girls left Beatty's Ranch was the day Uncle Harold cried like a baby. Mrs. Beatty was sad, too, and admitted that there were only two times her husband ever cried in his life, and that this was one of them.

Stanley and the Worthans were just as sad. Roger and Philip sat in their room quietly. Roger got up and looked out the same window he had peered out of the first day he moved in. He was debating whether or not he really wanted to leave the Worthan family. He remembered many things about the Worthans.

The food.

The trips.

The movies.

Then there was the time some young drivers nearly ran all of them off the road. Immediately, Mr. Worthan drove up to the laughing teenagers, who had pulled over for a moment. He slowed down next to them, and the boys noticed how the reckless teens became frightened as Mr. Worthan showed him his badge and told them to knock it off.

There were so many thoughts.

He looked down at Philip, who sat Indian-style on the floor, wiping his eyes, trying to look at baseball cards. Roger was beginning to doubt his zealous pleas to reunite his family. But he missed his sisters deeply. They were his friends as much as they were his family. Roger's emotions whirled around and around. Not even the fact that the Brooklyn Dodgers were about to win their first World Series could spin his thoughts away from this.

Mrs. Worthan knocked on the door, as if to have permission to enter. With a definitive mix of jubilation and sorrow, she said, "Roger, sweetie, your dad just called. He's on his way. He said to tell you both to have your things ready. He found a place for everyone. You're moving to Los Angeles."

$\mathcal{C}$ 5

Year of the Reunited Children

R oss had already been working as a truck driver, a salesman, a taxi-cab driver, and anything else that involved driving, sales, or missionary work. He had a passion for unifying churches in Los Angeles and for reaching out to minority populations, including Blacks and Hispanics. He desperately wanted several church denominations to be as one. He was absolutely driven day after day by his vision for people from all backgrounds to come to know God personally. Ross was notorious for, unconsciously or consciously, taking on the accent of those he witnessed to. For those who seemed Southern, he spoke with a drawl. For those who spoke Spanish, his words were tinged with an accent found south of the border. Perhaps it happened as a result of spending a lot of time around different people. In any case, it was comical.

Ross brought his family back to the mean streets of central Los Angeles, to an old rented house on the corner of 45th Street and Hoover Street, not far from the Los Angeles Memorial Coliseum.

Everyone in the Owens family was uncertain of the future they would have together. Mary was still at Patton State Hospital more than thirty miles away, and the baby, Paul, was watched by an older lady named Mrs. Ferguson. Paul, almost two and a half years old, would soon be joining the rest of his older brothers and sisters. Although the only Owens child never to have had the necessary bond between mother and baby, Paul would, in later years, feel what his other siblings already had felt, a lack of closeness with his own mother. All eight children would never know the depths of a genuine mother-child relationship. Mary was only well enough to visit her family periodically. For a few years, she did visit home every weekend. She would be in the hospital and away from her family for a total of seven years. These were the impressionable years for many of the Owens kids as they were developing into preteens and teenagers, while the three "babies," Elizabeth, Lois, and now Paul, turned to their older brothers and sisters for acceptance and guidance.

Roger enrolled in John Muir Junior High and started his first job, working for minimum wage as a stock boy at Lindsey's Drug Store. After some time had passed, he realized that he wasn't doing enough to help his dad financially. He thought of other possibilities. He liked the idea of finding opportunities that rewarded him for hustling and earning commissions based on his level of productivity.

So Roger found work selling the *Herald Examiner* on the corner of Hoover and Vernon, a busy intersection that boomed with potential buyers who had just exited the end of the Harbor Freeway. Roger made selling newspapers a somewhat lucrative business for himself, not just because of the proximity of the freeway, but because of his eagerness to sell every paper, running in and out of traffic, standing on islands between cross traffic, and dodging the old electric street cars. He did anything to get the job done, and he soon developed clientele that knew him and expected him every afternoon after school. In fact, they would have the exact change ready to throw to him as he tossed the paper into their cars.

As progress was made on the Harbor Freeway construction, Roger was unable to cash in on the busy afternoon traffic. The freeway was now ending further away, and he saw his profits dwindle.

On Sunday afternoons, Roger also began selling parking spaces on their front lawn and driveway, since the demand for parking exceeded the capacity of the Los Angeles Memorial Coliseum grounds, as more and more people showed up to watch the Rams play.

It was now January 1956, and all of this work matured Roger into a dependable young man. Even so, he was still a kid, and he did all that he could to find a balance between working, playing, and of course, daydreaming. Young Roger was witnessing his own metamorphosis, the inevitable process of growing up fast at the price of a unified but extremely poor Owens family.

Whether it was spending Christmas with his reunited family, watching how his five year-old sister Elizabeth was unaware that the man dressed as Santa Claus was really Ross, or celebrating his thirteenth birthday, Roger realized that nothing could match the family experience he had shared in the Worthan home. Even so, he was determined to find his place as the caring, loyal, highly emulated older brother, and the right hand man of his beloved father.

Ruth was in the sixth grade and loved going out in the yard and lassoing her rope. She was already a star with the rope among her classmates, even winning a talent contest. Ross was impressed with her efforts, but not as much on Sundays, since she wasn't allowed to do her roping, or anything for that matter, out of respect for the Sabbath.

Inside the house there was much work to be done. Ross was right to say that it was too much work for his girls to carry out by themselves. From the moment the family came together, Ross knew how necessary it would be to employ a competent, agreeable housekeeper. Over the next seven years, Ross and his kids would see an array of housekeeping talent and lack thereof. There were about six total that worked for the Owens household. As though recruited for military service, some dutiful housekeepers were honorably discharged, while others were just simply dishonorable.

Throughout the 1950's, Ross found that every one of the housekeepers he hired was a middle-aged black woman, no doubt trying to make ends meet with her own family, and probably living not too far away. It didn't bother Ross at all, and it didn't bother the kids either, since racism had little sting in the home of a Baptist preacher. Some stayed awhile, while some didn't last long at all.

One was a lousy cook who used too much spice.

One drank alcohol on the job and didn't like to mop, so she bribed the kids to do it for her. A few cupcakes always did the trick.

Another had a husband who had recently suffered a stroke, but was kind enough to let the boys listen to the Dodgers on his radio every Saturday.

There was even one who accused the kids of stealing money from her. The woman left, only to find that she had put the money in one of her own coat pockets.

Then, there was one who was the quintessential black housekeeper. She was as memorable and down home as her homemade, baking powder biscuits and scrambled eggs. Her warm smile was sure to make anyone love her. The Owens kids knew her as Mrs. Mattie Mae Johnson.

Endowed with a medium to large build by her Creator, Mattie Mae was built for comfort, not for speed. She had a soulful, unashamed, joyful pride that permeated her demeanor. More than that, she loved the Owens children as her own. Sometimes, she would round up the kids and drive them over to her house in Watts. She had a sense of style, often wearing a hat and fancy dress, even when taking the girls to church or a black hair salon. She cooked soul food that was the envy of every Owens stomach. But then again, if someone had asked young Roger, he would admit that any food at all was the envy of every Owens stomach. She was always more than a spoonful of charm and contentment. She was Mattie Mae Johnson.

Even with a caring housekeeper, living on 45th Street was tough. The streets were barren of innocence and cheerfulness. The neighborhood's good people were always susceptible to embracing the ways of the blighted. Day after dismal day, the hard, dark, gray asphalt vanquished all optimism, and all dreams that were conjured up curbside were plunged into the depths of water-filled potholes.

The only good thing Roger knew of the two years spent in this area was the huge, Olympic-sized swimming pool at Exposition Park. He and Philip would go down to the pool during the summer, preoccupied by their sense of excitement more than their sense of danger, since being accosted by troublemakers was always a possibility. They stood out in a sea of liquid blue and black skin as some of the only white kids in the pool. From high above, they must have looked like an incomplete constellation, as two white spots revealing their location in the pool.

Roger quickly learned about the rougher kids that plagued one's freedom to wander alleys and corners alike. He grew up, like his brothers and sisters, knowing how to be street smart in the heart of a growing metropolis such as Los Angeles. There were many times when one kid would approach another kid and brazenly demand that he be "given a loan." If the money wasn't handed over, or the kid pretended to have no money to give, the troublemaker would look him in the eye and ask, "Can you stand a search?" It would be a painful lesson if the kid admitted his poverty, only to have his bluff called.

Nevertheless, the Owens kids found safety in the faith that their father had in God to protect his children. Ross could only do so much, and he left the rest up to the Lord. The kids found living arrangements inside their home almost as aggravating as life outside. They had their typical bouts over living space and attention, over teasing, and over asking for silence so someone could do their homework. Many of the kids were still rather young, so they hadn't quite developed the fine art of teasing and meanness that would become prevalent in the teenage years still ahead.

Finally, Ross decided to move his family to a safer neighborhood.

$\mathcal{C}$ 6

Bums Play in L.A.

In early 1958, they moved west, but remained in Los Angeles. They took up residence in a racially mixed neighborhood on the corner of 41st Street and Western Avenue.

For 15 year-old Roger, life on 41st Street was a major improvement. He found a friend in a black kid who was his neighbor from across the street. His name was Celathio Ryan, or Lado as he was called. He had a younger sister named Marsha and another named Beverly. Roger and Philip began hanging around Lado on the street after school until they struck up a friendship. Ruth and Priscilla were soon friends with Marsha and Beverly, and nearly every day all of them would go over to the Ryan house to watch television. They all played games together, talked about whatever came to mind, teased each other, and just enjoyed being good friends.

Roger found other friends in two white kids, Nick "Banana Boat" Travis and Gary Gardener and, later, a tall, black kid named Frank Luster, who looked after his "gray boy" buddy, Roger. Gary introduced himself to Roger and the two quickly became friends. Roger enjoyed playing softball and sneaking into movies with his friends. However, it wasn't until Gary told him about his brand new albums that Roger knew he had found a gem of a friend. One day, Roger and Philip walked over to Gary's house. Together they went into his room and waited for him to find the records to play on his Victrola. Gary's father made good money driving an ambulance, and he bought him music albums and 45 singles now and then. Philip, however, ran out of patience and excused himself into the bathroom.

Gary found one of them and placed it onto the record player. The needle moved off its resting spot and glided slowly over the spinning, black plate. It landed. Audible scratches became even louder hisses and pops as Gary turned up the volume.

Roger sat in anticipation.

Suddenly, a burst of loud, rhythmically raucous music thrashed forth. Its hypnotic and steady beat was matched with a genuinely blended, edgy, yet soulfully southern voice. It was the voice of a young rebel who took the nation by storm. Blues artists and country and western aficionados alike found something about it vaguely familiar. It was like a cousin at a family reunion who looked unrelated to the kinfolk, but who shared the same last name.

It was the music of Elvis Presley.

They were listening to "Hound Dog," and Roger loved it.

They both began moving around, trying to keep time to the rocking music. Obviously there was an unwritten law between the two boys that no one would tell anyone else of their enthusiastic attempts at dancing. Suddenly Philip walked in, but he was captured by the music as well, and any memories valuable enough to tease Roger about were forgotten with each beat. But if Elvis songs weren't enough, there were other ones to be heard every day after school when they raced home and played songs like "Splish Splash" and some by Ricky Nelson.

From rock beats to street corner beatings, the Owens kids were growing up balanced. They were experiencing a life mixed with innocence and maturity, a storied concoction not unlike a Rum and Coke. However, Roger and his siblings struggled with starvation and with the desire to have enough decent clothes to wear. Nearly all of their outfits were from a secondhand store, but they were still appreciative. In any case, they were mischievous kids who found the rules of a Godly father much too strict. They often did things to satisfy their immediate needs, if not their devious impulses.

There were several times that Roger and Philip inserted a dime at a street corner newspaper rack, but instead of taking a newspaper, they would put gum on the end of a Popsicle stick and would insert it into the coin box inside the newspaper rack. The gum stuck to the dimes, and one at a time, they pulled the coins out. Whenever people walked by, they either whistled as though standing innocently or they pretended to take a long time getting the paper out of the rack.

One time, Roger went into a store and stole a Twinkie, an obvious temptation to a stomach that always ran on empty. Eleven year-old Philip ratted on Roger to their dad once they arrived home. Ross immediately took Roger into the bathroom and shut the door.

"Wait a second. Don't I get to pray first?" Roger pleaded.

"Okay, pray," he said. He knew his kids always asked that just to buy some time before getting spanked. Roger was taking a long time with his prayer, and Ross was becoming impatient. "Okay, that's enough. Drop your drawers and bend over."

Roger's dad promptly spanked him, while a laughing and taunting Philip waited outside the bathroom door. Roger was rubbing away the pain on his rear when he explained that Philip ate *half* of the stolen Twinkie. Ross finished with Roger and then took Philip into the bathroom, giving Philip the same treatment. Roger now stood in the living room laughing as he heard his brother yelping from Ross' straightforward discipline. However, sore rears and sore pride proved minimal deterrence when it came to food and clothes.

Roger and Philip were also known to go on "racking" adventures at the department store. Often, they went to the clothes racks that fit their size and style. One acted as a human periscope, while the other swiped the clothes. Shirts, socks, jackets, and just about anything else were game. Some times they put them in their shopping bags and exited the store. Other times they grabbed two pairs of identical clothes and repeated this until they had quite an assortment. They then went to the fitting room where one shirt, for example, was wrapped inside another identical shirt so it would seem they met the allowed number of garments to try on.

One day, they went into the fitting rooms with the clothes they planned to shoplift. A pair of department store detectives, working undercover as husband and wife, noticed something suspicious about the boys. They also noticed the boys were carrying shopping bags from a department store that was more than five miles away. They knew the boys were way too young to drive, so the shopping bag was one more reason to follow them into the fitting room. They sat quietly while Roger and Philip stood in the next stall. The boys were talking about the clothes and not having to pay for them. The two security guards then followed Roger and Philip as they walked out of the stall to return the clothes they didn't want.

Suddenly, the boys were caught. One of the undercover security guards went to notify the manager, and the other detained them, questioning them about their deeds and asking for their father's phone number. Ross got the call and drove out to the store.

"Hello, Mr. Owens?" the officer said as Ross quickly walked through the store's entrance.

"Yes, that's me," replied Ross.

"I work as a store security officer. Are these your boys?" he asked.

"Yes, sir, they are. What did they do wrong officer?" asked Ross.

"They were caught stealing these clothes here. They admitted their guilt, so the manager wants me to take them and establish a record on them at the police station," he added.

"Well officer these are good boys. I'm a Baptist minister, and believe me, you can be sure they'll learn their lesson," Ross explained.

"I understand that Mr. Owens, but I'd also like to respect the manager's right to protect his merchandise. Hold on Mr. Owens," the officer said. Just then the man waved toward the manager to come over, but he was busy with several customers and a few employees. He nodded as if to say he would be right there.

"Sir, can I ask you a question?" Ross interrupted.

"Yes sir, go ahead," the officer replied, wanting to expedite this matter.

"Are you right with God?" he asked.

"Huh?" the officer answered.

"Since we have a few minutes, let me explain how man and God are apart. You see, man and God can't settle their differences because sin is in the way. The only way we can have a relationship with the Heavenly Father is to ask forgiveness for our sins," Ross continued sincerely.

"You are preaching to me sir?" asked the officer, now completely puzzled.

"Yes sir. Like I was saying, if we acknowledge Jesus as the Christ, then....," Ross explained.

"Oh God," he sighed in disbelief.

"I can show you better with a drawing," Ross said, pausing to search for something. "Looks like I don't have any blank paper on me. Do you have any on you? Oh, you have some right there on your writing pad," he said, reaching for the pad.

"No, you can't have that" he replied, swatting the air to keep Ross' hands away. "You know what sir? Go. Just go. Take your boys. I'll tell the manager you'll teach them a lesson in stealing, or something, anything. Just leave already," begged the man.

"But I didn't finish," Ross added.

"I'm sorry Reverend, but church is letting out early today. Go already before I lock you up along with your two little disciples," the officer answered while escorting them out of the store.

Roger and Philip wanted to laugh out loud but that would have ruined the moment. As they walked out to the parking lot, the boys looked up at their dad and beamed with pride at how they got out of that one. But when they got home, the only thing that was beaming was the red, hot glow of a good spanking on their behinds. Their sniffles and tears quickly became hysterical laughter once again, but only when they were sure their dad had left them alone to pray, insisting they ask God to forgive them for stealing.

Roger and Philip weren't the only ones in the Owens family to try a hand at stealing. The Owens girls, with no hint of good, hearty cooking at home to show on their beanpole frames, were not immune to such waywardness either. Ruth was able to leave town to visit a girlfriend in San Diego, lying to her dad about some "class reunion," and even watched *Jailhouse Rock* with her friend once they got to San Diego. Although Ruth also helped herself to a swiped bottle of 7-Up from a vending machine, her sisters fared better on a different occasion at a local supermarket.

One morning, Priscilla and Esther walked into a grocery store and grabbed a shopping cart. They didn't bother to check their pockets for money, since buying food was never the agenda. It started out as a make believe shopping game, whereby they pretended to have enough money to buy anything. They gleefully glided down the aisles, pausing to peruse only damaged or opened food items, which they carelessly flung into the cart. Thoughts of consumption danced in their heads as they smiled at every row of delectable treats and blissful sweets. In their eyes, they were simply relieving the store of obviously unwanted or unmarketable products. The cart was now filled to the top. Their game had ended. The devious duo looked around and made off with their collection of cookies, candy, and chips. With all the sugar consumed from one cent Bazooka gum, 20 oz. Bubble Up sodas, and all kinds of candy, the Owens kids were a hyper bunch, with pockets full of lint and nothing, and mouths full of rotting teeth and smiles that just screamed cavities.

Arguing and fighting were also commonplace in their house, as space was extremely limited. All of the girls shared a room, and Roger and Phillip slept in the living room. Fighting over a pancake one morning before school, Ruth and Priscilla found themselves in a heated exchange that could have sizzled bacon and fried eggs for their hungry siblings. In a fit of anger, Priscilla picked up a butter knife and flung at her sister, slightly grazing the side of Ruth's face, narrowly missing her temple. Notwithstanding their good intentions, the Owens kids never ran out of reasons why they should beg for forgiveness on Sunday mornings at the Salvation Army Church. It was at this church that the kids had realized the previous Christmas that there were plenty of compassionate people from that church who provided for them.

After many Sundays attending the Salvation Army Church, the kids were starting to attend Sunday school at Hoover Street Baptist Church. They carpooled with a friendly couple named Rex and Elizabeth Harris. The Harris' were members of the church and fell in love with the Owens kids from the first time they met them. Sometimes after church, Rex treated all of them to as much ice cream as they could eat at a nearby Foster's Freeze.

As always, Ross continued to visit his wife in the hospital, driving out twice a month. He brought her toiletries, candy, and writing material. After spending some time alone with her, trying to get through to her, sometimes consoling her, other times updating her on the family, but always praying for her, he would finally leave half the man he was when he arrived because of the emptiness he felt in his heart. Mary would lie there in bed recalling Ross' wonderful, deep, and sincere voice. She would sometimes feel tired and hopeless. It was obvious that she wasn't well, yet the tears that quietly rolled down her cheeks attested to a genuine, if not sane, awareness.

Still attending John Muir Junior High, Roger loved to write. He wrote persuasive essays, as well as original, dramatic screenplays. In his spare time, he read newspapers and magazines, like *The Sporting News* and *Sports Illustrated*, to catch up on his favorite baseball players, Mickey Mantle, Willie Mays, and of course, Duke Snider. He was beside himself the first time he learned that Walter O'Malley had made plans to move his famed Dodgers to the sunny, tree-lined hills of Chavez Ravine in Los Angeles, California. As a matter of fact, the entire West Coast was thrilled to learn that the Dodgers would no longer be associated with the urban dankness of the Atlantic Ocean and the sprawl of New York's hustle and bustle, but instead with the Mediterranean climate of a desert-turned-oasis known as Los Angeles.

There was a charge of excitement in the springtime air with the Dodgers beginning a new life in Los Angeles. His favorite team would soon be playing their home games at the L.A. Coliseum, just two blocks from where he would soon be attending classes at Manual Arts High School.

Roger, who dreamed of someday making the baseball team as a pitcher at Manual Arts, still had to find time to help his father support the young family. Roger was becoming a handsome young man, and was already getting teased by friends and family because of his hairstyle and resemblance to Wally Cleaver from *Leave It To Beaver*.

His dirty blonde hair was turning brown and, although the wave in his hairstyle might have added an inch to his height, he still had a way to go before surpassing his dad's height at six feet.

He found work again selling newspapers as well as the *Los Angeles Times'* short-lived tabloid *The Mirror*. He found a street corner on 41st Street and Santa Barbara Boulevard, which would be renamed Martin Luther King Boulevard many years later. On the corner, he noticed a newsstand managed by an elderly man who planned on giving up his work there. Roger pleaded with him to let him take over, and the man agreed. Roger surveyed the busy intersection from under the shelter of the stand, and he smiled. Then he grabbed his papers and went to work, selling quickly to earn desperately needed income for the family.

Ross was consumed with his work too and depended heavily on the Lord for strength and patience. Good news came when he received a phone call one evening. It was Patton State Hospital. His wife was doing well enough to visit on weekends, and even during the week if she did better. Ross was overjoyed.

He made plans to bring her home, and the kids made plans to be on their best behavior. From then on, Mary was scheduled to stay with the family every weekend, from Friday to Sunday.

Although Mary was around more often, there was an eerie feeling in the air. The woman in the house was a stranger. Nearly five years had gone by since they had last seen her. Some of them back then were too young to even remember her. Now, they were a family, by name but not by feeling.

They were much closer to their dad who, on Sundays, would take them to church and then to a picnic. Before Philip, Elizabeth, Lois, and all the others could go play at the park, Ross made them read a scripture or two from the Bible. Then as night fell, they were like happy puppies, licking their Sav-On ice cream cones, which they bought for a nickel apiece.

The kids, even though they were practically starved more than half the time, still had all kinds of fun, whether they saw scary movies at a friend's house, played jokes on younger sisters, went trash digging, went "bottle hunting" and on adventure walks, played church, or had tent meetings. Mary, however, showed signs of relapse. Even though the kids tried to balance their time between school, homework, and after school mischief, they weren't too busy to notice how differently their mother was behaving during her visits.

Mary became aggressive and said things that made little sense. She ordered Roger around and uttered curse words, unbecoming and entirely unimaginable of such a woman, a woman whom Roger still held in high regard. She resented that a new housekeeper, a white lady this time, was needed to help out. Bitter and still mentally disturbed, she strolled around in the middle of the night, waking up Ruth and demanding that she dust and clean areas of the house before she could go back to sleep. Ross wrestled with his conscience regarding her actions. He was left with no recourse but to take her back to the hospital. She resisted. Anywhere was better than that wretched place, full of the chilling voices from those haunted beings that sat around her bed.

Everyone, from Roger and Ruth, to young Lois and Paul, felt the strain of their broken relationship with their mother, who was still a prisoner of her nervous breakdown. It made each one afraid and, with each passing teenage year, that much more embarrassed.

Each afternoon, Roger arrived at his post at the newsstand. Many times he was tired from being in class all day. Before getting to work, he would quietly stare at the dark, gray strip of boulevard. He was entranced with the torn newspapers flying down the forsaken streets, and with how the wind howled an octave higher than poverty's loud mockery of everyone that lived there. The streets were noisy and busy, yet Roger noticed that the scorn of the city was heaped upon the idle. Roger's thoughts of his mother grumbled like engines from cars passing him by. He finally gathered his senses, like a stack of newspapers, and began selling at the stand and forgetting his troubles.

One bright afternoon, Roger perked up. His attention was fixed on the nonsensical wanderings in and out of traffic of a medium-sized brown dog. The dog, a mix of boxer and pit bull, looked ragged and mean, but judging from the fresh wounds of a fierce dogfight, it was a survivor. It looked up and saw Roger at the newsstand. Roger's fixation with dogs overcame him, and he resisted all temptation to be afraid. The dog slowly walked up to him, sniffed him intensely, and without warning licked the top of his hand.

The dog seemed to have been searching for something, and Roger was intrigued. His scent and lack of tension disarmed the animal. It looked up at Roger. Capable of only seeing shades of gray in his eyes, the dog gazed intently in futile desperation to find the true, hue of blue in them. As Roger stroked the dog's short hair, the dog closed his eyes as if dreaming of life in front of an air vent that sent generous blasts of warm air or, better yet, of catching the breeze while leaning out of the window of a fast moving car, as he had seen other dogs do on that street.

Roger loved the animal.

The half boxer, half pit bull showed up every afternoon, sniffing out Roger's scent at the newsstand, as if clocking in for work with Roger. He stayed next to Roger, becoming his friend, and watching over his hoard of dollars and coins. Roger named him "Bert," and he took him back to the Owens house as the newly appointed king of their grassy lawn. The kids rejoiced at the affable Bert Owens, who panted and basked in their warmth.

Young Roger increased his newspaper selling by walking around town looking for people who might want a paper. He went inside various stores and shops, coaxing a coin or two from them in exchange for the daily events. His efforts paid off more when he began selling papers with a man named Ted. He allowed Roger to increase his routes while riding in the back of the man's white, Ford station wagon.

Roger knew that his future wasn't going to be in selling newspapers, and the money he earned from it certainly reinforced that decision. Although the income helped considerably, it wasn't until a grocery store manager noticed his hard work, hustle, and likeable personality that he finally had a real career opportunity.

The coveted newsstand Roger ran, with Bert's help of course, stood in front of a huge supermarket called Better Foods. It was full of shoppers all day long. The manager kept his eye on Roger, waiting for the day he could finally offer the young man a job. The store employees got used to seeing the hard working teenager and his dog on the corner. In fact, whenever police or fire truck sirens blared nearby, poor Bert would howl loud enough to let the whole world know of the terrible ringing in his ears. If shoppers asked who or what was making that "God-awful sound," the check stand attendant would confess it was just old Bert Owens.

Finally, the manager hired Roger.

It was a promotion for him. He stopped selling newspapers and started out as a box boy for the store. Instantly, he made new friends and felt very successful. He seemed to be heading into a promising, new career in the grocery business. There was even mutual consent that when he turned 18 years old, Roger would make an excellent grocery clerk, with a chance for advancement.

It was 1958, and the Dodgers were ready to start the season in Los Angeles. By April, the organization had installed a huge screen in left field at the Coliseum. That screen, approximately 50 feet high, compensated for the drastically short distance from home plate. If not for the new "wall," sluggers would have salivated at the thought of all the homeruns they could have hit, and legends would have been made of otherwise, mortal players with .200 averages.

Roger now wanted to work at the Coliseum. Like so many caught up with the Dodger frenzy, he quickly learned that countless other people were also searching for employment at the Coliseum. Realistically, he knew he was just one individual in a sea of raucous, unemployed men. In spite of this, Roger was determined to find work there. After completing all of the day's obligations, he would go over to the ballpark on game day, as early as possible before the game. Many times he waved his hands and hollered like the rest of them, trying to get the attention of the food concessions manager for Coliseum events. The man would point to an individual, and that person would hastily make his way to the front. The manager would continue doing so until he met the quota for day laborers. There were no contracts. Nothing was binding. Work offered was for that day only, and the whole process of fishing for labor started over the next game day. However, anyone that worked there before had an edge over the others, since the manager was good at remembering faces and work ethics of those he previously hired.

As for Roger, he left every Dodger game empty handed. Somewhat discouraged, but not out of ideas, he began finding entrances to the Coliseum's stadium seating in left field. During batting practice, Dodger players would send high fly balls into the seats with every loud crack of their bats. Roger was only one of a handful that raced to gather the souvenirs, clean them up, and begin selling the baseballs to the growing mass of baseball fans that showed up closer to game time. Weeks passed by, and he soon saw his profits swallowed by intruders. Now everyone was there, collecting baseballs for money. Roger was again out of work at the ballpark. He slumped back home, kicking dirt and soda cans along the way. Roger now felt hopeless, thinking he was only meant to be a drudger rather than a Dodger.

Months passed, but Roger hadn't given up. He continued to see the great opportunity to work there for his favorite team.

All he had to do was to show up.

All he had to do was to get hired just once.

Then he could show them.

He believed that his hard work would pay off, and the manager would be sure to remember him.

$\mathcal{E}$ 7

And the Pinnacle is Peanuts

R oger was ready again. This time, the manager had all of the eager workers lined up against a fence. The usual people were picked, and finally the manager stared at Roger. He eyed the young man up and down and then flicked his thumb into the air and flung it backwards in the direction of the new hires who were already running and jumping in excitement. Roger leaped off the wire fence, as though it were charged with a thousand volts. He ran toward the others, waiting at the concession stand. All the while, the manager barked out demands for more workers, as he eyed the restless bunch.

Roger was immediately given a crate full of 7-Up bottles to sell. Instantly, he felt the weight of his new responsibilities. He knew he was fortunate to be in this position, yet the burden of carrying full soda bottles in large crates up and down steep steps nearly overwhelmed him. But he took his mind off those things and collected his thoughts. He looked back in the distance, where the voices of the angry, work-starved mob carried like dispersed clouds that intermittently blocked the sunshine. Roger stared down at the cold, cement floor near the concession stand. He paused to think of his two brothers, five sisters, and his dad and mom. Then, he peered into the heavens, as though they would part like two huge curtains, spreading to reveal some divinely projected course of action. It was the same sky that he once canvassed for its opinions of the terrible Mrs. Naylor. It was the same sky that heard him ask what he should do about leaving the Worthan family. It was the very same sun that strolled around on its own prerogative, watching the young Owens boy grow into a diligent, worthy young man. Roger tried to resist the feeling that he was being shoved into adulthood, but that was too late. His happy-go-lucky ways were still present in his character, but he was no longer a kid. As sweat broke out on his forehead, Roger realized something. More than at any other time in his life, he was ready to go to work.

Within an hour, the players took the field.

"Play ball!" cried the home plate umpire.

Roger worked hard all day long, and he finally went home. Awaiting him were his rowdy younger brothers and sisters, and his faithful pal, Bert. Roger slowly made his way to the living room and plopped himself down on the sofa, which doubled as his bed. The immediate drain of energy made him feel like he was a block of ice, melting into a careless slush of empty stomach and exhausted mind. He found the sofa to be more refreshing than all of the 7-Up and Coke sold in all of the concession stands put together. He looked up at the ceiling, blocking out completely the noise of everyone else in the small house. He closed his eyes and then suddenly groaned to himself at the thought of having all kinds of unfinished homework due the next day.

The next afternoon, after he was done with classes, he went to Better Foods, put on his work clothes and apron and went to work. Roger's attention was divided as he thought of the excitement of working the crowds at the Coliseum versus the more stable career opportunity with the supermarket. He knew he had a decision to make soon if he continued to work at the ballpark. For now, it could wait. It was almost time to get off work, but before he left, he bought some sliced ham and wrapped it in a bag to take home. It was a simple dinner, which he ate on the porch of his house. He sat there eating the meat, often tearing some to hand to his companion Bert, who sat begging for any scraps that could be spared.

Several months had passed, and Roger had been consistently finding work on game days. He had built up his stamina and, while carrying the crates wasn't easy, he was getting used to the work.

One late afternoon, Roger showed up at the ballpark to stand in the vendor line. It was in this line that each vendor could request to sell any product sold at the ballpark. However, seniority determined who was allowed to choose to sell what, and for those at the top, it always meant peanuts. They were lightweight and quite profitable. By the time the vendors with less seniority got to the front of the line, all of the peanut positions were filled, as well as most of the ice cream gigs.

Roger's hard work had paid off. It was the first day in which he moved far enough up the line to be allowed to sell Coca Cola.

It was Roger's first promotion.

He was well aware that after every Dodger home stand, the concession food supervisor checked who was producing and who wasn't. The goal for every aspiring vendor, or anyone that just wanted to stay working for that matter, was to move up the pecking order, past soda and past ice cream, to finally reach the pinnacle and sell the crowd favorite.

Peanuts.

Roger now showed up at the concession stands and was given crates full of ice-cold bottles of Coca Cola. He gleamed with pride as he realized how immediately success could be achieved when he put his mind to it.

He was eager to please and eager to sell.

If selling Cokes made the crowd that much happier, then he was all for it. It was at this point that Roger first believed that he could become the best in what he did, if he only tried and worked hard enough. The advancement inspired him to bigger and better things. His sights were now on the sidewalk sundaes and the chocolate malts sold at the ballpark. After that, he knew he would be on the way to the big time, the major league of ballpark vending, the show, yes indeed, the bags of salted gold.

Roger's world was changing dramatically, but he still depended on his friendship with Lado, Gary, Nick, and Frank Luster to keep his sanity. He often found life at home to be boring and uneventful, except for the arguments of his younger siblings. His dad wasn't home much at all, and the likelihood of finding food in the house to snack on was so low, so improbable, it was like telling Sandy Koufax to throw a fastball underhanded or asking Gil Hodges to bunt with the bases full. It just wasn't going to happen. So Roger often stayed at one of his friend's house for hours, and when it came to be dinnertime, in the back of his mind he hoped he would be invited to stay for supper. It almost always worked.

The year was 1959, and Roger was now in high school. He enrolled in Manual Arts High as he planned. Some of the few friends he had made there were also lucky enough to find work at the Coliseum. Like everyone else working there, Roger realized there was good money in working at the ballpark, all the while catching every home game for free and watching his baseball heroes play in person. He couldn't beat that working at a grocery store.

Roger stood at the crossroads. Should he stay at the market with a guaranteed salary and chance of promotion, or should he take the opportunity with Dodger food concessions with an income that was strictly commission-based? It was a gamble. He had no certainty of how much he could earn, but he knew one thing for sure. The promise of big crowds and daily excitement during the long baseball season kept him dreaming at night. But if his nights were filled with thoughts of being a vendor for the Dodgers, then his days were filled with ambition for being a top pitcher on his high school baseball team.

Roger had tried out for the basketball and baseball teams and made it on both of them. In basketball he was a defensive force rather than an unstoppable scorer, and he knew his keen sense of passing would always play a pivotal role in game time, especially his behind the back passes. With a passion for passing that would have made Bob Cousy proud, Roger did his best on the court to shake his defender like jelly and play as smooth as peanut butter. He continued to grow as if he had secretly swallowed lawn fertilizer as a closet addict. He finally reached his dad's height at six feet, and started to grow into his frame. He played with the idea of having sideburns like Elvis, and the wave in front like Wally Cleaver. He was a good-looking kid if he did say so himself, but he wouldn't have, since his modesty kept him in check. He was still much too shy when it came to girls. As he continued to mature, he got plenty of attention but displayed little, if any, response. Timid and awkward at displaying his emotions, and with no foundation of a loving mother-and-son relationship to fall back on, he did little to show affection or concern to the opposite sex, unless they were his beloved sisters.

As his high school team's season progressed, he had aspirations of becoming a professional baseball player. He wanted to be a pitcher, but had he reached such stardom in the pros, and if he had signed with a team by the mid 1960's, he would have been in the same major leagues as young, intimidating, prototype hurlers like the Bob Gibsons, the Tom Seavers, and the Nolan Ryans. Well, realistically, what he couldn't offer the world with true, baseball pitching ability, he would make up for with an ironic, whimsical, and captivating version of the same hurling talent. However, it would take a new remarkable facility known as Dodger Stadium before such talent could breathe life into its own serendipitous soul and find full bloom.

Roger was ready to decide. He walked into Better Foods and gave them notice that he was leaving the store. Now he only had to manage his time between classes, homework, and work at the ballpark.

Ross admired his son very much for the sacrifices Roger made.

Roger's mother was slowly doing better in the hospital, but Ross was buried with his work and had little time for the kids.

The Owens household had changed drastically over the last decade. Those who were once babies and toddlers in 1949 had now grown into kids and pre-teens. Ruth, the shy, pigtailed, little city girl who could lasso circles around any sixth grade country girl, was now fast approaching 5 feet 7 as a 15 year-old. Even her sisters, who ranged in age from nine to thirteen, were maturing quickly and were an obvious cause for alarm under Ross' roof. He became stricter with them, allowing no make-up and no television shows that went beyond his stern guidelines, and he made sure they still napped on Sunday.

Ross was the one that they bonded with, obviously. He was the one who dutifully explained away the ignorance of a 12 year-old girl's conception of menstruation, and the one who indulged his kids with the occasional luxury of groceries on Fridays. He also was the one to stay up all night, praying for and comforting eight year-old Elizabeth, who had pneumonia, until they could go to the doctor in the morning. It was Ross who prayerfully gathered his strength to be a good father without his best teammate at his side. He loved Mary only a fraction less than he loved God and the Word. However, the Owens kids had missed much of that ride with their mom.

The dreams of the Owens children, vacant of any lasting remembrance of their mother's Italian countenance, called upon vague faces to fill the part. From the third to the eleventh grade, Priscilla, for example, depended on the harsh regulations of her father to also be the softer side of motherhood. The bond that should have been there had slipped her by, like a wind-blown leaf sailing past her brown, wind-blown hair. That same leaf was the only tangible remnant of the train that had raced by the station years ago. All the children stood waiting for that train to somehow circle again, bringing with it a promise of some kind of renewed ties between them and their mom. They didn't realize that they would only find happiness with their loving mother as young adults and eventually as parents themselves.

Someday.

From the distance, a familiar train slowly pulled into the station.

Ross heard from the hospital that Mary was doing very well. He was loud and happy with the kids, but they struggled to appreciate the news. By the end of that same month, Mary was allowed to stay at home on a permanent basis with her family. It was the first time in seven years that Mary was free to be at home and not have any obligations to return to the hospital. It was early 1960.

Even as the naiveté of American culture dissolved and made way for the moral and political challenges of the 60's, so, too, the 60's had brought the testing of the very foundation the Owens family had built upon.

Roger made his decision to be a Dodger vendor. He was convinced that if he just worked hard, he could forge a possible career. Of course, he had to think of something to do in the off-season. Almost 17 years old, Roger had moved up the concession ladder and sold ice cream by the time the Dodger season was over. By autumn, Roger was out of work, and it worried him. It began to hit home that possibly this wasn't the career for him, unless he could do something else to bring in money.

One day, he found a spot to sit down on the porch next to Bert. He talked with Bert and wondered. He became charmed with the idea of being a police officer or highway patrol officer. That wasn't too much of a stretch for his career goals, since his thoughts were already permanently branded by early, childhood memories of the *Lone Ranger* and how, in that show, justice always prevailed. He still smiled as he thought himself a baseball pitcher, but that smile quickly sank into a modest frown of self-doubt. He petted Bert, who had a tennis ball stuffed in its mouth. Roger took it from the dog and threw it. Bert leaped up and chased it. He brought it back, ready for another toss. But Roger just held onto the wet, fuzzy, green tennis ball. He squeezed it while he stared himself into a trance. Then Philip interrupted him. They both went inside and managed to find enough food to make sandwiches.

The next day was Saturday, and Roger decided to ride his bike around the neighborhood. It wasn't as tough as the places he once lived, but it was getting there. In fact, that afternoon, as Roger was pedaling, he saw two other boys approach him. Looking like ghetto versions of a mafia on bikes, they faced Roger, roughed him up, and stole his bike. That was that, and Ross had had enough of that neighborhood the minute Roger explained what happened. Roger made his way through the yard, taking out a sack full of garbage. He walked right by Bert, who looked puzzled with the lack of affection.

"Where were you today when I needed you, huh?" Roger asked forcefully, as he heaved the garbage sack. Bert knew his tone and groaned deeply in shame. Roger walked back inside and shut the door.

It was spring, and a new season had started for the Dodgers. Dodger Stadium was still being built, so they had two more seasons to play at the Coliseum. Roger was already dreaming of selling ice cream. He knew the next step was peanuts, and he wasn't far off from that. At home, Roger, like everyone else, tried hard to get used to his mom being around. Mary resented the presence of the housekeeper, and so the lady's services were no longer needed. Mary began to take pride in finding herself as a mother of eight children. Within just a couple of months of being home, at the age of 45, she found herself expecting her ninth little blessing. Although the total time of being pregnant throughout her life had amounted to seven and a half years, Mary hadn't been this emotionally ready for a baby since the 1940's.

Roger was a junior in high school, but at the Coliseum he was about to graduate to peanuts. It would take several months of selling ice cream before that honor would be realized. At home, Mary had plenty of help around the house from her daughters. The girls tried to feel comfortable around their mother, but they were detached and ashamed. The Owens kids had both of their real parents, but they struggled with the balancing act of respecting their mom and of becoming growing adolescents. Roger, however, enjoyed life being a pitcher for his high school team by day and an ice cream vendor for the Dodgers by night. In fact, he was so enthusiastic about his work that his brother wanted to help bring in money by working at the Coliseum too. When Philip turned 15, he started out selling soda, just as Roger had.

Roger earned enough extra money to buy a '52 Plymouth. He paid between two hundred and three hundred dollars for the light-blue car, which continuously leaked oil and brake fluid. One afternoon, Roger wanted to get some food at the store. Forgetting that he was low on brake fluid, he started the car. He slowly pulled away a few feet from the curb when he remembered to check his brakes. The pedal went all the way to the floor, but the car kept moving. Even at 10 miles per hour, Roger panicked. Instead of turning the front wheel into the curb to stop the jalopy, Roger opened his door and put his foot down on the pavement. Roger's shoes began to smoke from the friction, but he was successful in bringing the car to a stop. Sweating from the anxiety, Roger paused. He couldn't believe why he didn't simply turn the wheel into the curb, *and* how he could forget to add brake fluid. As he sat with arms folded over the steering wheel, he felt his foot burning, quickly removed his left shoe, and examined it. The friction had seared a large hole that went completely through the cheap, rubber sole. He couldn't have been more embarrassed, all the while looking around to see if anyone had noticed. Thankfully, no one he knew saw what happened, but he was disgusted at himself for ruining a pair of shoes while burning rubber at 10 miles per hour.

It was already summer, and the Los Angeles heat soared. During afternoon ballgames, the wave of its intense warmth caused even the most conservatively dressed to rethink the politics of their attire. In any case, cries for chocolate malts and sidewalk sundaes rang out above all the chatter, cheers, and charges to victory.

"Ice cream here. Ice cream here," announced Roger, yelling just to be heard.

"Right here," one fan replied.

"Over here," yet another said.

Roger delivered the frozen goods, resuscitating the overheated patrons with cooling refreshment. By the end of the long summer, Roger had done what he only had dreamed of. He earned the promotion to begin selling the prized bag of peanuts. Roger would someday learn that what he did in the span of one year, climbing to the top of the vendor pecking order, would take nearly 20 years today because of the number of vendors, their rank, and the vast number of marketable products sold on any given day at the stadium.

For young Roger Daniel Owens, it was only the beginning.

₡ 8

Breakfast with the Baritone

W ith a new baby due in a month, and the neighborhood getting rougher every day, Ross had enough of the area and moved his family to the dairy town of Paramount, about 20 miles away. The town's unmistakable stench of grazing cows soured the air, especially in the late afternoon when feeding time brought the rustling of dirt from under their heavy hooves. Living in a somewhat larger house on 16333 Orizaba St., the Owens kids, ranging in ages from seventeen to thirteen to ten to seven, now fell asleep listening to the guttural moos of mother cows instead of intermittent police sirens. By morning, they woke up excited at the idea of having a new baby brother or sister. Despite the move, the Owens family still searched for sustenance beyond their poverty. It seemed as though the only thing rich in their neighborhood was the cow manure a few blocks away. Ross continued with his missionary work in Los Angeles and with truck driving, but he now added vacuum cleaner salesman to his long list of occupations.

It was almost Christmas 1960, and many of the neighbors and church members at the Paramount First Assembly of God had heard of a new family in town. The pastor's son, Steve Singleton, had visited the family and had noticed how extremely poor they were. As he talked with Ross, he saw Mary, ready to have their ninth child any day, eating beans and fried onions. When the young man had counted a total of eight children living there, he couldn't wait to get back home and tell his father, Pastor Ted Singleton, about the underprivileged Owens family. Early Christmas morning, when the air was still chilled, Ross heard a knock at the door. These same people showed up on the front porch to bring gifts and groceries. Ross stood motionless, and Mary joined him at the door. The pastor's son silently lifted up one of the grocery bags and smiled at Ross. The unassuming little moment, like the brown paper sacks of offerings, was stretched full of good will and love from

67

friends, and as Ross and Mary stood hugging, tears fell the great distance from eye to floor, like light drizzle. By dinnertime that evening, just as the Christmas dinner was ready to serve, Ross called his family into the living room. He asked his wife and all the kids to stand in a circle and hold hands. Ross began to pray out loud and to give thanks for the food and for all they had. He then gently laid his hands on Mary's stomach and prayed for the baby. Ross had finished, and everyone broke for the dinner line in the kitchen. Poor Bert was howling outside, so Roger let him inside just for a while. Bert's sniffing was uncontrollable as he smelled the turkey and ham and bugged every Owens kid for handouts. The kids inhaled the dinner and left no scraps, so old Bert had to be content with licking the plates clean.

In January 1961, the Owens family received another special present, but this time, they were expecting it.

As Mary's contractions became more frequent, she knew the time had come to have the baby. At 3:00 a.m., the kids were awakened and Ross hurried to get all the things ready. Ross desperately tried to start his '49 Plymouth but couldn't, so he had all five girls and three boys push the car until the engine finally revved up. They made it to the hospital in time, and by morning, Ross and Mary had their last child, a blonde baby girl they named Grace Evangeline.

It was a new year, and the spring season had also given birth to a new baseball year. The Dodgers had younger stars like Don Drysdale, Sandy Koufax, and Willie Davis. The team also had aged veterans like Duke Snider, a slugger who now epitomized a dying era in baseball, a time that sent its players off to war in the 40's and, in the 50's, bred hometown heroes, such as Mickey Mantle and Willie Mays, like farm raised produce. A newer time was ahead, a time of secret agents and frontiers into space and mini skirts. The baseball world of players, owners, managers, Hall of Famers, writers, analysts, and vendors all maintained their passion for the simplicities of the game. The Dodgers were about to begin their final year within the steep walls of the Coliseum. Members of the grounds crew were on the field preparing for the afternoon game. Some were raking the infield and some were trimming the grass. Others were busy chalking the foul lines and batter's boxes. At the commissary, cardboard boxes full of peanut bags were being stacked. From behind the boxes, young Roger pulled out a piece of paper and kept track of the number of bags he would attempt to sell that day. There was a buzz throughout the entire place. It was early still, and the fans were only now starting to arrive. Finally, it was game time. The once empty seats had flourished into a sea of roaring fans at high tide. They were easily excited and emotionally charged from sharing the same city air as their Dodger idols cavorting in the dirt and grass below. With their inventory prepared, the vendors took their places, as the sonic grumbling of over 40,000 stomachs echoed in response to one child's open bag of fresh peanuts.

"Peanuts here! Peanuts here!" Roger shouted triumphantly.

Roger soon got used to the drive from Paramount to the Coliseum. After a few ballgames, he didn't mind the forty-minute commute and, furthermore, he didn't mind the new setting of Paramount High School, where he finished out his senior year. At 18, and a pitcher for his team, the Paramount Pirates, young Roger began thinking of moving out on his own. As the early baseball season progressed into May, Roger prepared to graduate. With his mind set on attending college at Compton Community College and earning a degree in Police Science, Roger became more certain that, despite his great job at the ballpark, he felt called into the life of police service and the highway patrol. He had always felt strongly about helping others, and the prospect of such job stability only further charted his course in that direction.

Summer arrived.

Roger officially graduated high school, and his sister, Ruth, had just one more year until she too would graduate. At home, family life was still burdened by poverty. The kids, although young, were old enough to feel the crushing weight of what being poor did to a child. If not for their father's efforts, evening prayers, and plenty of help from church friends at nearby Paramount First Assembly of God, the Owens kids would have had to collect a lot more than soda bottles to buy their stale, powdered donuts. Besides, it was bad enough that they went to school with their lunches actually wrapped inside the noisy, orange sandwich bread packaging that doubled as their lunch sack. Armed many days with only buttered bread and a nickel for milk, Priscilla, Esther, Elizabeth, Lois, and Paul fought the embarrassment of their financially battered way of life. They found some comfort in occasionally eating ice cream, which could only be afforded the times they renounced their cravings for milk all week long and saved their change to pay for the 25-cent treat on Friday. As the kids continued to miss their friends, the Ryans, back in Los Angeles, and as Ross still drove back to the church he worked with, so, too, Mary began to show signs of falling into the darker depths of her mental prison camp. She was held captive, and again she gave into the voices that spoke to her. As she suffered from her relapse, the train that had courageously pulled into the station now stirred its wheels. Coals were shoveled into the heated engine. Gray smoke bellowed out of the train stack. The kids, standing at the station in nice clothes and combed hair, stared at their long shadows and felt the freezing autumn wind gently whip against their falling tears.

They knew their mom was sick once again.

Mary was readmitted to Patton State Hospital.

After a few weeks had passed, Ross visited her and brought Priscilla as well as baby Grace. While Priscilla watched her baby sister in the waiting room, Ross and Mary had time alone. As evening approached, Ross knew he needed to get Priscilla and little Grace back home. He said goodnight to his wife, but Mary remained in bed, motionless, until she fell asleep.

Roger, attending Compton Community College, did very well selling the 25-cent bags of peanuts, and he loved every minute of it. Even at six feet tall, he nearly disappeared into the mass of Dodger fans at the Coliseum. For those who were desperate for a bag of goobers, however, he was well within sight. In spite of Roger's hard work and success selling peanuts, it wasn't enough to help his father avoid falling behind in rent. As Roger truly needed much of his money to help with his college and car expenses, it was expected that Ross and Philip would cover most of the family's expenses. Within a few days, they realized it was too late. The landlord unmercifully evicted the Owens family. Ross quickly found a small house in Paramount on 6608 East Compton Blvd., not far from Compton. It was affordable because the landlord, an older gentleman named Mr. Kane who oversaw smaller apartments built around the larger house, allowed Ross a discount on rent. The discount would only be applicable if Ross would take over that management position, which included collecting rent from tenants.

Quickly, they settled into their house.

Within the same month, the hospital called, and the doctor told Ross that Mary was doing so well that she had permission to go home again. Ross was overjoyed and told the kids the news. Ross drove out to pick her up the following day. Without much fanfare this time, and with the kind of harsh realization that maturity and experience foster, the kids calmly waited for her return. They stood in silence. As their small handfuls of confetti fell to the ground, they solemnly watched her to step off the train. They were both happy and indifferent at the same time. Only time would bring them confidence, and only time would nurture a motherly relationship.

Upon Mary's return, Ross wanted to give her the chance to have responsibilities that would help her feel wanted, valuable, and proud of herself. Ross asked if she would manage the apartments, and she agreed. Mary, who never had driven a car, was once an active, working, registered nurse. Although she would get back into the nursing field in 1965 and work until 1977, this was the first time in decades that she had had so much responsibility outside the home. In any case, it was good therapy.

Several weeks later, with the holiday season just a couple of months away, the Owens family was in for a surprise. On one Saturday around noon, Roger was washing his car with help from his little brother Paul. Even if Bert could have been of some help with washing the car, it was evident that he wouldn't have budged one bit. Bert was sprawled on his back, rubbing against the wet lawn and finding the laziness of soaking up all the unusually warm weather much too irresistible.

Suddenly, a shiny black Cadillac pulled up alongside the curb, directly in front of their house. Calmly exiting the car was a somewhat older man, not quite 50 years old, wearing dark sunglasses and a glistening smile, with teeth as polished as his automobile. Two young teenagers, one a girl and the other a boy, piled out of the back seat and walked over to Roger. Roger quickly calmed Bert down, who was barking ferociously.

"Hi Roger. Remember me?" asked the girl, dressed in blue jeans.

"Yeah, I think so," Roger said, fumbling in his thoughts to recall who she was.

"It's me, Cynthia."

"Oh, of course," he replied, embarrassed that he could forget his own cousin.

"Hey Roger," said the boy.

"Hey Johnny. How are ya?" Roger asked, shaking hands.

"Doin' okay," Johnny answered.

The older man was dressed in a light-beige, short-sleeve, golf shirt, black pants, and black, shiny leather shoes. He walked on the grass, approaching Roger, and gave Roger a big smile. Roger smelled the cologne as they shook hands.

"Hiya Roger. How have you been? Is your dad here?" the man asked.

"Hi Uncle Jack. I'm doing okay. Yeah, he's inside," Roger said.

"And who's this?" the man asked.

"This is my youngest brother, Paul," Roger answered.

"Well good to meet ya Paul. You know I'm your uncle, huh?" he asked.

Paul just smiled and nodded his head.

"Paul, go get Dad," Roger ordered.

Immediately, Paul went into the house like a dart, but the other siblings raced out like rockets. Their famous Uncle Jack Owens and two of their cousins had decided to pay them a very unexpected visit.

Ross made his way outside, squinting heavily from the intense sunlight.

"Hi Ross. Long time no see, huh?" Jack said.

"Sure has been a long time. Not since I took some of the kids to your house a couple of times," Ross answered his brother, who was two years younger than Ross.

"How old were you, Roger, when you went there? About seven or eight?" asked Jack.

"Yeah, that sounds about right," Roger replied.

"Boy, look at you now. There's a contract in Hollywood with your name on it," he said as they laughed. As everyone took turns hugging Uncle Jack, he couldn't help noticing how attractive all of Ross' daughters were. "Ross, I'm just floored. You have a beautiful looking family."

"Well, thank you Jack," he said, somewhat embarrassed.

"Where's Helen?" Ross asked.

"Oh, she wasn't up for all the driving and the whole trip. She's at home with our other kids," he responded.

"That's too bad."

"As you know, we're in Phoenix, now. I'm doing well with real estate, and plus my doggone allergies don't feel so bad out there," Jack continued.

For a moment, there was silence.

Sensing the lack of conversation, they both walked inside, and Jack warmly greeted Mary. Jack and his two kids visited the whole afternoon, but they didn't stay for dinner. It was exciting to have Uncle Jack visit, but it was unbelievably awkward for him as well as for Ross, and they both knew it. Both men were born to the same father, Ross Wheeler Owens, Sr., and the same mother, Emeline Louise French, and both were born in Tulsa, Oklahoma. They even had one sister in common, the youngest of all three, named Evelyn, who lived in Los Angeles, but that's where all the similarities ended. The two men could not have been any more different.

Ross Owens was a devout Baptist Reverend with an A.A. Degree, but he struggled unimaginably to bring money home and put clothes in the closet and food on the table for his large family. He was a simple man who put his life into outreach and evangelism to help people come to know God on the streets of Los Angeles. He always wanted to do more. In fact, as an example, he always promised to treat Roger to steak dinners in some downtown restaurant, but that never happened. Always well dressed, with an even blend of self worth and humility, Ross nevertheless lived a meager lifestyle, not once owning his own home.

A graduate of Wichita State College, Jack Owens was a handsome baritone singer who started out in radio in Chicago. Jack, a Roman Catholic and member of St. Thomas the Apostle Catholic Church, found work at an experimental television station in the early 1930's as a piano player. He was also a general-purpose singer and sometimes held up the "applause" signs for the audience. Then he became a featured vocalist on the *Pennzoil Parade*, *Real Silk Hour* and *Paradise Girl of Chicago* radio shows. By 1932, at the age of 20, he married the star of *Paradise Girl*, Helen Streiff, and soon he established the Owens-Kemp Music Co., a publishing business, when they moved to California.

In 1934, they moved back to Chicago, where he joined a new radio program called *The Breakfast Club with Don McNeill*. Looking at it now, it was part National Public Radio, part Saturday Night Live. Thousands upon thousands woke up every morning and started their days with the famous "March Around the Breakfast Table." There were plenty of acts, singers, news, and comedy, all delivered by the show's regulars. It was a radio show unlike any other, and it helped support NBC in a major way during the early years. By the 1940's, it brought in revenue for newly established ABC, a legally required offshoot of NBC that was sold and which grew into a huge competitor of NBC. *The Breakfast Club* continued to run well into the late 1960's, before signing off the air for good.

Jack, who was the regular male singer for nearly two years, once proved himself quite a character by agreeing to sing on a high trapeze, all in the name of a good show. But by 1936, he was charmed by Hollywood to become an off-screen singer for lead actors like Jimmy

Stewart. In 1944, one of the main male singers on *The Breakfast Club*
left to join the armed forces and was replaced by Jack Owens. Jack and
Helen packed their bags and headed back to Chicago.

He rejoined the cast and, soon after, created a unique singing style
that unintentionally caught on like wildfire with the women in the studio audience. With his wife, Helen, sitting among the audience, Jack
grabbed a portable microphone and casually walked over to her. The
crowd, growing anxious with every moment, waited for Jack. He began
singing to his wife, and as the words of the song "Love Is The Sweetest
Thing" poured like sunlit, amber honey over laid-out blue velvet, the
women in the crowd went wild. The reaction was so overwhelming
that, every morning, Jack walked into the audience and sang to the at-
tentive women, one by one. He often sat on their laps, crooning his way
into their hearts. Having deserved his new nickname, "The Cruising
Crooner," for the way he cruised through the audience, Jack Owens
fluttered female pulses but flustered some media critics. One such
critic, John Crosby of the *New York Times*, saw the special 1948 tele-
cast of *The Breakfast Club*, and he wrote his reaction.

> I strongly object to a singer named Jack Owens who cruises
> around the audience singing love songs to girls. By radio this is
> painful; by television it is excruciating. Mr. Owens kisses the
> women, musses their hair, and sits on their laps. Why some irate
> babe hasn't broken his neck is beyond me.

By the mid to late 1940's, Jack continued to hit it big with his song-
writing ability. He had written a song called "The Kid With The Rip In
His Pants," and as soon as Roy Rogers and The Sons Of The Pioneers
recorded it, it became a favorite of many, including Gabby Hayes. At
the same time, Jack wrote other songs, such as "Hi Neighbor," which
was featured in the 1941 movie, *San Antonio Rose*. He also co-wrote
the silly tune "The Hut Sut Song," and wrote the million-selling, number one Hit Parade song, "How Soon" performed, most notably, by
Bing Crosby. If that wasn't enough, Jack outdid himself by penning the
most intoxicating, fun, and popular Hawaiian hula song of all time,
"The Hukilau Song." With its contagious lyrics, like "Oh, we're going
to a hukilau, a huki, huki, huki, huki, hukilau," the song was destined
for greatness.

However, Jack wasn't the only Owens writing classic, Hawaiian-
themed music. There was, indeed, a more famous songwriter, who not
only wrote a slew of great Hawaiian songs, but who co-created an improved version of the island drink, the Mai Tai. Born in Nebraska in

1902, Harry Owens became known as "Mr. Hawaii," but according to Roger's family, there was no known relation to Jack and his brother Ross.

Jack, who was America's 10th most popular vocalist from 1937 through 1944, finally left *The Breakfast Club* in 1949 and moved with his wife and kids back to the West Coast. While in California, Jack and his wife bought a mansion in Beverly Hills. Within a year, they moved to an equally impressive estate overlooking the beach in Pacific Palisades.

During the first few years of the 1950's, Jack had his own television show called *The Jack Owens Show*. In the first year, the weekly show featured Jack as the host, as well as his wife and three children. In the next two years, he shared the camera with his eldest daughter Mary Ann. The half-hour show was filled with songs, celebrity interviews, and discussions held at the kitchen table regarding family problems mailed in from viewers. In 1957, they all moved to Phoenix, Arizona, where Jack retired from show business but continued to work in real estate.

In a somewhat twisted bit of irony, Ross did have his own radio show, *The Baptist Hour*, for six months on a local radio station in San Diego County. The simple, almost hokey but sincere, program aired locally during the early 1950's, the same time as Jack's television show. Furthermore, in 1968, Ross himself would make headlines on the front page of the city section in the *Los Angeles Times*, complete with story and a large photograph of him, but for a reason no one would have ever dreamed.

With the warmth of the sun beating down, Roger, wearing blue jeans and a white t-shirt, washed the windows of his car, while everyone else was inside with Jack. He recalled the two different times he visited Jack's elegant homes. It was around 1950, when Roger, age seven, Ruthie, age six, and Philip and Priscilla, both age three, first tagged along with Ross to take up Jack and Helen's invitation to visit them in Beverly Hills. They drove up and were taken with how unbelievable the place was. The pristine, white mansion, on Sunset Blvd. sat on property lined with huge trees. Once inside, they were overwhelmed by the presence of maids, a cook, a baby grand piano, nicely decorated living rooms, and a scenic view of two Cadillacs parked in the driveway.

Excited to have the kids over, Jack was in a playful mood.

"Hey Roger," Jack said, trying to get his little nephew's attention.

"Here, try and stop the monkey," he added as he produced a sparkling, clean, silver dollar and rolled it on the floor toward him. The visit only lasted for the afternoon, but nearly a year later, they were back at their uncle's new house. Jack and Helen had moved to a palatial home overlooking the beach in Pacific Palisades. The new place actually had a swimming pool in addition to all of the luxuries of the previous home. Roger was blown away by the presence of the pool, an obvious sign of wealth and privilege in those days. He could hardly believe his dad and Jack were brothers. In fact, it would require getting older to understand why the two men seldom spoke to each other. Roger was done with cleaning his car and leaned back against it, standing with arms folded, and looking up into the blue sky in a contemplative manner. With the sights and sounds of splashing water and childhood screams of excitement still fresh in his mind, he wondered how two brothers could be so distant and so different. Perhaps, he thought, Jack must have wondered all those years why Ross had so many kids with very little income to raise them. Jack did help him out a couple of times, but probably decided not to go too far with that, possibly because lending money all the time wouldn't have been a good idea. Whatever the reasons, Roger let it go and walked back inside, starving for a sandwich and a soda.

$\mathcal{C}$ 9

Young Man's Dreams in Blue

Finally, life was back to normal at the Owens house. With Mary running the apartments and Ross finding additional work collecting money for the L.A. Mission, they found some stability, long overdue in their household. All of the kids, except for Roger and Ruth, were enrolled either in middle school or elementary school. Even though Dominguez High School was literally just around the corner, Ruth nevertheless insisted on attending Paramount High with her brother. Before she was allowed to take a yellow school bus to Paramount High every day, she first needed to obtain a special permit that allowed her continued enrollment, since she was out of the school district. So her father took her to get the permit. Every day at school, Ruth loved working at the student store, stuffing down free popcorn and candy bars.

At age 17, Ruth had outgrown her middle school years and her rowdy *pachuka* buddies and had blossomed into a young woman before her dad's eyes. The time had finally come for Ross. He could no longer avoid it, and so, he faithfully assumed the role of enforcer. As the father of six young daughters, he had to keep a wary eye out for their safety. Even the next youngest daughter, Priscilla, was already 15 years old. At a moment's notice, Ross had to possess the keen instinct of deciding between the capable, worthy young men who planned on courting his girls and the run-of-the-mill, unpromising, good-for-nothing street boys.

Ruth's new boyfriend was hardly a run-of-the-mill, unpromising, good-for-nothing street boy, but already, he was putting Ross to the test. The slim 21 year-old, named Bob Green, with jet-black hair shaved into a flat top, had a great job in carpet cleaning and was a youth leader for his local Church of God of Prophecy. He had spent plenty of time around the apartments because he knew both the Meyer family and some friends, the Alexander boys, all of whom were ten-

77

ants. However, when Ross met Bob, he realized that Bob lacked a college education, something Ross was adamant about. Ross sat him down on the sofa and covered several topics, grilling him like a New York steak.

"You say you are a Christian, huh? Well, start talking," Ross said.

Despite Ross's serious doubts about him and his education, he reluctantly allowed Ruth to date him. On Friday evenings, Bob showed up with other young people in his '49 Plymouth, picked up Ruth, and headed to the church youth service. Roger, sensing Bob's easy manner, got along with him, but was somewhat reserved in interacting with him.

It was now 1962, and Roger had reached the point where he could no longer live in the same house anymore. As a college freshman, he began looking for his own place, a place that was somewhere, anywhere, just as long as he could study quietly and, for once in his life, feel independent and self-supporting.

So he looked around the area and found a small place to live in Lynwood. The house was owned by an elderly lady who charged Roger $25 a month to rent one of the extra bedrooms in a back part of the house. Not long after settling in, he noticed a man standing on the backyard grass, answering nature's call.

Baffled at the man's audacity to do that in the woman's backyard, he opened the window to yell at the supposed intruder.

"Hey, what do you think you're doing?" Roger said.

"Say, man, I live here in the garage. Out here is my only restroom. Lady charges me ten bucks a month in rent," replied the man. So Roger walked outside and checked out the garage. After seeing and smelling the garage, he immediately quit worrying about the somewhat high rent of $25 he had to pay for his "hole in the wall."

In college, Roger did well and made several friends. He spent his time watching movies and sports and going to house parties. Still somewhat shy, he started to hang out with some of his more outgoing, black friends, and every week they would check in at the student union on campus to hear the word on the latest location for the weekend house party. As he relaxed more and gained more confidence, he became as outgoing as they were. One of Roger's friends, Fox, as he was known, had been seeing a girl and knew that she had a sister named Carolyn. So Fox set Roger up with the light-skinned black girl, and the two hit it off. They started showing up at the house parties, dancing the "Bugaloo" and declining most of the Ripple offered them every few minutes. They even double-dated with Fox and his girl, Laurel, a few times at the drive-in. But all of them were always unsure at the end of the night exactly which movie it was that was showing.

During the major league baseball off-season, Roger collected unemployment to get by. He also worked at Rams and USC football games, but since there were only a few homes games for either team, he didn't make much money during the football season.

Even with a steady girlfriend and an active social life, there was no equal to the excitement building inside Roger, as he counted down every passing day until the beginning of a new Dodger era in their new home at Chavez Ravine.

Finally the wait was over.

It was Opening Day, April 10, 1962, at Dodger Stadium.

There it stood in the middle of Los Angeles, with its embryonic, four years of gestation finished. The peerless, stately cathedral of sport rose up out of the placenta of dirt, wood, and steel. It was now prepared to be the beating, pounding heart of the city, pumping blue Dodger blood into the circulatory system of the Los Angeles economy. The breathtaking and spectacular Dodger home was complete with a rainbow of red, orange, yellow, and blue seating that contrasted with the beautiful white architecture and the earth tones of the playing field. It looked as though the design was one, huge collaboration of pure baseball fans and a big-budgeted, Hollywood movie studio. Even more, it was owned and managed by a family. It was that perfect.

Roger showed up the usual two hours ahead of game time to stand in the vendor's line, requesting to sell peanuts. Sometimes he had the approval to sell peanuts and other times to sell ice cream, depending on whether the higher ranked vendors showed up and if the Dodgers needed more peanut vendors. In any case, he was in awe of the stadium. His job had a brand new charm and electricity, and that didn't even take into account the massive number of fans about to pour in.

Night after night, home game after home game, Roger worked the crowds in the right and left field pavilions, and other times, in the orange, loge level. Sometimes he satisfied people's desire for frozen, chocolate malts, and sometimes he handed or tossed bags of peanuts that left them with an uncontrollable urge to wash it all down with a large soda. It was a cycle of consumption that was multiplied well over 50,000 times by those in attendance every game, and that was even before the players took the field.

Roger still planned on becoming a highway patrol officer when he became 21, but he was content, nonetheless, to earn a living at Dodger

Stadium, supporting himself by his consistent effort and hard work during the busier, first five innings of every game. He continued his studies, getting closer to earning his degree and perhaps graduating in another year. As he worked on his college assignments in his one room pad, he listened to music on his portable transistor radio that he had just bought. News about increasing hostility in some small, poor country called Vietnam began to worry him, as it worried others across the country. Such reports became more frequent and, at the age of 19, Roger was a prime target in the crosshairs of Uncle Sam's draft. There were several days when, alone in his dimly lit place, doing homework for stern, unapproachable professors, he wondered about this Vietnam War. He looked out of the window and noticed how the overcast weather produced a rumbling in the heavens and brought clouds of rapidly deepening gray. He looked down as faint raindrops collected on the windowsill. He stared at the rainwater as it slid down innocently on the side of the glass until the rain picked up and came down with the intensity and weight of a tidal wave falling from the sky.

As spring became summer, Roger couldn't think of a better place to work. There were so many happy people at the ballpark, each and every one of them enjoying the afternoon game, and content with their sunny Dodgers and their shaded seats. Holding Dodger Dogs in one hand and cracking peanut shells with their teeth, young Dodger fans looked up at their parents with expressions of gratitude that went beyond words. Roger noticed these quick, affectionate glimpses all the time, and they made him feel good. Not to be outdone by cute appreciative kids, the Dodger heroes on the field had plenty of market-share in the hearts and minds of fans, as well as vendors who took a minute to absorb the truly happy moments that the stadium offered. Even Roger was in awe of the fact that while he sold peanuts with simple overhand tossing, Sandy Koufax, Johnny Podres, Don Drysdale and Ron Perranoski, just to name a few, were on the mound a few hundred feet away, hurling their best stuff at quaking Giant, Pirate, or Reds batters.

Then, on one late-summer evening at the stadium, there was magic.

For Roger Owens.

He showed up to work as usual. Armed with his large cardboard box of peanut bags, Roger began making the rounds of the orange loge section of the ballpark. It was early, but fans were already arriving. As usual, his dexterity was sharp, as he had to catch tossed quarters from every fan who bought a bag of peanuts. Since they were 25 cents a bag, catching the tossed quarters was always as much a part of the skill of being a vendor as selling the peanuts themselves.

Roger just finished handing a bag to a customer when he turned around at the cry of another fan several rows away. More people now made their way down the stairs, carefully reading the ticket stubs for row and seat number. Suddenly, they stood still, obstructing the travel path of a simple toss to the seated customer, who was yelling a second and third time for his peanuts. Young Roger stayed calm and instinctively surveyed the situation.

He couldn't put too high of an arch on the toss, because he noticed how the concrete rafter above, from the next highest level of stadium seating, was not high enough to allow a throw like that.

Some fans were already seated and, sensing the tension of the moment, they sat there grinning devilishly, as if watching a show. They sat back comfortably, but with undivided attention, to see what this young peanut vendor would do about the situation.

Before panic set it, he whimsically and nonchalantly poised the bag of peanuts to throw behind his back in one sweeping motion and let it fly.

The bag soared with a slight curve to it, sailing past the indecisive roadblock of people that caused the dilemma, and into the waiting hands of the shocked man.

"Hey. That was cool," the customer said in amazement, holding the bag in his lap.

The group of fans perked up on the edges of their seats and stared in silence with jaws hung open, as the bag flew straight to the man several feet away. They began to cheer, whistle, and clap for Roger.

"Did you see that?" one fan told another. "The peanut man just threw it behind his back, and it went right to the guy, like a sling shot."

Roger's heart raced from the sudden burst of adrenalin, both in response to their emotion and to the uncanny accuracy of his peanut toss. He blushed from all the attention.

It took a minute for what he had just done to sink in.

While the majority of those in paid attendance knew nothing of what had happened, those who were fortunate enough to be there counted themselves as witnesses to the conception of a realized new talent and, with it, the binding in marriage of professional obligation and childlike improvisation. Roger's peanut pitch was indeed a miraculous throw. But it needed to be. It was a pitch that made everyone look. It made them smile. It made them ask him to do it again. It made them enjoy their peanuts even more. It made them want to come back to Dodger Stadium again and again.

It was the *perfect* pitch.

$\mathcal{C}$ 10

Sharing Songs in the Key of Life

By the end of the year, Roger was thrilled by the impression he had made with fans. He thought about how he had slowly worked his new, trick, peanut-pitching ability into his vending routine and how he gained confidence with every toss. He couldn't wait until the beginning of the next baseball season.

At the Owens house, Mary did well with her large responsibility of managing, and Ross continued to lay down the law of the household. Many times Ruth could not call her boyfriend because of the phone bill, or see him because her dad was home, so Bob set a time when he would call a pay phone from his house. If Ruth was in her bedroom, she could hear the pay phone ringing from across the street. Then she would cross Compton Blvd. knowing it could only be Bob calling for her.

On Sundays, Ross made all of his kids take naps, as always, but that included Ruth and Priscilla, who were both reluctant to comply. Whenever Bob drove up in his new, white '59 Chevy Impala to their house on Sundays, Ross always saw him coming.

"Go away, Bob. She's taking a nap," Ross boomed forcefully from the doorstep. So Bob, who had taken just a few steps toward the house, quickly turned around and got back in his car, snapping his fingers in disappointment. Ross stood and watched the young man drive off. As he stared, his mouth turned into a grin. He didn't like the boy that much, but he was starting to. Besides, he didn't have too many things to hold against him.

Ross found life to be rewarding, even in the daily routine. His personal convictions motivated him, and it brought him joy to help others spiritually. Even though his family was still quite young and lacked so many material possessions, he kept the faith in his God that everything would eventually turn out just fine. Whether at work, or before he went to bed listening to Billy Graham Crusades, or while watching baseball games on television, he realized how much his kids and wife meant to him. Ross cherished every moment with them and, as he walked to their rooms and watched them sleep, his heart melted at the idea of them staying that age forever. But that was impossible, because they were growing so quickly.

One night, Ross stopped at a nearby Laundromat to count all the money he had collected for the L.A. Mission during his routes. Ross sat down and patiently and carefully laid out all the money to count. Others around him eyed him suspiciously.

Within a few minutes, an officer showed up in the doorway.

Ross felt uneasy as the cop walked toward him, almost wearing his accusation of Ross on his sleeve. They figured they caught their man, the one who had been robbing the Laundromat recently.

The officer handcuffed Ross, arresting him on robbery charges. Completely puzzled, Ross spent the night in jail, but he made the most of the opportunity. During that night and again in the morning, he witnessed to the jailed men of a risen Savior, until he was cleared of all charges and released. Ross' kids were surprised when they heard he was in jail for the night, but when all was explained, they soon went back to studying and playing games.

By now, it was early 1963, and Roger prepared mentally for a new season at the stadium. He went out often with his girlfriend, Carolyn, but he also found time to study and write research papers. Roger had formed sincere opinions about the times in which he lived. Whether he picked topics like smoking, Volkswagens, or race relations, Roger was able to convey his thoughts with passion. His impressive writing ability was noticeable in excerpts from two different essays, the first one entitled *It Relieves Gas Pains* and the second, *Somebody Different*.

> The best car for me is a Volkswagen! Why? In the first place let's consider gas mileage. I work at practically every sports event in Los Angeles and therefore I am always driving to and from Los Angeles almost all the time. A Volkswagen that is in good condition should get at least thirty miles to a gallon of gas. Here I can save money, which I like very much. But there are many other advantages in a Volkswagen besides just gas mileage. A Volkswagen is a car that's easy to keep up. That's because every Volkswagen is designed and built to be serviced efficiently, quickly, and economically. Take parts, for instance.

Most parts for the Volkswagen are interchangeable from one year to the next. Even when a part is improved the new part is usually designed to fit previous year Volkswagens as well.

It seems to me that my life would be changed in many more ways, than just the color of my skin. Many Whites seem to assume that U.S. Negroes are better off financially today than ever before, but although Negroes made substantial income gains during World War II, they were not permanent. In the past decade, the median family income for non-Whites (now $3,191) has slipped from 57% of White family income to 53%. The non-white unemployment rate is now 10.7%, almost double that of Whites. In such a situation, the Negro has had little incentive for self-improvement. Until recently, Negro children didn't think about being an engineer or a scientist. So they didn't study calculus, algebra, physics or electricity. And then people turn around and say, 'Why don't those Negro kids study hard like everybody else?' You wouldn't think a plumber's job was much, but it is. A plumber doesn't work too hard or too long, but he gets paid big, and Negroes who have that skill would like to get that pay. But Negroes cannot even become plumbers because of the arrant discrimination of many of the nation's craft unions.

Almost half of about 900 civil rights demonstrations staged since last May have revolved around the right of the Negro to eat in any place that he can afford, to sleep in any hotel or motel, to play in any park, or to enjoy the facilities of any other so-called "public accommodation."

These things, which the Negro is fighting for, are privileges I just take for granted. I could think of nothing that would be more humiliating than to get out of my car, and have one of my [hypothetical] daughters ask to go to the bathroom, and have to tell her, "No, we can't stop at any of these places."

Having recently celebrated his 20th birthday, Roger began the baseball season selling peanuts, while his brother Philip sold soda. The two kept busy at the stadium, but at the end of the day, Roger was concerned about Vietnam.

As news poured in over his radio, he sensed that the turmoil in that part of the world would not diminish any time soon. He sat in his room one night, along with Philip who was visiting, and thought about joining the Army National Guard to fulfill his military obligations, instead of enlisting to serve in a battle that became more deeply entrenched each month. He shared his thoughts with his brother, who was not quite 17 years old. Without dwelling on serious topics too long, Roger tuned the radio to listen to some music. He stopped when he heard the Temptations and turned up the volume. While the song played, the two then talked about the ballpark, girls they saw in the crowds, and their plans for the weekend. Besides talk of work and girls, Roger and Philip concluded that they would also have some fun by taking Elizabeth, Lois, and Paul to the mountains, the beaches, and to Marineland in San Diego. Even when they treated her to a simple ice cream sundae, Lois felt like she had the best big brothers any girl could have. Lois, the youngest of the Owens daughters until Grace was born, felt lonely much of the time. With Roger out of the house, a hard-working father away from the house, and a distant mother inside the house, old Bert Owens became her confidant. Bert sensed when chasing tennis balls and little birds had to wait. So he sat quietly and attentively looked up at Lois' sad face, knowing it was time once again to listen to her feelings.

She spoke of the happy moments, like the times when Dad would leave the house, her brothers and sisters would turn the radio on and play loud, rock music. Then there were times they snuck food into bed, like the two weeks in a row they had nothing but fried onions and potatoes. But then she remembered how Mom was such a stranger and how it made her feel confused when Mom acted the way she did and how Dad was careful to explain that Mom was "sick." Lois also remembered how embarrassing it was to bring to school that horrible, orange sandwich wrapping that left her no recourse but to eat her lunch alone in the bathroom.

Bert continued to listen.

She recalled the time Dad ran into her and her friends at a local store. She was on a budget of five cents a day to buy milk since there wasn't much at home. Occasionally, she saved that money for three days to buy a 15-cent package of Twinkies. On the day she stood in line to buy Twinkies, Dad caught her and completely embarrassed her in front of everyone. Before she could go on with her stories, tears filled her eyes, like two brown boats drifting across a lifeless, blue ocean.

Bert had a feeling he knew which story she was about to tell.

Lois continued.

She confessed how she saved her milk money, enough to pay 35 cents for her class pictures. When she finally received them, she looked at them and sighed. Suddenly, her eyes welled up with tears. She knew she couldn't keep them and risk Mom and Dad finding out that she hadn't been buying milk for herself in almost a week and a half. Barely able to see well enough through her watery eyes the detail of her pictures, she tore them to shreds in a matter of seconds.

Lois had more to tell that afternoon, and Bert had nothing but time.

$\big\{$ *11*

Arsenal of Pitches

I t was almost the summer of '63. On a Saturday in late May, Roger drove to the Paramount First Assembly of God to meet the rest of his family and some friends there. All of them were there for a wedding rehearsal. Ross and Mary were standing near the altar talking with Ruth as Roger showed up. Bob had already proposed to Ruth, after going together for nearly two years. The couple had full approval from both sets of parents, and so Ruth worked and began saving her money for the wedding. As Ross saw how much money was being spent on flowers and everything else for the wedding, he became upset and told Ruth he would not walk her down the aisle during the ceremony.

Ruth was extremely hurt.

A church friend offered to let her husband do the honor, but with a month remaining before the special day, Ross changed his mind and apologized. He walked her down the aisle, proud to give away his "number one" daughter.

On June 1, 1963, Ross' little Ruthie, all grown up, got married. Ross finally saw the promising, responsible, young man within his new son-in-law. Like his new wife, Bob also fought the odds by growing up on Century Blvd. and San Pedro St. in Los Angeles, with a poor family, and a mother who also had suffered from a nervous breakdown. In the wedding, one of Bob's brothers, David, was the best man, while Roger and Philip were two of the other groomsmen. Roger, standing at six feet tall, and Philip, at six feet two inches, appeared in their tuxedos like towering handsome heroes of the silver screen. Philip, with his dark brown hair and deep blue eyes, had the cool hand look of a very young Paul Newman. At age two and a half, Baby Grace, with her curly locks of platinum blonde, was not in the wedding, because she was still too young to be the flower girl. Priscilla, however, was the

87

maid of honor. Elizabeth, almost age 13, and Lois, soon to be age 12, were also in the wedding, making their way down the aisle to light the candles behind the altar. But as they did so, Lois eyed her sister anxiously and whispered to her to hurry up because Elizabeth's candle wasn't lighting. Nevertheless, it was a memorable ceremony, full of emotion, especially for Ross and Mary. Everyone was happy for the newlyweds, but Roger was especially proud of his beautiful sister. Soon, all eyes were on Priscilla, a talkative brunette like Ruth, who looked like a mix between Donna Reed and Sally Field as *Gidget*. Having caught the bouquet at the reception, "Buttinski," as she was known for always interrupting others, was next on the list to find love, and, with it, the ticket to finally leave home.

With Roger and Ruth now out of the house, the rest of the family continued with the daily grind of futility in finding privacy and finding food. It seemed as though even Bert wanted to leave the house too, as he stayed away sometimes for days at a time. It was a known fact that he liked to get in dogfights now and then, but when any of the kids called for him lately, he seemed to be distracted somewhere in the neighborhood. One night, at nearly 11:00 p.m., there was loud scratching at the front door. With the kids not quite asleep yet in bed, they heard a familiar howling outside. Elizabeth sat up and peeked outside her bedroom door. She saw her dad dragging Bert inside. Chewed up and covered with blood, poor Bert Owens managed to sit up and humbly look up at Ross. The kids raced to the front door and helped clean all the wounds they could find on Bert, whom they hadn't seen in three days. They were determined to make sure he would be okay, and after a few days, Bert was almost like new.

As the baseball season came to a close, Roger realized that his new peanut pitching ability excited fans as well as himself. He loved his job with a passion. He had used the behind-the-back toss somewhat sparingly throughout the entire year, because he wanted to master the entertaining throw. By 1964, however, Roger began developing a full arsenal of pitches.

With emotional trauma still lingering after Kennedy's assassination, the country found itself, almost overnight, engulfed by the escalation of fighting in Vietnam. Roger registered with the Army National Guard as planned. It was depressing to hear of young servicemen coming home as casualties of both war and poorly defined military objectives. But even so, Roger had to live life as best as he knew how, and that included the therapeutic, wonderful job of being the crowd's favorite peanut man at Dodger Stadium.

During the first two months of the '64 Dodger season, Roger began showing off his new skills. He had spent many hours practicing his peanut pitching by trying to hit the pillows on his sofa or by throwing them to friends who were willing to climb monkey bars at a local park.

Fans who showed up expecting only a Dodger game were treated to a triple threat of entertainment, which included Roger's outgoing, joke-telling salesmanship, his live peanut pitching, and the thrill of being on the receiving end of the trick-thrown bags. All game long, Roger worked the crowd with his behind-the-back tosses. As one fan stood up to be his target, Roger swept his arm behind him, and in a quick, wrist-snapping swoosh, he let the bags go. They sailed every time to the waiting hands of the peanut-craving fans.

Suddenly, with the people thinking another patented behind-the-back throw was on the way, Roger quickly kicked up his left leg and threw the bag of peanuts under his leg, straight to a fan.

The fans went wild.

The place lit up with enthusiastic cheering and whistling for Roger's amazing, under-the-leg toss. They couldn't believe the fun they were having in the stands. If there was any doubt that Roger was *their* peanut vendor, the peanut man of the orange loge level on the third base side, or of the entire stadium for that matter, then it vanished the minute Roger unleashed the incomprehensible, behind-the-back, double bagger.

With pinpoint accuracy known only to heat-seeking missiles and other advanced trajectories of military science, Roger zoned in on his targets. Two different people, standing in entirely different places, were the beneficiaries of a skilled double bag pitch. That pitch really brought down the house but lifted Roger to a level he never before imagined.

"Can you believe this guy?" one fan said to his friend. "Did you see that?"

"No, I missed it. What happened, man?" the other man replied.

"The peanut guy just threw two bags of peanuts at the same time, behind his back, and they landed in the hands of two different---," the man answered, interrupted by the crowd's sudden burst of loud cheering.

"See? He just did it again. Is that cool or what?" he said in excitement.

"Yeah I saw it. They went to two different people. Far out," he said.

"Hey let's buy some. Lend me a quarter."

"Okay here man."

"Hey over here, Peanut Man!"

"Did he hear you? Say it again man."

"Over here, peanuts right he---. Damn, here it comes."

Just then the bags of peanuts thwacked against the man's clumsy hands, and fell to the ground. Both men were rolling over, hysterical with laughter.

"Ahh, you idiot. He sent you an under-the-legger and you dropped it," the other man said, barely getting the words out beyond his uncontrollable laughter.

"I know, I know," the man replied, laughing too. Both of the bearded, long haired hippies continued to laugh and giggle at the dropped bag of peanuts the rest of the night.

Roger enjoyed his life working with his brother Philip and his vendor friends, Jay Bieber, Mort Rose, James, and Jordan. James and Jordan lived near him and carpooled with Roger and Philip. Roger was paid fifty cents from each person for gas money, and since he had a gas saving VW, he considered it extra spending money. At first, James complained about the fifty cents, asking Roger if he would get charged another 25 cents just to turn the radio station. Sometimes they would drive in Roger's car to Jordan's house to work out in his garage so they could handle the vigorous work of selling soda, ice cream, or peanuts up and down the steps at Dodger Stadium. Other times, they carpooled to work, looking out of the car windows, feeling the cool blasts of wind against their faces, and bobbing their heads back and forth as Roger turned up Little Stevie Wonder's "Uptight," on the radio.

Despite Roger's new success at the ballpark, duty called him away from college and work when he was ordered to report to the local Army National Guard office. With his A.A. Degree on hold, Roger said goodbye to his family and girlfriend, who promised to write him all the time. Roger showed up, unsure about what he had gotten himself into but certain that it was better than actually serving in Vietnam.

He was off to basic training, or two months of boot camp, in Louisiana's Fort Polk. Life there was absolutely nothing like it was at home. But Roger, with his happy go lucky manner, had been through boot camp once before at Naylor's Ranch, so he did fine. It didn't help, however, that the drill sergeant, Sgt. Rye, was so tough that he made Mrs. Naylor look like Mrs. Beatty holding out a tray full of freshly baked cupcakes.

After boot camp was over, he was ordered to fulfill the remaining part of the sixth month commitment by selecting a specialty and then receiving training. Naturally, he selected Military Police. So, he was immediately sent to Fort Gordon in Georgia, to further train as a Military Policeman.

Roger bunked with a bunch of guys who quickly became his friends. In the few quiet moments he had to himself, Roger recalled the basic training in Louisiana and how, in rural areas surrounding the fort, he had been shocked to see signs above water fountains saying "Colored" and "White Only." He even saw an ice rink that only allowed white people, not that too many non-Whites ever had the inclination to go ice skating in those days, but it was nevertheless appalling, especially to a forward thinking Californian.

Roger had a few letters from Carolyn that he opened and read as soon as they were delivered. However, even before he left to join the Army National Guard, there was a measurable drifting apart between Roger and his girlfriend, and despite the letters, the training that kept him away for several months only accentuated it.

Every evening, Roger relieved his fellow officer atop the platform, overlooking the prison stockade. Standing guard in full uniform, complete with white helmet and white band around his left arm with the bold initials, *M.P.*, Roger paced back and forth, breaking the dark, eerie silence of night with his portable transistor radio. He was a fan of all kinds of music, so he didn't need to change the station too often. On his watch, he felt lonely, sometimes tired and homesick. The tough exterior of poise and uniform belied his insecure and irrepressible inner thoughts. On the radio, he heard the usual array of feel good songs, love ballads, rock anthems, and social protest numbers. While one song pleaded for people to smile on their brothers, and to try to love one another, the next one cued Roger's feelings of emotional distance from Carolyn. Of all the songs the station could have played that moment, it had to be "You've Lost That Lovin' Feeling" by the Righteous Brothers. Roger stood on his watch, stoically hiding his cascading emotions, and while the rain silently started to fall, he listened to the sharp lyrics delivered by the smooth, soulful duo.

At the stadium, the Dodger fans were dismayed at Roger's absence. His brother, Philip, told the people that despite Roger being called away for basic training, he would be back soon.

Six months passed, and Roger was set to return. Roger simply had to attend seminars held in Los Angeles on a monthly basis, and had to report for two weeks of training camp each summer at Fort Irwin in the Mojave Desert. This added commitment to a five-year program with the Army National Guard was nothing compared to a tour of duty on the other side of the world. It was like comparing the minuscule weight of a hobo's knapsack to the burdensome, army canvas bag, stuffed with gear and loaded down by the trauma of young Americans sent to fight in mine-strewn rice fields and jungles steaming more from smoke and ammunition than from the Vietnamese humidity

When Roger arrived, his family greeted him joyfully.

For 22 year-old Roger, 1965 was indeed another eventful year.

He had enough of the shack in Lynwood, and moved to an apartment rented out by Philip and Philip's friend Gene Turner. Located in Compton, the apartment was easily a step up for Roger, especially when he had all of Gene's Beach Boys albums to listen to. The three young men took turns with household chores and enjoyed life together. Roger was busy much of the time with classes and preparing to graduate that year.

After graduation from Compton Community College, Roger considered joining the California Highway Patrol. With the beginning of the baseball season, Roger was once again excited to greet his faithful fans. They welcomed him back, along with his entertaining, unique style and approachable personality. He took his time, talking with the fans, especially before game time. He hammed it up, told jokes, kidded them, and listened to their stories.

More than just the peanut man, he was their friend.

Philip, on the other hand, was friendly but reserved. He already made the switch to selling ice cream, but he wanted to someday sell peanuts, perhaps working the same area as Roger and splitting the profits. Philip savored the idea of trying his hand at some trick peanut tossing too, and giving the grateful fans not one Owens boy, but two.

Roger, however, could not entirely savor the taste of jubilation that marked his return to the stadium. There was yet the bitterness of the sudden uprising and racial rioting in the Watts area of Los Angeles and, being in the Army National Guard, he was instructed to be near a phone after work, should he be called upon for duty on the streets. As he sat on his couch, transfixed by the live news of riots, fires, and chaos, Roger dreaded the possible scenario of hearing his phone ring while watching on television, the armed guards pushing back crowds, and knowing it was the National Guard calling. How the imaginary ringing continued incessantly in his mind gripped his conscience. Roger leaned back into the sofa, turned off the television, and thought of his friend, Mort Rose. Mort hadn't been quite as fortunate. Mort, who did his basic training at the same time as Roger at Fort Polk, was called to hit the streets and bring order to the neighborhoods. Literally quaking in his boots, he was terrified that he was out patrolling the streets, night after eerie night, trying to silence the rage erupting in the forsaken communities. Roger was thankful, but he continued to think of his friend. Roger lay down in bed, sinking into the depths of warm sheets and buoyant pillow. A smile suddenly appeared on his face. With his eyes closed, he thought of the time he realized that Mort was doing his basic training at the same place as Roger. The two had no idea they were in the same region, and when Roger heard a tip that he was there, he drove out and found Mort doing kitchen patrol, with stacks of dishes towering above his short stature. Roger couldn't stop laughing at Mort being there at the same time. It tickled him to think of the odds of that happening, and after Mort's tour of duty in K.P., Roger invited him to his barracks.

One evening, Mort came by the barracks late at night. From outside, through a window near Roger's bunk, came soft whispering.

"Owens? Hey, you in there? Are you up? It's me, Rose."

Roger fumbled around to gather his senses. He hadn't been asleep too long, so he managed to recognize Mort's voice, even as a whisper.

"Owens? It's Rose. You there?"

"Yeah, I'm up," Roger answered, leaning out of the window.

Suddenly, there was some noise and movement amongst the other men.

"Rose, huh, what, who's Rose?" asked a few men, groggy, but coming to their senses.

"There's a girl named Rose around here, around our barracks?" another private asked.

Roger wanted to laugh, so finally he let out as much as he could of his laughter under his breath, as though containing it.

"Naahh, guys, it's my friend, Mort Rose. Go back to bed," Roger said in a disappointing manner.

"Ahh man, woke up for nothin'," said one man as he leaned out of the window to look at Mort.

With a huge grin on his face, Roger stopped thinking of his friend Mort, eased into the sheets more, and quickly fell asleep.

By mid-1965, Priscilla became the second Owens daughter to get married. At 18, she stood at the altar alongside her best friend and husband to be, 18 year-old James Solomon. Priscilla's sisters, Ruth and

Esther, were in the wedding, and four year-old Grace was the flower girl. After Ross and Mary had spent all their tissue paper on tears of joy for their second daughter, they wondered when Roger would ever find someone to settle down with.

Roger hadn't even been thinking of marriage just yet. Besides, the times he shared with Carolyn were over, and more often, he was the object of attention from many of the female attendants at the ballpark. During some of the warm, summer, afternoon games at Dodger Stadium, people of all backgrounds and ages, especially young men and women, showed up to forget their worries, stuff down Dodger Dogs, crack open some peanut shells, and take in some Dodger baseball, complete with Vin Scully's plethora of colorful stories told over any portable radio. Like many of the guys out for a summer day at the stadium, countless college women and even younger high school girls bought tickets to relax the afternoon away with their girlfriends, talking, laughing, and watching pro baseball players on the field. Obviously, soaking up some Los Angeles sunshine was a priority. But even though the sun warmed just as well at the local beaches, the young men and women found enjoyment in variety and with the sights and sounds that were uniquely Dodger Stadium.

During one afternoon in particular, near the end of the '65 season, Roger found the courage to start a conversation with a young, white girl sitting in the crowd. The girl was from Pomona and her name was Susan Hoblit. Within a few minutes, the handsome, young vendor had her phone number.

On the drive home, Roger was beside himself. With only the VW bug and the Good Lord above aware of his new feelings for this girl, Roger showed up to his apartment and cooked dinner, humming songs all the while. Philip, who arrived from the ballpark before his brother, moved some clothes off the sofa and sat down. Gene, sitting on the floor watching television, paused in mid-sip of his can of soda and looked up. Quietly, the two looked at each other and then eyed Roger. He stopped for a moment, sensing that they were looking at him. After a few seconds trying to hold it in, the two roared with laughter, knowing full well that only a girl could do such a thing to a grown man.

"When Dizzy and Paul Dean were winning 49 games between them for the 1934 Cardinals, their elder brother, Elmer, was peddling peanuts in the stands at Houston, then a member of the Texas League. 'He was as good as us,' said Ol' Diz, ''cept Elmer threw his arm out pitching them damn peanuts.'"

-from *The Sporting News*, July 4, 1981

$\mathcal{C}$ *12*

Mission Road

I t was late 1965, and Roger and Susan had become inseparable in just
a matter of months. They went on a few mountain trips to the cabin
with her parents, with whom he got along nearly as well as, if not better
than, Susan. The couple went with Susan's parents, again, to *Theater In
The Round*, in West Covina, where the live comedy featured the whole-
some, family-centered hilarity of a young, up and coming comedian
named Bill Cosby.

Susan, with her long, blonde, light-brown hair, enjoyed Roger's
company every minute they were together. On many nights, her parents
insisted Roger not make the long drive from Pomona and allowed him
to spend the night in one of the guest bedrooms. Before long, Roger
knew that the high school senior, resting in his arms on the sofa and
falling asleep to late night television, was the girl he wanted to propose
to. Before the year ended, Roger did ask her, and they were engaged.

In 1966, Roger wanted to live closer to Susan, so he moved to a
nice apartment complex on Mission Road, in the city of Alhambra. At
the stadium, Roger developed friendships with some of the vendors, but
it was his friendship with Eddie Young that was special. Young, whose
name fit him well because of his youthful face, was the number one
peanut vendor at Dodger Stadium. The two had worked together in the
Coliseum days. By the time they made the transition to the stadium,
they had become friends. Working on the yellow, more expensive field
level at the stadium, he had the highest rank of all the vendors, and because Roger and Eddie were easy going, they became best friends.
Young, a 40 year-old, black man with a wife and two kids, and graduate from UCLA, also worked as a social worker in the daytime. He was
financially astute and loved helping Roger to read and understand *The
Wall Street Journal* and to learn about buying and trading stocks. He
also dabbled heavily in real estate, borrowing loans to fix up properties

and sell them. Eddie's interests in land included Palmdale, where there was talk of building an airport, and in Orange County, where the southern portion was absolutely ripe for growth and investment. However, Young had one habit that was more than likely his downfall, falling in debt from gambling on horse racing.

Whenever they could, Susan and Roger took time to decide on the specifics of their wedding day. Susan didn't want Roger to be a police officer, a highway patrolman, or anything else in that line of work. She didn't want him to have that kind of stress, nor did she want to deal with it when he brought it home. She also didn't want him to be away for six months of C.H.P. training in Sacramento. Roger thought it over and agreed. So the two looked for other occupations for which Roger would be suited when he wasn't working mostly evenings at the ballpark.

One Saturday afternoon, while the Dodgers played a game in the best weather in nearly a month, Roger met a businessman who was enjoying the game. The man loved Roger's energy and likeable character. The man handed him a business card. Roger read the company name, *Westransco*, and then saw the salesman's name, *Bill Woodling*.

"Pleasure to meet you Mr. Woodling," Roger said.

"Pleasure's all mine," the man replied. "I've been watching you sell those peanuts. You do a damn good job at it. I'm a salesman with Westransco, a freight shipping company. You have a day job?"

"No sir, but I'm looking," Roger answered.

"I'll just get right down to it. Roger, we would love to have someone like you, someone with a lot of energy. Working in sales could be a great opportunity for you."

"Well, sir, I don't think I would be good at being a salesperson. I mean selling peanuts to hungry people isn't too hard."

Mr. Woodling smiled. "Well that's true, but I see how you make the peanuts your product. You take pride in working the crowd and making sure they catch the bags and have a good time. I know a salesman when I see one, Roger. Here, you have my card. Think it over, and please give me a call. We could *easily* use someone like you, Roger."

"Well, what comes along with working there?" Roger asked.

"For one thing, we give you a salary of five hundred a month, a company car, an expense account, and of course, your own sales rep card. Like I said, think it over and let me know, okay Roger?" the man continued.

"Okay Mr. Woodling."

"Please, you can call me Bill."

"Alright Bill. I'll call you tomorrow."

Roger got back to entertaining the fans, and by the end of the night, he drove over to Susan's house but was reluctant to tell her the good news. Hesitant about the sales job, Roger dismissed it. The only other job he had given consideration was one he saw in an ad for a Sparklett's water delivery route, but that would have interfered with his game schedule. Nearly a month later at the ballpark, the same man was enjoying the day at the ballpark.

"Hey Roger. Can you believe that rally? The Dodgers better get a rally going of their own if they wanna win this game. How are ya?" Mr. Woodling asked.

"Hey Bill. Doing well. Sorry I didn't call about that sales position. I wasn't too sure I could do well with it," Roger answered.

"Hey that's okay. But you know that job offer still stands. We could really use someone like you Roger. How about you not think about it too much and just call?" Bill added.

"Well, sure, this time I will," he replied.

"Okay then. Go ahead. Get back to your fans. They're hungry."

"Okay thanks. Talk with you later," Roger said enthusiastically.

Roger indeed made the call. The day arrived, and he made quite an impression. He was offered the job, and he accepted.

With Mr. Woodling now his boss, Roger settled in easily as their new salesman. He still couldn't believe the expense account and the company car. They paid for the gas, and even on the weekends, he was *still* allowed to use the car. He even had his own business card. It was just a small, rectangular piece of slightly heavier than normal paper stock with his name printed on it in black ink, but to young Roger, it was a sign of self-improvement. He showed it to his dad, and Ross was extremely proud of him.

At work, Roger made new friends and was filled with pride that he was engaged. The salesmen congratulated him and shot the breeze with Roger a little longer before getting back to work. After just two months on the job, Roger was called to sit in on his first sales meeting. The room was full of much older white men, dressed in suits and black, horn rim glasses, but they acknowledged Roger and gave him a warm welcome aboard. It was an open session for Roger to ask away about anything regarding the company, benefits, or anything else.

Roger sat anxiously in his seat. Finally he raised his hand.

"Yes, Roger?" the man asked.

"What about a retirement plan?" he asked.

Everyone who was writing notes or thinking of meetings with clients instantly perked up. Suddenly, the whole room howled with laughter.

Sinking in his seat, Roger let out a few laughs along with them, just enough to hide his embarrassment.

"Retirement plan? Already thinking of retiring? But you've just started?" the man continued, laughing even as the words came out.

As the room took a couple of minutes to quiet down, the man admitted it was a perfectly worthy question and went into detail about their current retirement plans for the salespeople.

At the end of the meeting, Roger was relieved to go back to his desk. The other salesmen, however, continued to amuse themselves with his comment. They loved Roger. They loved him not necessarily for his potential or innocence but for making them laugh so damn hard.

When Roger got to Susan's house, she was waiting for him in the living room. She was happy for him, especially since they had some extra money coming in. But one time, while making out on the couch together, Roger said something under his breath that nearly cost him their wedding. Roger's errant mental wanderings led him to utter the name of his ex-girlfriend, Carolyn.

"What did you say?" Susan asked, pulling back from him. "Did you just say 'Oh Carolyn'? You did, didn't you?"

"Uh, well, I don't think so," he responded, knowing full well he blew it. In his defense, Roger was in fact over and done with Carolyn. He was puzzled why he even said it. With no answer or reason good enough, Susan stormed to her bedroom and slammed the door, yelling at Roger to leave. After apologizing and admitting he had no feelings for anyone else but her, Roger stood still until she finally opened the door. All was forgiven, for now.

One evening, during the week, Roger and Susan talked about who would be in their wedding.

"So have you been thinking about who's going to be your best man?" she asked.

"Yeah, I thought I might surprise Eddie and ask him to be it," Roger answered.

"Your friend, Eddie Young?"

"Well yeah, Eddie from the stadium."

"Roger, no. That's not gonna work. There's no way mom and dad will let him be in our wedding. Besides, isn't there someone else?"

"There's nothing wrong with Eddie."

"Yeah well, try explaining that to all the Hoblits. The answer is no, and that's that."

Roger stayed quiet. He saw past skin color, but he was obviously dealing with people who couldn't. He loved Susan, but he worried this issue was indeed no small matter, and that it could come between them as a source of contention in the coming days, weeks, and perhaps even years. But what finally brought the slamming of matrimonial brakes and skid marks right in front of the church door was more than just the Eddie problem, but the fact that the Carolyn incident wasn't an isolated event.

The minute Roger uttered Carolyn's name a second time, while making out with Susan, he knew it was over between them. Susan ran to her room in a fit of anger, but this time she would not open the door to forgive him. After insisting he just go home already, Roger got his jacket and drove home. The blunder proved to be too much, and so the wedding was called off. They allowed their feelings for each other to fade, and the two went their separate ways.

Disillusioned by his cancelled engagement, Roger did the only thing he could do to keep his sanity. He dove into the swimming pool at his apartment complex. It was quite warm outside, and Roger leisurely swam laps back and forth to both ends of the pool. He swam to the edge of the pool and paused. He folded his arms across the wet concrete to support himself while he rested, and immediately noticed a curvaceous, brown haired, twenty-something woman wearing a white bikini. She was sitting on one of the light-blue, chaise lounges. She noticed the strikingly handsome young man looking at her, and walked over to him, sat down, and put her feet in the pool. The water went all the way up past her shapely, smooth, light-brown calves.

"Hi. You live here?" she asked.

"Hi. Yeah I do, right up there," Roger answered, pointing in the direction of his apartment door.

"Same here. Well, not exactly where you pointed, but in the apartments." The two laughed for a moment. "My name's Vena, Vena Garret. What's yours?" she said.

"Good to meet you Vena. I'm Roger."

"So what brings you to the pool, besides the great weather?" she asked.

"I got a lot on my mind. Thought maybe it would help to go swimming," Roger responded. "And you?"

"You see that stack of papers next to my towel?" she asked.

"Yeah."

"Well, I have to get through at least half of that today. I'm a paralegal, and as you can tell, we've been a bit busy lately," she added. "Would you like to help me?"

"Sure."

As he got out of the pool, he grabbed his towel and dried off, but not before she took a long look at him, bit her lip gently, and smiled. They walked up to her apartment, and she took him by the hand as they went inside. She offered him something cold to drink. After nearly twenty minutes of talking and looking around her place, she picked up her stack of legal papers and walked up to him. She took the drink out of his hand and threw more than just the papers onto her bed.

From that day on, the two were a highly combustible couple, full of physical attraction for one another that had the drive of a chemical dependency. One evening, there was a party in the complex. With some of the people drinking heavily, Vena sat on Roger's lap kissing him. One of her male friends, barely able to walk in his drunken stupor, became hostile toward Vena and blurted out degrading comments about her. Nearly in tears, Vena held onto Roger. She let go of him as Roger stood up. Having considerable more size than the middle-aged man, he stood in front of him. Upset over the man's taunting of his girlfriend, Roger heaved back his right arm and clocked the man right on the jaw. The man yelled at Roger, and swore to him that he would be back with his gun. The party continued, and Vena confessed to Roger that he was her "hero." The man never came back.

In spite of the two being such a hot item, Roger quickly sensed that even in the short time he knew her, their relationship was bound to be more of a shallow, physical adhesion than anything else. Although the relationship lasted into early 1968, and despite her growing desire to marry Roger, he knew that there just wasn't enough in the mix to make the spiritual connection between a man and a woman.

It was the summer of '67, and Roger moved from the Alhambra apartment. He found a tattered, old apartment building on Tularosa Ave., in the Silver Lake area near Downtown Los Angeles. It was close to his sales job and to Dodger Stadium. He stayed there for just a few months, but Vena visited occasionally to help him fix the dingy place up a bit.

By the end of the baseball regular season, during one particular game, Roger noticed that his friend Eddie Young hadn't showed up for work yet. It was uncharacteristic of him, and Roger became a bit worried. The next few games also brought no sign of him. Roger finally called his house and learned from his wife that Eddie hadn't been home in over a week. Roger felt his stomach drop. After doing his best to comfort his friend's wife over the phone, he hung up the phone and sat down, sick to his stomach at the sad possibilities that raced through his mind. Less than a month earlier, Eddie asked Roger for a ten thousand dollar loan for a real estate deal. Without any question, Roger was there to help.

His good friend Eddie was never heard from again, and Roger got burned on the ten thousand dollar real estate deal.

Perhaps somewhere between his gambling, real estate ventures, and borrowed loans, he ran into sour deals. In any case, he left an immeasurable void in the lives of those who knew him, especially his wife and two boys.

After some time had passed, Roger went out more often with his two vendor friends from the stadium. Mort Rose and Jay Bieber enjoyed going out with Roger to watch movies, to go people watching while hanging out in various places around Los Angeles, and even to visit a nightclub in Santa Monica called *The Oar House*. It was a somewhat hokey club that played a lot of Creedance Clearwater Revival music during the early 70's. Mort, Jay, and Roger were best buddies, but even they didn't realize that they were forming friendships that would last nearly 40 years. It was at that same nightclub in early 1968 where Roger, not with Vena any longer, first noticed a very attractive black woman named Bernadette.

The two began talking in a quieter part of the club and took an immediate liking to one another. Soon they were dating, and as Bernadette realized what she was working with, she knew some change was in order. Bernadette told him that he should try spending a little more money on himself, including buying stylish clothes, a newer car, nicer furnishings, and better yet, finding a nicer apartment. She was caring and thoughtful and put Roger first. She even bought him a leather jacket, something he had never owned before.

Roger, with his new girlfriend's prodding, moved to a wonderful, beachfront apartment in Manhattan Beach. With the beach sand within toes reach, it was a great place to throw a party.

So they did, all the time.

She helped him buy and set up a new stereo system, which sat inside a hand carved piece of wood furniture that looked like a coffee table. To pay her back for her generosity, he planned a surprise birthday party for her, inviting many of their friends over to their new digs. As she unsuspectingly unlocked the front door to come in, a crowd of familiar faces leaped up from behind sofas and from behind walls. With the speakers blaring out the song "Bernadette" by the Four Tops, Roger approached her and danced with her on the spot. She was overwhelmed and loved Roger for making her day.

During the winter of '67, Roger worked the football games at the L.A. Coliseum, as he always did every football season. No matter if they were USC, UCLA, or Rams games, he was there to sell peanuts and thrill the paying customers.

One unusually warm day in January 1968, Roger and his vending buddy, Jay Bieber, were working in the aisles at the Coliseum as the fans trickled in. Suddenly, a few men approached them. The men were with a major movie studio.

"How are you two fellas doing today?" asked one man.

"Okay," Roger and Jay replied.

"I just wanted to find out if you two were interested in a small role in an upcoming movie that we're filming right here on location. The role is simply to act as stadium vendors. Not much of a stretch for you both, I know, but what do you think?" the man asked.

Roger and Jay looked at each other, squinting from the sun, and smiled simultaneously.

"Well, sure. What's the movie about?" Roger asked.

"It's called *The Split*, and it stars Jim Brown and Ernest Borgnine. Their characters are thieves, and they're attempting to steal all the money brought in from food concessions and souvenirs at the Coliseum. You guys have a good look, so if you'd like, show up tomorrow, and the whole crew should be here already. Pay isn't much, about 29 dollars for the day, but it's a whole day's work. Interested?" the man continued.

Again, Roger and Jay looked at each other, knowing that they would have done it for free. "Sure we are," Jay responded.

The next day, the two were beside themselves at being on the set at the Coliseum. It was explained to Jay that he would be holding a huge handful of cash in one hand, and a stack of programs in the other. He would yell out for people to get their programs, and Roger was told to stand behind a souvenir stand, selling hats, pins, pennants, and anything else. With every one in place, the director yelled for action, the camera light went on, and the film rolled.

The part was nothing more than a few seconds, but Roger and Jay loved it.

In fact, they were so cooperative and acted so naturally on the set, that the film crew invited them to watch the taping the next day. They accepted without hesitation.

Later that night, they spent their money by watching the roller derby at the Olympic Auditorium, and thinking how cool it was to be in a movie.

The next morning, they were back on the set, even though they were done with their parts. Suddenly, Roger and Jay stood still as they saw none other than Cassius Clay walk onto the set. Like two boys stopping on their bicycles to stare open-jawed, Roger and Jay watched as the boxing legend stood only a few feet away, greeting the football hero turned actor, Jim Brown.

Roger and Jay didn't know what to say, so they just watched the two playfully hunched over, air jabbing one another as though sparring right then and there. Everyone on the set was in for a real treat having Brown and Cassius clowning around together. After just a few minutes, Roger and Jay realized they weren't dreaming and then heard someone on the film crew ask when Jim Brown and Cassius Clay would really get into the ring. Brown and Cassius just looked at each other and laughed.

Then, Jay, feeling a bit more comfortable around such famous heavyweights, teased Cassius.

"Hey Cassius, when are you gonna fight Wilt Chamberlain? That's what I wanna know," Jay asked.

Cassius took a step back, and said defiantly, "Man, that chump would rather go to Viet 'Nam with a BB gun than to step in the ring with me."

The whole crew, Roger, and Jay all cracked up with laughter.

Later that same year, Cassius changed his faith, and changed his name to Muhammad Ali, and was well on his way to becoming the greatest boxer of all time.

$\mathcal{C}$ *13*

A Testimony at Point Blank Range

B ack at the Owens home, Ross had saved enough money to take his kids out more often. He had already taken them a year before to Yosemite National Park, an event especially memorable for the time Ross' teenage son, Paul, moved in for a closer look at a curious little bear that wandered nearby. Ross quickly saw the mama bear snorting and walking faster toward its cub. Without warning, and louder than a drill sergeant who woke up on the wrong side of the cot, Ross yelled at Paul to get away. Paul instantly ran for safety in the opposite direction. While threatening events such as this proved avoidable, one such event was not. And this time, it made headlines.

On a Sunday afternoon on November 17, 1968, just an hour after service let out at Immanuel Baptist where they attended church, Ross asked if anyone was hungry. Elizabeth, Lois, and Paul all chimed in and asked for fast food. Ross, who was still dressed in his gray tweed suit from the service earlier, followed his kids to his parked car. They piled into the car, and after Ross pressed the push-button ignition, he drove them to a local Jack In The Box. Elizabeth, who was about to turn 17, stared out of the back seat car window and thought about attending classes at Compton Community College. Lois, age 16, sat next to her sister, watching people walk by on the sidewalks. Paul, age 14, rode shotgun and desperately wanted to change the radio station to anything besides the news.

As the three Owens teenagers got out of the car and made their way to the fast food place, two young men suddenly approached the attractive Owens girls. Ross was just about to leave to visit a fellow church friend for a few minutes.

"Hey, we haven't seen you around. You live nearby?" one of the young men asked, grinning as he checked them out.

Paul remained quiet, and Elizabeth and Lois felt uneasy over the flirting and questions. They also remained quiet, trying to avoid the almost threatening advances.

"Hey, did you hear me? I asked if you live nearby. What, you don't wanna talk with us, is that it?" the man asked angrily.

Suddenly, their hearts jumped, and their adrenalin pumped, bringing a cold sensation up and down their legs. Even at 5 feet 10 inches, Lois wasn't about to try any heroics, and Paul, still a few years away from his adult height of 6 feet 4 inches, was frightened just as much as his two sisters. Ross, sensing the hostility, ordered his kids to go to the car. In seconds, they were standing on the curb watching the two men getting angrier with their dad.

"What's the problem, boys?" Ross asked.

"You're the problem, old man. Do yourself a favor and leave so we can talk with the young ladies," he answered, looking at his friend for a quick laugh.

"Well, I'm a Baptist minister, and I'm their father, so bother me, not my girls," Ross said.

"You think we care about that, old man?" he answered menacingly, pulling out a .22 caliber handgun from his coat pocket.

Ross, who was prayed up for the day, eyed the young man pointing the gun. Ross inhaled sharply and stared at the gun, shining from the reflected sunlight at the tip of the barrel. From inside the fast food place, the manager saw the gun and called the police. Ross' kids looked on, unable to move or speak, as though they were on a set of a television program, watching as the director yelled action.

But this was no show. This was Dad, frozen in his tracks, standing at the mercy of an intimidating troublemaker.

The gun clicked.

It misfired.

The young man looked at his gun in disbelief.

Ross stood still, petrified that the trigger was actually pulled on him.

Again, the man pointed the gun at Ross at point blank range and fired, sending all six feet, 200 pounds of gentle human, husband, and father reeling backwards, as though slugged just below the chest by a heavyweight boxer contending for the world title. With the sudden gunshot ringing out throughout the neighborhood, screams were heard in the parking lot, and everyone ducked for cover.

But the gun-wielding perpetrator stood open jawed, along with his friend who also was in shock. Ross, who had not entirely fallen down, straightened himself, and while grimacing in pain, simply rubbed his chest. There he stood, with a clearly defined hole in his suit pocket over the right side of his chest. No blood poured out, just tiny bits of paper that the wind carried off of his suit.

Standing in awkward silence, Ross and the two men simply looked at one another. All three were completely baffled.

"Well, how about you hand over all your money?" the man ordered. Ross immediately produced his wallet and took out a one-dollar bill, the only paper money he had on him. Then he reached in his pockets and pulled out all of his change. He looked down in the palm of his hand and counted a measly twenty-seven cents.

Instantly, a police car pulled up to the scene, before the two boys could grab the money from the minister. The car skidded as it came to a fast stop, and as the side doors flung open, two officers jumped out and aimed their revolvers at the befuddled street bandits.

"Put your weapon down," the officer yelled several times before the young man complied. The two were immediately arrested.

Elizabeth, Lois, Paul, and a few bystanders rushed to Ross' side. Coughing and in pain, Ross sat down to gather his composure. Everyone, including the onlookers, his kids, and the officers, asked how Ross was doing. He seemed to be okay. He looked down at his suit and opened up the right side of his coat. Stuffed inside the coat pocket was a thick wad of Gospel tracts, pieces of paper with various Bible topics that evangelicals love handing out to people on the go. Among the bits of paper, torn by the path of the bullet, and sandwiched between the tracts, was the .22 caliber bullet itself.

The fateful placing of Ross' religious papers in his coat, together with the bullet stopping less than two inches from his skin, made the event nothing short of miraculous. Left with a powder burn and a huge, reddish purple bruise just below his chest, Ross insisted he was okay. As Ross was detained for the police report, a member of the press showed up for the unbelievable story. The reporter, Charles Hillinger, a staff writer with the *Los Angeles Times*, was there with newspaper photographer, Frank Q. Brown, to get the story. The police decided it was okay for Ross to leave, and once everyone was home, standing on the front porch, the photographer took a picture of Ross pointing at the hole in his suit coat. In his other hand, as also captured in the picture, was the initial Gospel tract that was first in line to begin stopping the bullet. On the cover of the tract were the words, printed in red ink on white paper, *The Blood Of Christ*.

While the two men were being held in jail, it was realized that they were the same two gunmen who had recently killed a man in a different holdup.

Finally, after the excitement finally started to recede, Ross went into his bedroom to lie down. Paul called his mom at the hospital where she worked as a registered nurse.

"Hi, Mom. Dad's just been shot. He's lying down in bed," Paul said.

"Lying down? What do you mean he's lying down?" she asked in shock. Before he could respond, Ross took the phone and explained to his wife what had happened.

Later in the day, Ross called the station and asked if he could go down to the station to see them. The authorities allowed it, and when he saw them again, they showed a quiet disdain for his presence. Even so, that didn't keep Ross from praying for them and witnessing to them about a forgiving God.

Hanging out in Las Vegas for the weekend with his friends, Jay and Mort, Roger was unaware of his dad being shot in Compton. After a weekend of fun and great eating in Vegas, Roger was ready to get back home for work the next morning. After a few hours driving back to Los Angeles, Roger arrived home late at night and slept soundly.

Early the next morning, Roger washed his face in the bathroom sink. The water splashed in his hands, and as he wiped cold, refreshing water all over his face, he looked into the mirror and realized he'd better shave. His eyes more open now, and his mind more alert, he began to shave, but not before he turned on the radio, which was placed beside him near an outlet on the bathroom sink.

Over the radio came a familiar voice. It was Paul Harvey's. His news program on ABC radio was one that Roger heard almost every morning while getting ready for work at Westransco. He enjoyed the broadcast because Harvey always told all sides of the story.

Roger set the razor under the warm water to clean off the hairs. While the small facial hairs fell into a circling whirlpool of running water, he placed the razor back on his face and continued.

"And good morning everybody. Did you hear about the miracle in Compton over the weekend?" asked Harvey.

Roger turned up the radio.

"On Sunday afternoon, a white Baptist minister from the Los Angeles area was shot at point blank range in Compton. Two assailants held up the reverend and two of his daughters in front of a fast food establishment, but even after the shot was fired, the minister was still on his feet. Apparently, the bullet was stopped by a large wad of gospel tracts, placed in his front coat pocket."

Roger's heart nearly stopped as he heard the news. He was convinced that it was his dad in the story. He toweled off the extra shaving cream on his face and called home. The line was busy. He tried again. The line was constantly busy, no doubt tied up from reporters calling to get the story. Finally, he called his work and told them he would be late, and that his dad was shot.

Roger quickly got into his car, but realized there was little gas remaining from the long road trip. Without any hesitation, he revved up the Chevy and took off, counting on the gas fumes alone to get him to the nearest gas station.

Within minutes, he saw one and pulled in.

"Hey, I don't have much time. Here's a few dollars," Roger told the attendant.

"What's the hurry?" the man replied.

"My dad's been shot. It was on the news. I'm gonna go find out what happened," Roger answered frantically.

"Hey, well hold on a minute fella. Slow down. Does your dad happen to be a minister named Ross Owens?" the man asked.

"Hey, yeah!" Roger yelled in excitement.

"Well, here it is in the morning paper. Read it."

Roger walked quickly over to the counter, and there it was, an article in the *Long Beach Press Telegram*, telling the story of the miracle in Compton. Roger read it hastily, filled his car with just enough gas, and sped off toward his parents' house about 35 minutes away. Meanwhile, at work, his friends heard the news, bought the *Los Angeles Times* paper, and saved the article from the front page of the city section so he could read it when he arrived.

When Roger reached the Owens house, he realized everything was okay.

The Owens kids, actually not really kids as much as they were young adults or twenty something adults, all found the news of their dad both shocking and remarkable. Ruth was already quite busy with family life, with her second child born just months before, and Priscilla was busy, living in Alameda, California with her husband, who joined the Navy in 1966 and who wouldn't be discharged as a Vietnam Veteran until 1970.

After some time had passed, a sense of the familiar, the routine, and even some tranquility had returned to the Owens household. As for Roger, he looked forward, as usual, to the fast approaching baseball season and, in addition, to the last summer he would be obligated to serve in the California Army National Guard.

It was spring 1969, and 26 year-old Roger was thrilled that opening day at the stadium had arrived. Already an established Dodger icon in the hearts of the small crowds of Dodger fans fortunate to sit in his area of the ballpark, Roger still couldn't imagine a better place to work, eleven years after the Dodgers had moved West. While he wasn't as familiar a face to the thousands that filled the various, other parts of the stadium, his following of friends and the warmth they felt for him as their peanut man was as genuine as the smile and sweat that Roger brought to the ballpark every inning of every game.

$\Big\{$ *14*

Nearer My God to Thee

Throughout the first half of the year, Roger continued to spend time with his girlfriend Bernadette, as well as with his best friends Jay and Mort. Roger also kept busy with his day job, impressing everyone with his top salesmanship. In fact, from the time he first started there in '66, it took him less than 10 years to be the number one salesman with regard to volume of sales. Roger always knew that his work at the ballpark, as well as his outgoing personality, sincerity, and honesty, all contributed to his success for his company. In fact, one time he sent a bag of peanuts to a potential customer. Immediately, it charmed his customer and, as a result, it became his trademark in sales. He learned how to start and end a sales offer, when to talk and when to listen, and he realized just how meaningful two simple words, "thank you," could be.

By June of 1969, Roger had to report back to Fort Irwin in the Mojave Desert. This was the fifth and final year of his duty with the Army National Guard. It was just two weeks worth of service and training that he needed to complete over the course of the summer, and he was excited about finishing it.

Roger maintained his work schedule as much as possible at the ballpark and with his sales job at Westransco., but occasionally he was required to miss some days while away on training. It was Friday, June 13th, and Roger had a busy day at work and at the ballpark. It wasn't an unusual day, but he was nevertheless exhausted by the time he went to bed at midnight. Three hours passed, and Roger's alarm clock went off. By 5:00 a.m., that Saturday morning, Roger had to be at the Army Depot in Bell, California, ready and reporting for duty.

He fumbled to get dressed and leave but made it on time to Bell, not far from Long Beach. Fighting off the sensations of heavy eyelids and body aches from sleep deprivation, he managed to gather what energy

he could with some morning chow. At almost 6:30 a.m., he and the rest
of his fellow M.P.'s were ordered to head out to Fort Irwin, so they
could be on duty by the time a large convoy of quarter-ton jeeps and
half-ton army trucks made it to the base that afternoon. Once there, the
M.P.'s would act as road assistants and set up traffic control points.
They would also be ready for service once the personnel of the convoy
settled in.

The officers, including Roger, all in full uniform, hopped in their
jeeps and rolled out. They expected to reach Fort Irwin in several
hours, keeping a pace of about 40 miles per hour. With their lieutenant
riding in the lead jeep, the training personnel found the journey to be
hot, dry, isolated, and unbearable. Soon, the expanse of urban commotion became mere specks in their rear-view mirrors, like the sand grains
emerging from the wind-whipped, rapidly approaching desert. The hot
air blew against them from the front and sides as arrogant gusts of wind
that blurred out any possible joy from the trip.

They reached Barstow.

Suddenly, Roger's jeep blew a freeze plug, resulting in loss of water and overheating. The small convoy quickly came to a halt when
news reached the lieutenant. He walked over to Sergeant Andy Grueter
and ordered to him to connect Owens' jeep to his and tow it for the re-
mainder of the trip. Grueter did as instructed, and Roger hopped aboard
Andy's jeep. Before the trip resumed, all of the officers complained
that they needed a rest, obviously wanting to take advantage of the
pause for Owens' jeep. The lieutenant looked at his watch, hesitated for
a second, and then agreed.

The men looked around them and spotted a nearby cemetery, in the
middle of the desert.

It was 11:00 a.m.

The cemetery had patches of cool, inviting grass, swaying in
rhythmic, ocean-like waves. The wind continued to stir it gently, like a
child running its fingers through the grass. Planted around the place
were palm trees, towering in unchallenged isolation and providing
much welcomed shade. The men couldn't believe their luck to find
such a place to rest. They walked off the hot pavement and collapsed in
relief upon the damp earth.

Ten minutes passed.

Time was up.

It wasn't long enough to make out more than a few shapes from the
clouds, nor to tune in more than a moment's worth of daydreamed

sports. It wasn't long enough to slowly close one's eyes to imagine for a second the cycle of humanity told in every headstone, nor to imagine a skyline out of the alternating heights of those same stones. It wasn't enough time to imagine a long, cold drink of water chugged from brim to bottom or to feel the wind cool one's face in the sleep inducing shade.

"Okay men. Get moving. We have a schedule to keep," barked the lieutenant.

Roger looked above him and saw the palm leaves hanging high over him. He closed his eyes for one last moment of calm. Everyone got up and stretched, heavily sedated from the peacefulness and light headed from standing up quickly after their solemn rest. The men walked slowly to their jeeps and got in. With their green, Army-issue, soft, ball caps on their heads, they started their jeeps.

"Hey Andy, I'll drive if you want," Roger asked.

"No, that's okay. You said you hardly had any rest last night. Besides you look beat," Andy insisted.

So the two drove off, towing Roger's jeep.

Andy and Roger had become good friends, especially because they went to the same National Guard workshops, held every month throughout the year. They could be attended in various locations, but they were a mandatory part of the five-year training. They took notes while watching videos about first aid and crowd control, and during lunch break, Andy and Roger would hang out outside the room, talking and snacking before they had to go back inside.

By now, Andy, Roger, and the rest of the convoy were heading down a long, straight highway that stretched nearly 50 miles. The landscape was a showcase of desolation for as far as the eye could see. Nothing but gray road ahead, baked, beige sand on all sides, some green plant life, clear blue sky above, and blistering beams of intense desert sunlight, which reflected off every piece of glass and surface of the jeeps ahead. The dry heat was intolerable, but these men, these troopers, found some solace in the blowing wind, which seemed almost cool as they sped along.

It was exactly this combination of oven heat and somewhat cool driving breezes that put Roger to sleep almost instantly from the time they left the cemetery. Andy glanced over at Roger, who was partially slumped over in slumber, with his head bowed in exhaustion and hat tilted further to keep the sunlight out. Any slight bounces in the jeep were carelessly disregarded by Roger's senses. Andy looked back at the road and the jeeps ahead.

Andy's eyelids became heavy.

The desert air heated to a merciless 110 degrees, attempting to parch the reserves of every man and machine crossing through its forsaken land. Vast mirages of glimmering sea and melting highway toyed with their minds. Duty pushed them forward, but the elements bent their resilience to a slow crawl upon the desert floor.

Andy nodded his head, bowing in submission to the demands upon his body, until he finally fell asleep at the wheel.

With both men in their seats, hunched over in ignorance and helpless to the awaiting danger, the steering wheel turned slightly in its independence to the left and then to the right. Its unguided course gave way to the direction of the jeep's front wheel alignment, and quickly the jeep headed off road at 40 miles per hour toward a five feet tall sand embankment. With Roger's towed jeep bumbling driverless behind it, the jeep advanced onto the shoulder, and the feeling of soft sand under the tires replaced the firmness of asphalt.

Instantly, there was a jolt.

Andy and Roger, now startled and awake, felt the chilling warmth of surging adrenalin, as they were about to slam into a large mound of firmly packed sand. They instinctively grabbed the steering wheel and turned it simultaneously with the intensity of two teenagers mindlessly turning their spinning cup into a circling frenzy at an amusement park. The wheels locked, and the jeep flipped over onto the hot, unforgiving pavement. The flip freed Grueter's jeep from the towed jeep, but not before the towed jeep rammed into it and fell on its side.

Roger was thrown instantly like a sling shot, crashing head first into the windshield of the towed jeep and landing hard onto the pavement.

Andy was thrown ahead of the jeep, also landing hard onto the pavement. With the jeep's momentum propelling it forward, it caught up to Andy and dragged him along the road, cutting and ripping off parts of his skin, uniform and boots. Finally, the jeep came to a stop, and Andy lay there moving slowly and soaked with blood.

Roger was cataleptic.

Suddenly there was a loud explosion. Just a few feet away, a small fire blazed under the hood of the jeep. Consequently, the jeep's battery had blown up. With Roger lying motionless and his uniform soaked with battery acid, the other officers rushed to get him away from the jeep and put the fire out. From under his green Army hat, trails of blood slid down his head and neck. He had suffered a basilar skull fracture, not far above his spinal cord, as well as several bruises and contusions on his scalp and back. Some of the officers used water from their canteens to wipe off battery acid and gasoline from Roger's skin.

The personnel maintained their composure as much as possible, reacting quickly under pressure to get desperately needed medical attention for their two friends. They noticed Roger's dog tag, found out his blood type, asked for volunteers to donate blood, and called for an ambulance to be dispatched from Weed Army Hospital at Fort Irwin. Within a short time, the ambulance arrived. On the way to the hospital, Andy was in pain, but even more, he was hysterical over Roger.

Once there, Roger was rushed to the emergency room. Not one neurosurgeon was staffed there, and time was running out. Roger was in a coma, diagnosed with severe head trauma. He appeared stable after the first thirty minutes, but developed a fever and continued in a coma, not responding to the simplest of commands.

By evening, a telegram was sent to the Los Angeles Sheriff's Department. The telegram was handed to a deputy sheriff.

It was the summer of '69, and while other young kids, teenagers, and young men and women were out buying the latest Beatles records, buying their first, real six string guitars and wanting to start a band of their own, or just enjoying the best years of their lives, young Roger was fighting for his life. At home, it was another lazy Saturday for the Owens household, but within an hour after dinner, there was a knock at the door. Elizabeth got up from her comfortable spot on the sofa and answered the door.

"Hello, young lady. Is your father home?" asked the sheriff.

"Yes, sir. Just a minute," she answered.

"Thank you."

"Dad, there's a police officer at the door for you," she calmly told her dad, who was studying Bible verses in his room.

Ross walked to the front door, removed his reading glasses, and greeted the sheriff.

"Hello officer," Ross said.

"Sir, are you the father of Roger D. Owens?" asked the policeman.

"Yes, sir. What happened?" Ross inquired, uneasy about the telegram the man was holding.

"I have a telegram for you. I urge you to read it at once," stated the officer respectfully. He looked into Ross' squinted eyes, and then he looked down at his shiny, black, police shoes, tipped his hat and walked back to his police car.

"Thank you," he replied in a barely audible tone as he put on his reading glasses and shut the door.

The telegram, dated June 14, 1969, read as follows:

Mrs. Ross Owens, Report Time Delivery ASC 04 to Ft. Macar-thur,

Do not fwd
6608 Compton Blvd Paramount Calif
06-077 I regret to inform you that your son, Roger D., has been hospitalized for a skull fracture, his condition warranted placing him on the seriously ill list. Your presence is not required unless you so desire. You will be notified in the event of any change in Roger's condition. Letter will follow Commanding Officer WAH W2RJAA-01

Immediately, Ross' heart sank, almost dropping the telegram from sudden nausea. Ross stood in silence, shot by this bulletin, but this time no large wads of paper or gospel tracts could dispel this penetrating wound to his heart. He found a seat in the living room, sat down, and called Mary at work about the telegram. After trying to calm his wife's anxiety, Ross made a handful of other phone calls and then went into his room, knelt down by his bed, and poured out his heart to the Lord.

On Monday, he called the freight company where Roger worked and informed them. Ross explained to them about the family car not being so dependable should they plan to visit Roger. They dispelled his worry by granting Ross permission to use Roger's company car at any time to visit him. However, they begged Ross to keep them updated on his condition.

Roger was kept at the hospital under close surveillance. While their knowledge and training was as modern as possible, doctors, or neuro-surgeons in this case, relied on proven medical practices regarding methods of detection and diagnosis. By comparison with 21st century technological advances in medical science, even the most advanced hospitals and astute physicians in 1969 were using archaic methods and tools. They did not have computer-based instruments, nor did they have the technology that changed medicine forever, and which has been taken for granted ever since, the CT scan.

After two days of observation, doctors noted that Roger was still in a coma. They debated about how they should proceed. They decided to wait out the coma. Doctors tried every way possible to snap him out of it. They resorted to shaking and slapping his body, yelling his name loudly, and when some of them were told he worked at the stadium, they even made loud cheering and ballpark sounds that might stimulate familiarity in Roger's brain. All of these efforts failed; moreover, later that same morning of June 16th, they first detected signs of papilledema in his right eye, or the yellowing of his eye due to increased blood clotting and pressure on his brain.

Plans were immediately made to transfer him to the Neurosurgical Service at Naval Hospital in San Diego, California. They considered taking him by helicopter, but fearing both the delays for the necessary security clearance as well as the risk of increased movement, they ordered that he be rushed by Army ambulance, with a police escort, all the way to San Diego. Ross was present by that time and rode along in the ambulance, praying agonizingly and tearfully for his son, who lay motionless and unaware of anything or anyone.

$\mathcal{C}$ 15

The Life Worth Embracing

The rest of the Owens family had already been informed about Roger, and although powerless to help him directly, they made it a priority to pray for him, asking the one Friend that had provided for them year after year to help their oldest brother, whom they loved greatly. They asked God to once again perform a miracle like He had done with their dad. They were raised to have such faith, because their dad lived what he preached. Whether God even existed, whether God was indifferent, or whether God had the power to do anything about anything, these were questions that would have been much harder to answer without such a faith instilled in them and without a father who exemplified the kind of character they admired. In return, Ross and his wife, Mary, had given their children the gift of an anchored character that would help them cope spiritually with life as growing adults and as parents themselves. The Owens family had grown beyond the stages of childhood, except for Grace at eight years old, and even the three "babies" were all within the age range of starting college. They were maturing and enjoying the independence of adulthood. But even in their lives, separated by busy schedules and many miles, they found that the heartache of Roger's serious plight only reminded them of how they were so fortunate to have a caring family such as theirs.

Philip heard the news, and in his contemplative, quiet demeanor, he became depressed over the possibility of losing his brother and best friend. Philip couldn't bear to hold his feelings inside. While Roger lay quietly in the hospital bed, still in a coma, Philip hand wrote an endearing letter to his brother.

Caring?

Caring is the most important thing there is; my brother lays not knowing how I care now. If only...if only-oh how common do we say...if only he could be well again...please God...please make him well...so I and others might see life for what it truly should be in

118

him, to care for others, to feel love and to express it...caring now brings a silent move. Tears shed now...why? For something precious...life and love. Roger may it never be said I never said or felt love for you. I do care for you. I love you. Watching you in your wrestless [sic] slumber made me wonder. What is life? How hopeless man seems at times. He awake[s]...then he's gone, no songs to sing, nor stories to tell, Roger-just sadness of heart for a good person.

> God is here-God is there.
> God is everywhere-except
> Where you need him.
> He is so big and I am
> So small that it seems
> I can't see him at all.
>
> He makes the worlds and
> Controls the heavens;
> He receives the dead
> And keeps on giving-but
> Why oh why can't he help the living?
>
> God is a friend, who
> Knows no malice,
> Perhap[s]

The letter Philip wrote seemed to be unfinished, but even so, it contained the essence of his feelings for Roger.

The ambulance reached the U.S. Naval Hospital, and Roger was rushed into intensive care unit of the Neurology Ward. Most of the beds were filled with severely wounded soldiers sent back home from the fighting lines of the Vietnam War.

Once there, his medical report was handed to an extremely gifted and experienced neurosurgeon, Lieutenant Colonel Dr. Victor Schorn. He was the best the military had to offer, and incidentally, he was the same Dr. Schorn who was on call as the personal neurosurgeon for President Lyndon B. Johnson.

Not long after admission to the hospital, on the evening of the 16th, nearly two and a half days after the jeep accident, Roger slowly came out of the coma. Finally, the shock that had confined his body to an outward silence now sent him upwards and out of the abyss. As it abated, Roger's body, mind, and soul merged together into an awareness that was agreeable to his traumatized body.

He woke up with an excruciating headache.

"Where am I?" Roger asked groggily, with modestly swollen eyelids, cuts, and bruises on various parts of his head and body.

"You're at the Naval Hospital, Roger," one doctor answered.

"Can you take me to the window? I'd like to see the water outside," Roger responded. "We're on a ship right?"

"No, Roger. We're at a hospital, the Naval Hospital, on dry land," he said.

Roger held his head and grimaced.

"Can't you take me to the window to see the water?" he asked, looking down in pain.

"Nurse, help me strap him down. Roger, we need to strap you down okay, son? Relax and get some rest," the doctor said.

Later, Roger was able to give a past history, but he had little, if no, memory of the accident. After a day of lab work, X rays, and careful observation, Roger seemed to improve, taking in fluids by mouth. X rays were negative regarding his skull, chest, and cervical spine. As Roger lay in bed, he looked around him and quickly became depressed. He could see the hideous countenances and hear the haunting groaning of young men dying in intensive care. The voices, muffled by blood soaked bandages, and the limbs no longer recognizable or even present, all saddened him immensely.

Then, Dr. Schorn walked in.

"Hello, Roger," he said in a soothing, warm tone as he reached his bedside. "My name is Dr. Schorn." He smiled at Roger. Roger hardly moved, and just managed to open his eyes wide enough to see the man. "Looks like you took quite a spill son," he said affectionately in a low voice. Roger nodded his head slowly.

By the 18th, doctors noticed increased yellowing in his right eye, and now there was yellowing in his left eye, a huge tip off that things were not going well. After also noticing nerve damage, Dr. Schorn ordered an echoencephalogram. The test revealed further problems, a slight shift of his brain and bilateral hemotympanum, or bruising and contusions on both sides of the brain. Roger then underwent a special X ray study known as a cerebral arteriography. It revealed that there was marked elevation with the right, middle region and a shift to the left of the right anterior cerebral region. It was the physician's impression that he possibly had a severe temporal lobe contusion, or a severe wound and bruising. Emergency brain surgery, as unbelievably dangerous as it sounded, was the only option.

Roger's mother and father were called, and the two drove out to the hospital.

Once there, doctors approached Ross and Mary, took them aside, and quietly explained to them the circumstances. Then they calmly told Mary that they were almost certain Roger would not make it. Mary suddenly felt an immense burden within her chest and stomach. While talkative and gregarious at times, she found herself speechless and silent, standing still as the words sank in, that her cherished son "would not make it." Streams of tears fell down her cheeks as she thought how the sweet young man she had been so privileged to call "son" always managed to make his Italian mother so proud of him. He was generous and affectionate with her, and she was happy for him for his work at Dodger Stadium. She quietly sat down, gathering her strength for Roger, for Ross, and for all of her children. But even though she shared the same strong faith in her God as her husband, and enjoyed seeking refuge in her God by writing poetry and playing piano, there was only so much courage one mother could have.

Dr. Schorn arrived in the room, and shook hands with Roger's parents.

He explained to them the nature and risks of the operation and asked Ross to sign release papers that granted them permission for the brain surgery. After the papers were signed, the doctors and nurses began preparing Roger for surgery. Ross walked over to his son's bedside, knelt down slowly, and began to pray for him. He asked God to protect his boy, to help the doctors every step of the way, and to simply perform another miracle the way He did less than a year earlier during the holdup. Ross trusted firmly that everything would be okay, if he just believed God was bigger than the jeep accident, just as He was bigger than the stopped bullet. Ross wiped the tears from his bloodshot eyes, took out his handkerchief, and blew his nose. Mary still had her head bowed. Then she stood up, took Ross by the hand, and they left the room.

Roger was taken to the operating room, where Dr. Schorn and his staff performed the surgery.

There were at least two operations, which included using a surgical saw to drill burr holes in his skull, in the frontoparietal and temporal regions, as well as actually having to cut away a tip of his brain in the temporal region, because of severe contusion. The swelling of the right temporal lobe went down only after removal of the tip as well as the use of Mannitol. After the surgeries, they closed the wounds on his head and monitored his recovery. He was started on Decadron and Dilantin and was gradually weaned off the Decadron.

As Roger rested with lazily opened eyes, Dr. Schorn approached his bedside.

"How are you doing, 'Roge' babe?" he asked.

Roger, who was caught off guard from the warmth in the doctor's tone and with the intimacy of the moment, slowly smiled and nodded his head.

Roger continued to rest while doctors and nurses monitored him constantly.

Roger's girlfriend, Bernadette, heard about Roger, and like the rest of Roger's family, she drove to San Diego and asked to see him. It was an awkward moment for Bernadette, who had never met his family. She felt uneasy, not only because she met his parents, brothers, and sisters, but also because it was news to them that she was also black. They quickly dismissed the superficiality of the issue and bonded with her, especially because of Roger.

Ruth, Priscilla, Elizabeth, Lois, Esther, Philip, Paul, Ross, and Mary walked in to see Roger, who was in stable, but guarded condition in intensive care. The medication given to him created senseless, audible remarks, and he couldn't recognize anyone. He complained of having headaches and was strapped down for his own safety. Roger lay motionless while being fed intravenously. With his completely shaven head and loss of more than thirty pounds, his brothers and sisters found it impossible to hold back their tears. Ruth glanced at her dad and saw him crying. It was the first time she had ever seen her dad cry openly. As they stood around talking quietly, Lois noticed one man hooked up to a countless number of tubes. He had a badly swollen face, the result of a grenade explosion.

With everyone's attention back on Roger, they began to pray. They could see first hand how their big brother was merely a shadow of his energetic, outgoing self. It burdened their hearts to see him that way, and on the trip home, the talkative family sometimes expressed their feelings about what they saw, and other times just looked out of the car windows, their souls weeping, their bodies empty, and their hearts holding fast that Roger would recover quickly.

Roger's friends from his sales job also visited him. They brought him a small token of love and admiration. It was a tiny, plastic trophy that read in tiny letters at the base, *World's Greatest Salesman*. They told Roger that every day at work a group of them stood in a corner and prayed for him. He also learned that Philip, for as long as necessary, would pay his bills and rent, using Roger's own money since the freight company saw fit to look after their own by compassionately keeping him on salary. It was a wonderful gesture of support and show of faith in their most profitable salesman. Roger's vendor friends also came by to show their support, encouraging a quick return to the stadium.

Back at the ballpark, Philip had the unfortunate duty of explaining what happened to Roger. Fellow food vendors and many season ticket holders were in disbelief and were saddened to hear of the accident. Philip simply asked that they pray for Roger, and he told them he would promise to keep them updated. They missed their peanut man greatly, and soon Roger started to receive mail from Dodger fans wishing him well. Some even visited him to ensure his spirits were up.

In the days surrounding the operations, Ross stayed in San Diego so that he could be at Roger's side as much as possible. Ross didn't have enough money to stay in a hotel or motel, so after learning that a local YMCA was filled to capacity, arrangements were made for him to stay at a nearby YWCA. Dr. Schorn was quite fond of Ross' display of affection and concern for Roger, especially when he always found Ross in prayer, kneeling beside Roger's bed.

Roger showed gradual improvement, but by June 22nd, he had severe anemia and was given 1000 cubic centimeters of whole blood. Roger continued to improve and began eating a full diet. His progress amazed the doctors.

During his time at the hospital, Roger's personality changed. His emotions became much more sensitive, he lost a great deal of self-confidence, and he approached matters of his health and future problems with increased anxiety. While he remained in the hospital, in the midst of dying servicemen in beds to his right, left, and in front, Roger couldn't help but be depressed. The uncontrollable salivating of one veteran, the groans of another, and the countless haunting of sights and sounds roamed like spirits through the hallways of his thoughts.

One afternoon, while resting in bed, Roger received a phone call.

It was someone from whom Roger least expected a call.

"Hello Roger. This is your Uncle Jack Owens. How are you feeling today?" asked his uncle.

"Hi, Uncle Jack. Just resting for a while. How are you?"

"I'm doing fine. I heard from your dad what happened. I know I never call you guys, but when I heard about it, I just had to see how you were doing," Jack said. "So how long do you think you will be there?"

"I'm not sure. I might be here awhile," he answered, still somewhat groggy.

The two talked for only a few minutes.

"Well, Roger, take care and feel better okay?"

"Thank you, I'll try. Thanks for calling me," Roger added.

"My pleasure Roger. Okay, get some rest. I'll check back with your dad to see how you're doing later on. Bye, Roger," Jack said.

"Bye, Uncle Jack," Roger replied.

Roger hung up the phone and fell asleep.

After two months of recovery, Roger gained a bit of weight and strength. He was coherent and enjoyed the gift of conversation with some of the patients. Despite these moments, Roger stared deep into the blankness of the walls, thinking about what future he might hold. He pondered how he would ever learn to cope with the fast paced lifestyle he knew before the accident. He thought of how energetic he was at the ballpark and at his day job, and he became depressed again to think that he would never measure up to the man he was before all of this happened. Roger's whirlwind of emotions swirled into a vortex, spinning and tossing his optimism back and forth, like a turbulent game of "monkey in the middle." He narrowly missed the breaking point, but nevertheless he allowed himself to entertain thoughts of suicide.

As Roger sank further into his melancholic stupors, his friends and family displayed a relentless show of support and concern. They continued to visit and send cards, opening Roger's eyes and moving him to tears. During such visits, fans would confess to Navy doctors just how happy-go-lucky Roger had been. The team thought it over, and Dr. Schorn agreed to let Roger go for a one-day trip to visit the ballpark.

Roger was thrilled.

Of course, he wasn't permitted to drive, sell any peanuts, or climb any stairs, but Dr. Schorn knew it would be the best therapy and medicine that anyone could prescribe.

Once at the stadium, Roger took a silent moment to breathe in the open air and gaze upon the glorious expanse of familiar scenery. Yet for Roger, to be amongst the joy and unbelievable cascade of warmth from the people at the ballpark, and to be counted among friends, was truly a gift from heaven. Word spread throughout the stadium that Roger the Peanut Man was standing in an aisle on the third base side of the loge level. Quickly, a stream of affectionate fans became a sea of friends, bringing waves of welcome that sent emotional surges through Roger, like bathing sunlight to his soul.

Suddenly, one man stepped forward, looked into Roger's eyes, and gave him a bear hug. The man smiled reassuringly, and with a strong, Yiddish accent, he told Roger, "I know baseball, and I know you're going to make it. I've got a rabbi praying for you on first base, a priest at second base, and a minister at third. I've got all the bases covered for you."

Standing with watery eyes, he realized that day how much life was worth living, and he embraced the treasure of a second chance.

It was, indeed, the turning point in young Roger Owens' recovery.

The DiRisio family - Mary, Joe, Josephine, and Daniel

*Mary's sister, Virginia, who died
from a fireworks accident, and Daniel DiRisio*

Roger's grandfather, Ross W. Owens, Sr.

Roger's uncle,
Jack, and
Roger's father,
Ross, Jr.
as toddlers

Evelyn, Jack, and Ross, Jr.

Mary, all dressed up – 1930's

Mary, not so dressed up – 1940's

Baby Roger, with Grandma
Emeline Owens

With mom

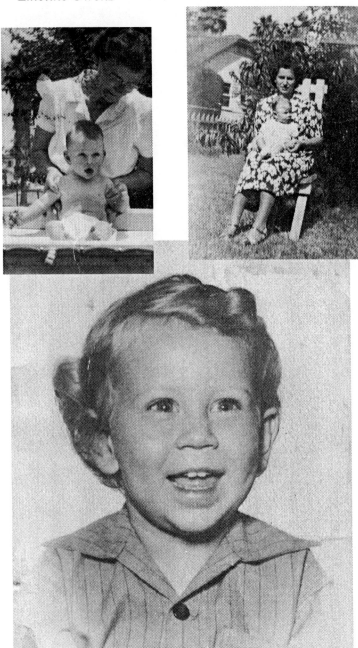

Roger Daniel Owens

Roger and Ruthie

Roger, Ruthie, and a friend – 1947

Gazing up in admiration, Ruthie and Roger – 1948

A happy family – Roger, Ross, Ruthie, Philip, and Priscilla – 1946

Your Family

is WELCOME to the BOYLE HEIGHTS BOYS And GIRLS CLUB which meets every SATURDAY AFTERNOON, Chicago and Michigan Avenues, 2:30 to 4. Group singing, Bible Stories, Religious Moving Pictures (Twice a month), Contests, Prizes & Refreshments. Parents and adults are also invited.

BEGINNING APRIL 22nd

You are also cordially invited to the following SUNDAY SERVICES:
Sunday School—9:45 a.m.
Morning Worship—11:00 a.m.
Prophetic Address—2:30 p.m.
(Guest Speakers and Special Music)
Youth Meeting—6:00 p.m.
(Friendly Discussions)
PRAYER MEETING Wednesday—7:30 p.m.

PLEASE BRING YOUR FRIENDS.

CHICAGO AND MICHIGAN AVENUES
BOYLE HEIGHTS
Ross Owens, Youth Director—Phone ANgelus 9-8601

TUNE IN K.G.E.R.
DIAL 1390 — EVERY NIGHT — 8:15

A family portrait - 1950

A friend, Ruthie, Philip, Roger, Esther, and Priscilla – 1952

Roger and baby Elizabeth – 1952

Esther "The Pester," Priscilla, Ruthie, Lois, and Elizabeth
– Beatty's Ranch – 1954

Lois and Elizabeth – Beatty's Ranch – 1954

Christmas at Beatty's Ranch – 1954

*Far back: Harold and Edith Beatty – three plaid girls:
Ruthie, Priscilla, Esther – matching overalls: Lois,
Elizabeth*

Beatty's Ranch – 1954

Ruthie – Roping the wind atop Half-Pint the pony

Little Esther and Edith with Becky the Donkey

Esther on the right, along with Uncle Harold

Harold and Edith Beatty – Postcard Advertisement for Beatty's Ranch for Girls – 1953

Harold Beatty, Ruthie and friends posing with War Paint, Half-Pint and Becky the Donkey – Beatty's Ranch – 1955

Reunited at last – 1956

*Back row: Roger – Middle row: Philip, Lois,
Ruthie, Edith Beatty, Priscilla – Front row:
Elizabeth, Paul, Esther*

Roger styling and smiling for the camera – 1958

Okay, not smiling for the camera

Esther – 1957

Ruthie – 1957

Lois – 1958

Priscilla – 1957

Paul – 1958

Elizabeth – 1957

Swinging for the fences –
Manual Arts HS – 1959

Shaking hands, or paws, with
good old Bert Owens – 1959

Mean exterior, lovable interior – Bert Owens

Don't mess with these two –
Roger and buddy, Bert – 1960

Back row: Esther, Philip, Priscilla –
Front row: Elizabeth, Paul, Lois – 1960

Roger Owens – 1960 – Teen idol? No, not quite.
Wally Cleaver? Perhaps

*Uncle Jack Owens
and one of Jack's
daughters, Mary Ann
– 1950's*

Jack Owens at home – 1930's

Roger's uncle, singer songwriter,
Jack Owens – 1960's

Standing in front of Ruth's boyfriend's 1959 Chevy Impala

Ruth, Lois, Priscilla, Philip, Paul, baby Grace, Mary, Ross, Elizabeth, Esther, and Roger – 1961

Ruth – 1962

Priscilla – 1964

Ruth and Bob – 1961

Ruth – 1958

Ruth – 1967

Ruth – 1962

Roger and Philip – 1961

*Roger, with sister
Grace*

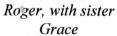

*Looking to pick a fight
with the camera*

*Handsome young
man*

The twins

Priscilla and Philip – 1963

Philip and Priscilla – 1963

Paramount Grad, Roger Owens Plans Policeman Career

This week's personality is energetic Roger Owens. Born in Glendale, California, February 14, 1943, Roger and his family later moved to Paramount, after several years. Attending John Muir junior high school, and Manuel Arts high school, Roger was very active in sports. At Manuel, baseball and basketball took up much of his time. In his senior year Roger attended Paramount high school where he graduated.

June Graduate

Roger has attended Compton College for two years, and plans to graduate in June of this year. Being a police science major, Roger plans to further his education at

Roger Owens

Long Beach State College with hopes of joining the Los Angeles Police Department. Roger's hobbies include listening to jazz recordings, and eating all kinds of "good" food. His favorite hobby, however, is selling peanuts! He sells peanuts six months out of the year at Dodger Stadium. Also, for three months of the year, he sells peanuts at the Los Angles Coliseum, at all of the football games.

CC Rates High

Roger thinks Compton College is a wonderful school to be a part of. He finds the teachers helpful, and the students friendly and amusing.

Roger in his Army best – 1964

Class picture –
Compton Community College – 1965

*Graduating from
Compton Community
College – 1965*

*The first five graduates in the college's new
Police Science Department*

Enjoying the night life with girlfriend, Vena – 1965

Roger in the Army California National Guard – 1966

Roger and Philip working the crowds at
Dodger Stadium – 1966

Basic Training with buddies -
1964

Leading song
service

In full M.P. uniform – 1966

At home on the couch

Lois, Philip, friend, Roger, Grace, Elizabeth – 1966

*Ross, Grace, Mary, Esther, Priscilla's husband
Jim, Priscilla, Ruth's brother-in-law Darrell,
and Paul – 1966*

Religious Tracts Stop Bullet Fired at Minister in Holdup

BY CHARLES HILLINGER
Times Staff Writer

Two youths twice jammed a 22-caliber revolver into the chest of a minister and shot to kill.

First, the smaller of the two squeezed the trigger. The gun misfired. His companion grabbed the gun and fired a second time.

"The gun went off," the Rev. Ross Owens, 58, a Baptist minister, related Monday. "I was supposed to fall over and die—but nothing happened.

"They were as confused as I was and didn't know what to do. So, instead of killing me, they decided to rob me."

Police, alerted by witnesses, arrived at the food stand where Mr. Owens was accosted as the minister was emptying his pockets of the $1.27 he had.

The two youths, identified as Marvin V. Smith, 18, of 613 W. Greenleaf St., and James Cole, 20, of 609 N. Evers St., both of Compton, were arrested and later booked on suspicion of robbery and assault with intent to commit murder.

As officers snapped handcuffs on the two men outside the Jack-in-the-Box stand at Compton Blvd. and Central Ave., in Compton, Mr. Owens felt his body for a wound.

There was a hole in his coat where the bullet entered. But no blood.

Reaching into his coat pocket he pulled out a thick wad of religious tracts—and in the bottom of his pocket, the spent bullet.

The religious literature stopped the bullet from piercing his body.

"It was a miracle. I'm sure it was and I'm sure those two young men believed it was," Mr. Owens insisted.

The shooting occurred Sunday afternoon shortly after he dropped his three daughters, Elizabeth, 16, Lois, 15, and Grace, 7, and a son, Paul, 14, off at the refreshment stand.

"They were going to get a bite to eat while I visited with Rev. Fred McElroy of the Beulahland Baptist Church, nearby," the minister explained.

Please Turn to Page 3, Col. 3

MINISTER

Continued from Third Page

The minister said as he was about to drive away from the food stand he noticed the two youths pushing his oldest daughter in a menacing manner.

"I went over to see what was happening and saw one of the young men had a gun in my daughter's back.

"I told them to let her alone, that I was her father, that I was a Baptist minister."

He said the youth with the gun then jammed it into his chest and squeezed the trigger. Nothing happened the first time. The tracts saved him the second time.

Police also were attempting to learn if the two youths were linked anyway with the weekend murders of South Gate barber Arnold Medina, 32, and delicatessen owner Gene Waxman, 45.

Medina was shot to death in his shop at 3077 Firestone Blvd. and Waxman was killed in his delicatessen shop at 4600 S. Central Ave., Los Angeles, Saturday night.

Two Compton youths were arrested Sunday night as suspects in the Medina slaying and also were being questioned by police about Waxman's death.

They were identified as Walter Harris Jr. of 1605 W. Arbutus St. and Jesse Philips of 1513 W. Spruce St., both 18.

RELIGIOUS TRACTS STOPPED BULLET—The Rev. Ross Owens, 58, shows hole in coat and a cut, circled, in the religious papers that stopped a bullet fired at him pointblank on a Compton street. "It was a miracle," Mr. Owens said. Two young suspects were arrested.
Story on Page 3, Part 1   Times photo by Frank Q. Brown

Story by Charles Hillinger. Photo by Frank Q. Brown. Copyright 1968, Los Angeles Times. Reprinted with permission.

WESTERN UNION
TELEGRAM
®

The filing time shown in the date line on domestic telegrams is LOCAL TIME at point of origin. Time of receipt is LOCAL TIME at point of destination

798P PDT JUN 14 69 LA219

L LLS584 MP XV GOVT PDB 8 EXTRA TDL PWS IRWIN CALIF 14

727P PDT

MRS ROSS OWENS, REPORT TIME DELIVERY ASC 04 TO FT MACARTHUR,

DO NOT FWD

6608 COMPTON BLVD PARAMOUNT CALIF

06-077 I REGRET TO INFORM YOU THAT YOUR SON, ROGER D. HAS BEEN

HOSPITALIZED FOR A SKULL FRACTURE, HIS CONDITION WARRANTED

PLACING HIM ON THE SERIOUSLY ILL LIST. YOUR PRESENCE IS NOT

REQUIRED UNLESS YOU SO DESIRE. YOU WILL BE NOTIFIED IN THE

EVENT OF ANY CHANGE IN ROGERS CONDITON. LETTER WILL FOLLOW

COMMANDING OFFICER WAH W2RJAA-01

(753).

*Photos of
Roger's jeep and
Andy's jeep –
1969*

INSTRUCTIONS

1. Instructions for completion and distribution are provided by Articles 18-20, 18-21, 18-23, and 18-24 of the Manual of the Medical Department.
2. When Statistical Coding is required, send the first copy of the cover sheet to the Naval Medical Regional Data Center.

1. TO: Convening Authority	3. DATE BOARD MET
2. VIA:	
	29 September 1969

4. FROM (Facility and location)	5. FACILITY AND LOCATION NO.
Naval Hospital, San Diego, California	00025911

6. DATE OF ORIGINAL ADMISSION TO SICKLIST (Day, Month, Year)	7. PATIENT REGISTER NO.	THIS BLOCK FOR NMRDC USE
14 June 1969	691459	

8. LAST DUTY 92311	LENGTH OF SERVICE (Days, Months, Years)	8A. DUTY	9A. LENGTH SERVICE MO / YR
EQ HQ CO., MP DET., 40th ARMOR, FT ___, CA	27das05mos04yrs		

10. PLACE OF ENTRANCE PHYSICAL (if less than one year)	11. DATE OF ENTRANCE PHYSICAL (Day, Month, Year)	10A. ENTRANCE PHYS.	11A. ENT. DATE MO / YR

12. PRIMARY DIAGNOSIS (Include Anatomic Part)	12A. DIAGNOSIS
Basilar Skull Fracture with Contusion and Hematoma of Right temporal lobe, #8019-116; Multiple Abrasions and Contusions of Scalp and Body, #9290-967; Bony defect, Acquired, Combined about 23 square centimeters, #7490-112.	8 0 1 9
	12B. ANATOMIC PART
	1 1 6

13. ORIGIN	14. EXISTED PRIOR TO ENTRY/AGGRAVATED BY SERVICE	15. PRESENT CONDITION
1. DUE TO OWN MISCONDUCT	1. EXISTED PRIOR TO ENTRY, AGGRAVATED BY SERVICE	1. FIT FOR DUTY
2. NOT DUE TO OWN MISCONDUCT	2. EXISTED PRIOR TO ENTRY, NOT AGGRAVATED BY SERVICE	X 2. UNFIT FOR DUTY
3. INCURRED IN LINE OF DUTY X	3. DID NOT EXIST PRIOR TO ENTRY IN SERVICE	3. UNSUITABLE FOR SERVICE
4. NOT INCURRED IN LINE OF DUTY		

16. PROBABLE FUTURE DURATION	17. INDICATED DISPOSITION	
1. PERMANENT	X 1. REFER TO PHYSICAL EVALUATION BOARD	5. RETURN TO DUTY
X 2. MAY BE PERMANENT	2. DISCHARGE, PHYSICAL DISABILITY	6. RETURN TO LIMITED DUTY
3. TEMPORARY	3. DISCHARGE, ERRONEOUS ENLISTMENT	7. CONTINUE INPATIENT CARE
	4. DISCHARGE, UNSUITABLE FOR SERVICE	8. OTHER (Specify under "REMARKS")

18. THE FOLLOWING SHALL BE COMPLETED BY THE MEDICAL BOARD PRIOR TO SUBMISSION TO THE CONVENING AUTHORITY	YES	NO
1. DID THE MEMBER APPEAR BEFORE THE MEDICAL BOARD IN PERSON?	X	
2. WILL DISCLOSURE OF INFORMATION TO THE MEMBER RELATIVE TO HIS PHYSICAL/MENTAL CONDITION ADVERSELY AFFECT HIS HEALTH?		X
3. HAS THE MEMBER BEEN ADVISED OF THE MEDICAL BOARD FINDINGS?	X	
4. HAS THE MEMBER BEEN OFFERED AN OPPORTUNITY TO SUBMIT A REBUTTAL STATEMENT IN WRITING (Not applicable if No. 3 is yes)?	X	
5. WHERE APPLICABLE, HAS THE MEMBER WAIVED HIS RIGHTS TO A FULL AND FAIR HEARING?		
6. IS THE MEMBER'S SIGNED STATEMENT OF REBUTTAL AND/OR CERTIFICATE TO WAIVE RIGHTS TO A FULL AND FAIR HEARING ATTACHED?		
7. WILL APPEARANCE BEFORE A PHYSICAL EVALUATION BOARD BE DELETERIOUS TO THE MEMBER'S PHYSICAL/MENTAL CONDITION?		X

19. REMARKS

20. BOARD MEMBERS AND SIGNATURES	GRADE	SERVICE	SIGNATURE
SENIOR MEMBER TYPE NAME W. W. HAMILTON	CAPT MC	USN	
MEMBER TYPE NAME V. G. SCHORN	CDR MC	USN	
MEMBER TYPE NAME S. TOLCHIN	CDR MC	USN	

21. IDENTIFICATION (Mechanically imprint or typewrite Name (last), first, middle initial), File or Service Number, Grade or Rate, and branch of Service)	21A. CODE NAME
OWENS, Roger Daniel SP4 ARMY, RA19868593	

EXHIBIT   A

(OVER)

DEPARTMENT OF THE ARMY
OFFICE OF THE ADJUTANT GENERAL
WASHINGTON, D. C. 20315

AGPO-R   25 Aug 71

LETTER ORDERS NUMBER D 8-1364

SUBJECT: Removal from TDRL

SP4 ROGER D. OWENS

1140 Strand Apt. B
Manhattan Beach, CA 90266

TC. 381. The above named individual having been determined PERMANENTLY
unfit for duty by reason of physical disability, is removed from the
Temporary Disability Retired list on date indicated and on the following
day is PERMANENTLY RETIRED in current grade.

Retired list: AUS
Authority: 10 USC 1201
Date removed from TDRL: 30 Sep 71
Percentage of disability: 60%
Special Instructions:

BY ORDER OF THE SECRETARY OF THE ARMY:

                                        Slone

                                  Adjutant General

DEPARTMENT OF THE ARMY
UNITED STATES ARMY HOSPITAL
FORT MACARTHUR, CALIFORNIA 90731

IN REPLY REFER TO

December 7, 1969

Dear Dr. Schorn,

    I just wanted to wish you a very MERRY MERRY CHRISTMAS AND
HAPPY NEW YEAR.

    I also want to again thank you for everything you have done
for me. I can still remember when the only time I ever smiled
is when you asked, " How are you doing Rog. Babe." I'll never
forget your name nor will my six sisters, two brothers and
Mom and Dad. Everyone is so Thankful and so am I.

    I am enclosing my business card although I have not returned
to work yet. It seems that my P. E. B. is being held up so I'M
still at Fort Macarthur Hospital.(2½ months) Maybe soon I'll
get out. I hope so.

    If you can remember I am the one who sells PEANUTS at all
Sports Events in L. A. I am asking a favor of you. If ever you
and your wife or children are in L. A. please call me so that we
may get together. It would mean very much to me. I receive many
tickets (Free of charge) to Baseball, Basketball, Football and
Ice Hockey. I also will be able to get you all the stale peanuts
(smile) that you can eat.

    Dr. Schorn, I know you are a very busy man and San Diego is not
close, but whenever possible please give me a call. Everyone at
the Company I work for knows your name so you will certainly not
be a stranger.

    May God Bless You Always.

Your friend,
Roger Owens

Roger

Roger selling before game time – Mother's Day, 1970

Back at the stadium nearly a year after the accident – with that big smile, no one would have ever known it happened.

*Top: with Elizabeth and
Lois – 1970
Middle: with Lois and
Paul – 1970
Bottom: Lois – 1971*

*Elizabeth, Ross, Lois,
Grace – 1972*

Ross, Esther, Roger –
1972

Roger and friend, Jay
Bieber, at Jay's
wedding

Roger and Paul at home in the apartment complex
in Los Angeles

$\mathcal{C}$ 16

Here is Not My Home

A fter three and a half months of hospitalization, Roger was ready to go home. On one occasion, he was allowed to go home for a weekend, to slowly dip his feet into the waters of rehabilitation. Then, he was allowed to go home every weekend. Each Friday, Philip drove down to San Diego, picked up Roger, drove back to Manhattan Beach, then returned to San Diego on Sunday to drop Roger off, and then headed back to Whittier that same day. Every weekend, Philip drove nearly 400 miles for his brother. Back in the hospital, Roger was up and about in the room everyday, but his doctors noticed that Roger found light and sounds irritating. He became less aggressive and complained only occasionally of a slight headache. He was also fully aware of time, where he was, who he was, and who everyone else was. Opthalmologists examined Roger's eyes and found everything was better, with the yellowing of his eyes completely receded.

By September 29, 1969, medical staff filed a report summarizing Roger's case, and it was Dr. Schorn's belief that Roger was well enough to be discharged.

As a result of the surgery, Roger no longer had his sense of smell.

Puzzled doctors thought he should have lost his sense of taste as well, since they were closely associated. From then on, Roger would only know from memory the smell of a fresh bag of peanuts, or anything else for that matter.

Although discharged from the hospital, Roger was still considered on active duty for the Army National Guard. Doctors instructed him to rest, but in order to fit back into the busy stream of every day life and work, they also advised Roger to receive rehabilitation through work at Fort MacArthur in San Pedro. Five days a week, for three months, Roger showed up to do light amounts of work, including filing papers and answering phone calls.

169

Doctors predicted that it would take three years for a full recovery, but Roger was showing remarkable progress. In spite of this, he began to suffer mental lapses, and short-term memory loss. Sometimes, when writing out sentences, he unknowingly left out entire words or phrases. He would then read what he had written, only to realize the large gaps in the sentences. He would crumble up the paper in frustration, depressed by his inability to write a coherent sentence. At night, he often found it difficult to fall asleep. He would wake up with chills and momentary depression. He told his doctors about it, and they gave him some medicine to help. With each passing day, however, he was improving.

It was early 1970, and the jeep accident, the recovery, and the rehabilitation had taken their toll on his relationship with Bernadette. They drifted apart, and Roger found life in his Manhattan Beach apartment to be solemn and emotionally burdensome. After all, it was a party pad. In fact, there were clubs and restaurants all along the strand, and the commotion from people having so much fun contrasted sharply with his sorrow. It was a lifestyle that ridiculed him, because his heart was not in it. He decided to spend as little time at home as possible, often calling on friends to stay at their place to hang out or spend the night. Sometimes he stayed the day at Jay Bieber's apartment in West Los Angeles. Other times, he relaxed a few minutes away at the house of a fellow Westransco salesman and friend, Taylor Haines. He had a family, a Great Dane that Roger loved, and a barbecue grill in the backyard. On at least two occasions, his boss, Bill Woodling, who also lived close by in Manhattan Beach, allowed Roger to hang out and spend the night. Roger couldn't have asked for a more supportive bunch than his friends from the ballpark and from his freight company. However, Roger knew he was straining their friendship, or at least straining their ears, with the constant mentioning of the accident and how he was doing better but not fully himself. He knew he was guilty of seeking sympathy and attention, but he felt the need to find reassurance from them and from within. He was grateful for their patience and for being kind enough to listen. They were just happy that they still had their friend.

Throughout the year, Jay tried to get Roger back into the flow of social life. Jay and his English-born fiancé, Pam, were soon to be married in a small suburb, south of London, England. Jay invited Roger to tag along in Europe for a week, to not only be with friends, but also to be the best man in the wedding. They knew that he needed a change of scenery, and not to mention the chance to meet the one girl who had been writing him letters from England, at the insistence of her friend Jay.

The time for the wedding arrived, and Roger enjoyed the ceremony. He finally met the lady, named Jill, when all four of them went out to a nearby restaurant. Roger's anticipation clanked loudly in his mind, like banging forks on fine china, awaiting the stimulation of some, in fact, any, conversation from Jill. As Roger sat recalling the rambling woman from the letters, he was convinced he should be mentally trained for their meeting in England. However, the garrulous and pretty woman he conjured with every letter mailed to him remained as vocal as a napkin, a victim of her own timidity, and consequently, the carefully-plotted place settings on their table retained more presence than she did.

Jay and Pam had agreed to spend their honeymoon in Paris, France. By the time Jay, Pam, and Roger arrived in Paris, they learned that all of the remaining rooms were booked in the hotel they requested. When they reached the hotel room, Jay and Pam looked at each other, and then looked at Roger.

"I know, I know, I'll just put my stuff away, and I'll go take a walk for a few hours," Roger said.

They smiled.

"We'll make room for you on the floor when you get back, or when we're done, whichever comes first," Jay said.

"Yeah right," Roger replied with a chuckle. "By the way, thanks for putting up with me."

"No problem, Roger," Pam said.

"Okay, see you guys later tonight," Roger added, closing the door behind him.

Roger was happy to be with friends that cared enough to bring him along, even on their own honeymoon. But Roger found the scenery of Champs Elysées, the countless cafés, pigeons, people, and of course the Arc de Triomphe, standing gallantly in the midst of the city, to all be reasons enough to be happy. The afternoon sun dipped below the horizon, skewing the long cast shadow of the Eiffel Tower across the landscape of grass and trees. The stars found their glowing glory in every night's sky, beaming as spots of inspiration and shining high above every street corner café that boasted aromas of éclairs and warm coffee. Such scents swept through the chilling, night air like a proud wave of flavor. These tasteful odors were like French waiters, standing in indignation in their futility to entice Roger's nose because of his lack of smell. Bundled up for the cold evening, he strolled down the narrow streets wherever his curiosity took him, and he found solace in the familiarity of a smile, even as the strangeness of language threatened that comfort with a deep longing for home.

It was spring, 1970, and the baseball season had begun. It was more than half a year since Roger had been discharged from the hospital, and he was well enough to return to the stadium. Upon his return, the fans enthusiastically welcomed him. They showered him with the same kind of love and admiration that he received on his day trip to the ballpark, less than a year earlier.

As the months passed, Roger noticed a different type of lifestyle and philosophy evolving within him. He steadily accepted a new mentality, filled with a sense of added purpose and meaning in life, and combined with a stronger faith in God and a gratitude for friends and blessings bestowed upon him.

His return to Dodger Stadium was glorious, as he sold peanuts and talked with fans once again. Roger couldn't believe how little time it took for him to get into shape climbing stairs and regaining control of his peanut pitching. However, he couldn't understand why he was able to approach his work at the freight company, and at the ballpark pitching bags of peanuts, with more gusto than ever before, especially considering all that he had been through. Although some worries lingered and some readjustment to the real world was necessary, Roger was convinced that he was on the road to recovery and success.

On a Saturday afternoon, near the close of the 1970 baseball season, while working at the stadium, Roger saw two young ladies smiling at him. The two girls were friends and often went together to see the Dodgers play on the weekends. They were close in age, but the younger of the two who had just turned 13 years old, introduced herself as Cindy Brazil. Roger paid no more and no less attention to her than any other girl or boy at the ballpark. Young pre-teens and teenagers found Roger to be easily approachable and occasionally talked to him and joked with him while he walked up and down the aisles tossing peanuts. But this girl was different. She admired him with an intimacy that was revealed only to her close friend, her parents, and in her new diary.

The girl's father worked as policeman for the city of Vernon, and he also worked part-time as security guard at the stadium as a way to enjoy baseball and meet the players. As a result, young Cindy saw several baseball games for free. With every passing game, Cindy's crush on Roger flourished. As for Cindy's friend, she was attracted to his brother Philip, and since she was as outgoing as Cindy, she initiated conversations with Philip. Cindy sometimes followed Roger around the loge level, watching his every move and paying attention to his mood and character. At the end of the day, she wrote about Roger in her diary and freely discussed such thoughts with her parents at dinner.

One day, she drove with her dad and her girlfriend to the stadium for an afternoon game with the Giants. On the way there, she sat thinking of Roger. She thought of how or when she would finally ask for his phone number. When she made it up the escalators, she began looking for him in the usual area.

Whenever she lost sight of him while tracking him down, she just listened for his voice, as he hollered, "Peanuts here. Peanuts here." He became louder with her every stride, and soon, he was within sight. Roger noticed her. She just waved at him, along with her girlfriend. He smiled and waved back. They walked to where Philip was, so her girlfriend could talk with him in the large walkway near the concession stands. Cindy was enthralled by Roger's presence, but even she sensed he was evasive and not very playful.

"Philip, can I ask you a question?" Cindy asked.

"Sure," Philip said, taking a break from work.

"Why does Roger seem so serious all the time?" Cindy inquired.

"Well, Roger's been through a lot in the last few months. He was in a military jeep accident last year, and I guess since then, his outlook on life changed. We weren't sure he would make it," Philip added. He continued to tell them what Roger went through, and Cindy listened and asked questions. Finally, when Philip had to get back to work, Cindy stood in silence, aware that she was falling even harder for Roger.

"When's his birthday?" Cindy asked abruptly.

"February 14th," Philip responded. Cindy couldn't hide her huge smile, as she thought how romantic it was for his birthday to also be on Valentine's Day.

"I was thinking of sending him a birthday card, but I didn't know when it was. I'd mail it to him, but I don't have his address. Do you know it?" asked Cindy.

Philip formed a wide grin on his face and gave out a chuckle.

"Yeah I know it. I don't see any harm in giving it to you. Besides, he could use some cheering up." Philip said. He paused, and then he let out another mischievous chuckle. "In fact, here's his phone number, too," he added, handing her a piece of paper.

"Don't tell him you gave me his number, okay?" she asked.

"Of course not."

"You're the best," she said, grabbing him down low enough around his neck to kiss him on the cheek. The two girls let out squeals loud enough to chase away pigeons on the roof of the left field pavilion.

It was February 1971, and on one Saturday afternoon, Roger planned to relax for a few hours by crossing the expanse of about fifty yards from door to shore, lying on a towel spread out on the warm sand, and watching the sunlit waves flow lazily onto the shore of Manhattan Beach. But first, Roger checked his mailbox. In it, he found an envelope sent from Cindy Brazil. He recognized the name and opened it immediately. Inside was a birthday-Valentine's card for him, and he was moved that she cared enough to send it.

In 1971, Roger decided it was time to move. According to Roger, the road to recovery and success that he was on could only be paved with new asphalt. He was fed up with his Manhattan Beach apartment, and he was desperate to find another place.

Aware of Roger's increased depression, due in part to the nightclub scene dominating the apartment, Jay Bieber invited him to just get in the car to drive around and look for a new place to live. They drove around West Los Angeles, close to Jay's place, and eventually, they found a small apartment complex on Barrington Avenue. It had a pool and tall, inviting palm trees.

Roger had found a new home.

17

Answering Love's Call and Other Such Interviews

B y now, Roger's parents, Ross and Mary, and his siblings Paul, and ten year-old Grace, moved into a larger, red-brick house on San Marcos Street in Compton. They managed to secure the house, which was a step up in status, despite being kicked out once again for falling behind in rent. At age 17, Paul found it extremely difficult to live under the same roof as his parents, especially his mother. Mary argued constantly with Paul. His teenage lifestyle only accentuated his idiosyncrasies, straining any attempts at a mother son relationship. Mary, already a grandmother, could have been Paul's grandmother due to their large age difference and, because of the extended lack of infant bonding many years before, it could be expected that Mary and Paul would feel little attachment to one another. Paul had enough and transferred from Dominguez High School, which many of his brothers and sisters had once attended. Ross, sensing his growing son's frustration, asked Roger if he could be the big brother and let Paul move in with him. It was an odd, yet symbiotic relationship that formed from the day he moved in.

Paul was handsome and tall, and he was still growing, even at six feet two inches. A lanky teenager with a mischievous grin and long, flowing, brown hair, he seemed to always have his arms around one girl or another, and the phone ringing for him when he got home from school at University High, which was just a few blocks away. Roger helped Paul get a vendor job at the stadium, and now all three Owens boys worked at the ballpark, two selling peanuts and the youngest selling soda.

When Paul moved in, Roger, who needed the company, let him set up a cot in the living room. Paul promised to keep his things together in exchange for using the living room, but he never quite mastered the art

175

of locking the front door at night. On several occasions, early in the morning, Roger found the front door closed, but unlocked. After a long night of carousing, an exhausted Paul let himself in and fell asleep. The next morning, after telling Paul many times about not just shutting the door but locking it as well, Roger approached the front door. Roger stared in disbelief. Grumbling under his breath, Roger grabbed the handle, finding that, indeed, the door was locked this time, but it was also half way open. Roger slumped over slightly at the shoulders and exhaled slowly, unsure whether to laugh or remain dumbfounded.

Throughout the baseball season, Roger continued to impress Dodger fans with his remarkable peanut pitching and down home personality. Game day after game day, Dodger fans sustained an insatiable desire for the taste of fresh peanuts and for the showmanship of the Peanut Man, who threw them bags of happiness overhand, under his leg, behind his back, and two at a time behind his back. He gave them the "give me five nut," where he placed the bag in the fan's hand as if slapping his hand to give that person "five." He also hurled the "fast nut," which people loved to see, and, if on any one of these tosses, a fan should drop it, Roger would often call them on it, and have the bag sent back to Roger for another toss. The poor, uncoordinated fan found redemption only on the second toss, when the fan grabbed the peanut bag out of the air, and as a result, captured the respect once again of taunting friends. These experiences brought more than tossed bags of peanuts, and bundled within every bag, there was more than just salted nuts nestled in vulnerable, little peanut shells. It seemed as though the label on the side of the bags included such eye-catching ingredients as charisma, humor, and the feeling of genuine excitement in Roger's voice. In fact, even compared with the lingering saltiness and flavor of the peanuts in one's mouth, the enjoyable time had by the fans lasted much longer in their memories, until the next time dads could bring their daughters, sons could bring their mothers, whole families, and groups of friends could all be so lucky to buy Dodger tickets once again, to be content with the day's simple offerings of Dodger baseball, Dodger Dogs, Vin Scully on the radio, and the Peanut Man in the stands.

Throughout the next two years, fan mail steadily trickled in to the Dodger front office. The letters praised Roger for his remarkable talent and for the joy he brought to every home stand. By 1973, Dodger officials working in public relations took notice of the appreciative letters, one of which called Roger's peanut pitching performances a "show within a show," and others stated how much fun the game was to watch, with Roger throwing packaged goobers left and right to hungry fans.

During this same time, Roger still had a difficult time fighting off depression. Doctors permitted him to see a psychologist in Long Beach, so he could air his momentary feelings of sadness and lack of self-confidence. The psychologist listened to him, helped Roger open up about such matters, and suggested he find a girlfriend to help cheer him up. Roger went every two or three weeks for six months, and was finally prescribed medicine to help him. Much of the depression subsided as a result, but nothing was as therapeutic as being at the ballpark.

It was late in the season, 1972, and Cindy and her girlfriend made their rounds in the orange loge level to find Roger and Philip. During the last several months, Cindy only showed up occasionally to the games, now and then to watch Roger from a distance. Roger didn't see her stop by as often in the last year or so, but he kept busy with pitching peanuts and catching the eyes of other twenty-something girls. By the time she was fifteen, Cindy already looked like a fully matured, attractive, young woman ready to attend college. She was interested in Roger more than ever.

One afternoon, Cindy and her friend drove to the ballpark with the intention of catching one baseball game and two peanut vendors. Her friend headed toward Philip, who looked forward to seeing her each time. Cindy strolled steadily toward Roger, eyeing him the whole way as she walked down the aisle. She was perhaps five feet, five inches and had long brown hair that reflected sunlight with the kind of sheen that must have taken four shampoo rinses to acquire. Roger showed off his sense of style with his huge, lamb-chop sideburns and large, shiny-framed, amber lens sunglasses. His cool shades, which looked as if they were handed to him by Elvis himself, protected his eyes from such a glare, but did little to guard against her lengthy stare. Her seductive brown eyes and smile even made Roger's thoughts stutter.

Roger eyed her up and down, judging her age to be no less than seventeen and no more than nineteen. It was the first time he had seen her in this way, and it was the first time he had a conversation with her that was more than just a few words.

"I'd like some peanuts," she said with pretend coyness. She had been watching him from a distance for nearly three years, all the while growing and maturing until the one day she was prepared to approach him in a more serious and intimate manner. She had been thinking how attractive a man he was, and now she was ready to talk with him, to find out all about him, to ask him questions, and to know what made him tick. Her diary was full of affectionate notations about Roger. Her parents knew about him and were proud of his work at the stadium. She treated her mother as her best friend and confidant, displaying a maturity that proved she was ahead of her time.

But, at 15, evidently she was *way* ahead of her time.

Roger handed her a bag of peanuts.

"Hi Roger, it's me Cindy" she said, pulling out some change to pay him.

"Yeah, I know," he replied with a bit of excitement in his voice. "Oh no, they're on the house," he insisted.

"Thank you. So, how are you?" she asked.

"Fine. How are you?" he responded.

"I'm fine. Good game today, huh?" she added.

"Yeah, it is. They have a rally going, and Wes Parker's at bat. They can get a few more runs if they keep it up," Roger said.

"Yeah," she said. She paused for a moment. "Nice brother you have, Philip, I mean."

"Thanks."

It was awkward, but they talked for a few minutes, until she let him get back to work. He couldn't believe how pretty she was, but he knew she was young, if not too young. During their brief conversation, Roger wasn't ready to tell her about his jeep accident, but she already knew.

At home, Roger and his younger brother Paul rarely were around together at the same time. Roger's friend, Mort, often called Roger to see what he was up to. Every time he called, he jokingly asked Roger how his "son" was doing, referring to Paul, who was ten years younger. Roger and Paul were quite different in many respects, but they got along as well as two brothers could. Sometimes, Paul found himself disliking Roger, and sometimes, Roger found himself disliking Paul. They were brothers after all, and while their squabbles were minor, they managed to find plenty of redeeming qualities in one another. At dinner, their schedules overlapped, and they ate together and watched *Sanford and Son* on television. It was their favorite show, hands down. Redd Foxx played "Sanford," beating up everyone's feelings on the show, including those of "Aunt Esther," like a title bout between Ali and Ugly. The two brothers laughed themselves to tears every time the show was on.

During the early 70's, Roger, Philip, and Paul were all very competitive in nature, and while their personalities clashed many times, they also found ways to bond. On some occasions, they played tennis against one another with such tenacity that it seemed as if the Wimbledon Cup was riding on the line. One time, they went on a boating trip near San Luis Obispo, and all three were so angry that their boat had tipped over and sent all three of them into the lake. The rundown, pest-infested cabin they had rented didn't help much either.

Even though Paul enjoyed some days at their apartment, especially when Roger played records with songs, like "War" and Marvin Gaye's "I Heard It Through The Grapevine," Paul also felt that Roger's overbearing, fatherly and protective ways were getting to him. He felt that sometime soon he would be better off moving into an apartment with his friend. For everything that bugged Paul about his older brother, he couldn't help but find things that he also admired about him. Even when Paul was a young boy, he remembered his big brother visiting the Owens house on San Marcos Street in Compton. Paul and Roger shared fried chicken on the curb and then went to a movie at a local drive-in. Paul also remembered the time Roger stuck up for the huge Latino crowds that were watching a soccer event at the Coliseum. Many of the vendors wanted to charge the people a dollar instead of a quarter for each cup of Coke. Roger put his foot down on the matter, but he was outnumbered, and so the cost of the sodas was hiked for the event. Paul also recalled with fondness many years later how Roger, during the late 60's, always made it a point to tell friends not to take the Lord's name in vain in his presence. Roger even helped Paul buy his first two cars. Despite their differences, Paul knew he had a good, older brother. Roger's sisters, especially Lois and Elizabeth, sometimes visited Roger and were paid to count all of his quarters from work at ball games.

At the stadium, Paul showed up to every game, but always made it to the vendor line at the last minute. Philip and Paul both knew they didn't have the showmanship or drive that Roger had for the vending business, so no lasting rivalry developed. In fact, despite a few arguments typical of two brothers, Roger and Philip were content to help each other out by splitting the profits equally, as they both sold peanuts in the same area of the loge level. During the day, Philip taught at a middle school in Whittier. A graduate of Compton Community College and then Whittier College, he had taught middle school kids for several years already, but with growing demands upon his schedule to help students and parents, he realized that he might only have a handful of years left to work at the stadium before calling it quits and dedicating himself fully to his students.

As more time passed, more fan mail poured in for Roger. Finally, at the end of summer of '73, the public relations manager at Dodger Stadium called the local ABC news station, and *Channel 7 Eyewitness News* sent their young reporter, Chuck Henry, to Dodger Stadium to cover the story about a talented, thirty year-old, peanut vendor named Roger Owens.

Roger was interviewed, and the story ran on the sports segment of the evening news on September 22nd. The coverage sparked two more interviews a year later, on September 3, 1974 with reporter Tom Kelly from CBS, and on October 8th, with Terry Phillips from ABC. Roger was excited that his peanut tossing earned him recognition enough to be on television, especially since he had no idea that people had written letters to the Dodger management, praising him for his unique abilities.

Cindy and her friend waited for Roger and Philip at the ballpark several times, either at escalators or at the commissary, where at the eighth inning, vendors picked up their money for the day's work. Cindy wore more revealing outfits and flirted with Roger, asking him questions and showing him considerable interest. Roger didn't embrace the idea of a relationship with Cindy with open arms, mainly because of the age difference of fourteen years. Although, his loneliness bothered him considerably, he wasn't sure it was a good idea to be an item with a teenager. Her advances were always met with hesitation from Roger.

One evening, while at home relaxing, Roger received a phone call.

"Hello?" Roger asked.

"Hello, is Roger there?" asked a young woman with the kind of voice that aroused his attention.

"Speaking," he answered.

"Hey, Roger. How are you?" asked the girl.

"I'm fine. Who am I speaking with?" inquired Roger.

"Oh you don't remember me? We met on the beach that day outside your apartment in Manhattan Beach. I remember you," she added.

Roger gathered his thoughts to remember who it could have been. There were plenty of people he talked with, especially people he told about his accident and how he managed to get through it, and how fortunate he was to still be alive.

"I think so," he said.

"Yeah we were hanging out, and you told me all about your jeep accident, and your work at the ballpark," she said convincingly.

"Oh yeah, that's right," said Roger, still unsure exactly who it was but thinking of one woman at the beach that could have been the one on the phone.

"Well, I was thinking. How about we meet up some time tomorrow evening for dinner?" she asked.

"Sure. Where at?" Roger replied, slightly excited at the thought of the woman he had pictured.

The two talked for nearly fifteen minutes.

"Roger, I'd like you to know something first, before we meet," the girl said with a noticeable sigh.

"Yeah, what's that?"

"Roger, it's me Cindy. Now, I know you might not want to go out, but I wanted to at least call," she said.

Roger instantly felt somewhat disappointed, because he felt that something like this just wouldn't work out, no matter how good Cindy looked every time he saw her, and no matter how caring and how mature for her age she was. However, Roger did need someone in his life, and because he felt comfortable around her at the ballpark, he considered going out on a date with her, but only if her parents agreed to it.

"What about your parents? What do they think?" he asked.

"My parents are okay with it. I talk about you all the time with them."

Roger didn't believe her that it was okay with her parents.

"So how did you know about the jeep accident, from Philip?"

"Yeah, he told me."

"And my number? Let me guess, Philip told you?"

"Right again," she said laughing. "If it will make you feel better, how 'bout you pick me up after the next game, and before we go eat, we can go to my place and meet my parents in Cypress?"

"Okay, that sounds better," said Roger.

Finally, the day came for the two to go out. After the Dodger game, Roger drove Cindy out to Cypress, stopping at a McDonald's, because she was hungry. They made it to her house, and Roger met her father, Ernie, and her mother, Beverly. They were a friendly couple, opening up their house to Roger with generosity.

They all sat down at the dinner table and talked.

"How are you doing Roger?" asked her mom.

"I'm doing fine. Keeping busy at the stadium," Roger answered nervously.

From the minute Roger stepped inside their house, he noticed how clean the place was and how nice the furniture was. Beverly eyed the sack of fast food.

"First date, and you take our daughter to McDonald's. Boy, Roger, you don't spend much do you?" she said teasing him.

"Yeah, it looks that way doesn't it? We stopped for a quick bite on the way over," Roger confessed, laughing along with her.

"Roger, do you feel strange at all about the age difference between you and Cindy," asked Beverly.

"Well, yeah, in all honesty, I have some concern about it." Roger answered.

"Well, to Ernie and to me, you seem trustworthy and the kind of man that knows responsibility."

"Yeah, Cindy's talked about you for years, so we feel like we know a lot about you already. We know you work at the ballpark, and we know your character, and if Cindy's okay with it, then we are too," her dad said.

"Well, I appreciate that Mr. Brazil," he said.

"No problem."

After meeting her parents, the two just stayed and talked with her parents. At the end of the night, Roger finally felt relaxed knowing her parents approved. Over the next several months, Ernie and Beverly developed a bond with Roger that practically rivaled the relationship between Roger and Cindy. At the police station, Ernie did a background check on Roger, and he checked out fine, but years later he laughed about it while telling Roger what he had done.

The family had a swimming pool in the backyard. The pool got plenty of use from Roger, who often fell asleep on the floating raft, soaking up sunshine after a long day of selling peanuts on a Sunday afternoon. Many times, he was invited to spend the night, only to wake up in the morning to a kiss from Cindy and her dad's homemade breakfast. Other times, all four of them went to the movie theater, and with a simple flash of his badge, Ernie got all of them in for free. During the off-season, Roger had more time to play tennis, a sport that had grown in popularity during the early to mid 70's. It helped his legs stay in shape, and as a result, he eventually hooked Cindy's parents into becoming avid tennis junkies.

By the end of 1973, Cindy Brazil, age 16, was engaged to Roger Owens, who was almost 31 years of age.

During that same year, a television producer heard about Roger from the recent interviews on the local news. He had a television show called *The Girl In My Life*, with the host, Fred Holiday. Roger received a phone call about it and then told Beverly about it. He wanted to surprise Cindy by having her in the live audience when Roger appeared on the show. So Beverly convinced Cindy to spend the day together going shopping and to a taping of that show. Cindy agreed.

The show was about how each couple met in unusual places or under unusual circumstances. The host had Roger act as though he was crashing the set by grabbing all the attention and throwing peanut bags to the audience. After Roger was on stage, and after Cindy was thoroughly embarrassed and shocked as she sat beside her mom, the host finally let Cindy in on the prank, and Roger shared their wonderful story of how they met at the stadium over a bag of peanuts. Everyone was happy for the couple and for their fairytale story of romance.

Not long after the show aired, Roger received another call from the people at the game show, *Truth Or Consequences*, with host Bob Barker. Roger agreed to be there, and when he was on stage, Barker offered money, sometimes 50 bucks, to contestants to throw bags of peanuts just like Roger the Peanut Man.

One night, during a ballgame, Roger was throwing peanuts and grabbing the tossed quarters out of the air as payment from each customer. Suddenly, a man in a business suit walked up to Roger and introduced himself as the Vice President of Montgomery Ward's department store.

"I sure am impressed with your peanut pitching talent, Roger. I'm sure you know of Peter O'Malley, the Dodger President, right?" the man asked.

"Well, of course, but I've never actually met him," he said, unsure about what the man was getting at.

"Is that so? Does he know about you entertaining the people like this?" he asked.

"Well, sir, I have no idea. He might know about me, but then again, as you could relate to, he's quite a busy man."

The man stood quietly thinking.

"Okay, Roger, if you have a minute, I'd like you to follow me," the businessman said.

The two walked up to the stadium club level, where the press box was. In the press box sat Vin Scully, who eloquently spoke to millions of Dodger listeners about one Dodger story after another, only interrupting himself to relay the action on the field. To the left of the press box was the office of Peter O'Malley.

The Dodger executive had taken a break for a few minutes from his paperwork to stand and watch the game. O'Malley turned around and recognized his friend from Montgomery Wards. He also saw the young peanut vendor, standing there a bit nervously.

"Hiya, Peter," the man said.

"Hi, how are you doing today?" O'Malley said.

"Doing fine. I just wanted to show you someone special working here at the stadium. I thought I'd introduce you two, to make sure you realize what an asset you have in this peanut vendor, Roger Owens.

Roger and Peter O'Malley shook hands, both of them smiling cordially. But Roger was easily the more awe struck of the two.

"Roger here gives quite a show with his peanut tossing. Everyone loves him in the loge level on the third base side," the man continued.

O'Malley felt slightly embarrassed that he had been so busy not to be aware of Roger's theatrics. Before the two left O'Malley's office, the man set up the scene for Roger to stand back and throw a bag behind his back to the Dodger president.

O'Malley smiled in anticipation, and caught the wondrous peanut throw. He would remember Roger from now on, thanks to O'Malley's friend. From that point on, for many years, O'Malley would often find Roger at a private party or fundraiser, and he would pat Roger on the back, affectionately telling him that he looked forward to another year with him in the stands.

"How's that arm holding out, Roger?" O'Malley asked.

"My arm feels great, Mr. O'Malley, and not a case of peanut elbow," Roger replied, bringing a chuckle from O'Malley.

Almost another year had passed, and more articles were written about Roger. Within sight, however, was the big day for Roger and Cindy. In September of 1974, during the Dodger home games, the huge, electronic scoreboard in left field displayed the news about Roger's upcoming wedding day. Lit up on the large board, several years before Diamond Vision was introduced, were the words, "Social note...upcoming marriage...Roger Owens and Cindy Brazil...they met when he sold her a bag of peanuts at Dodger Stadium..."

The following month, Roger and Cindy were invited to Los Angeles City Hall. On October 25th, they were presented with a special resolution from Robert Farrell and the entire L.A. City Council. One of the special gifts presented to them was a beautifully decorated decree.

It stated, "From the City of Los Angeles in the State of California. Happiness is falling in love at Dodger Stadium. Congratulations Roger and Cynthia." It truly was a happy moment for Roger, who was overjoyed to be recognized in such a special manner.

The next day, on October 26, 1974, the two exchanged vows during a memorable and glamorous wedding.

Roger's groomsmen included best man, Philip, good friend Joe Miller from Westransco, his younger brother Paul, and vending buddies Jay Bieber and Mort Rose. Roger's 13 year-old sister, Grace, was one of Cindy's bridesmaids. They tied the knot at Holy Cross Lutheran Church on Ball Road in Cypress, California, in front of approximately 500 people. Ruth, who was busy with her third son, a three month-old boy, was there but showed up after the wedding had started. Ross and Mary were there with watery eyes and tissue paper in hand, enjoying the festivities of their son's wedding day. Joining them in attendance were Lois, Paul, and Esther. Priscilla and her husband Jim were there as well as their four year-old daughter, Wendy Marie. Elizabeth was there, even after giving birth to her only son the month before. Even famous Uncle Jack Owens was on hand to celebrate, playing piano and singing many of his trademark songs at the reception. The reception was held at the Anaheim Sheraton Hotel, and it included a buffet for 300 people. Counted among Roger's friends were two prominent figures in the L.A. scene at the time. One was the respected and amiable Mayor Tom Bradley and his wife, Ethel. The other was one of the Dodgers' starting pitchers, and eventually one of the greatest pitchers in Dodger history, Don Sutton, who was there with his wife. Roger knew Mayor Bradley from the days Bradley was a city councilman and sat in Roger's section of the stadium, enjoying both the Dodgers and Roger's humor. Roger knew the Suttons because Mrs. Sutton often brought her two boys to the game, always sitting in the area behind home plate, at the border of Roger's section. The boys loved catching peanuts from him.

At the end of the ceremony, Roger and Cindy fled the scene but not without a substantial showering of peanuts, instead of rice, from friends and family. There were television news spots about the wedding and articles written in the local paper, thanks in part to Ross who submitted the information. The wedding was more than Roger and Cindy could have asked for, and their honeymoon in Hawaii was just as memorable.

One afternoon, while on their honeymoon, they decided to take in a game of football at the University of Hawaii football stadium. One of the officials working in the stands recognized Roger and asked him to stand up and toss a few bags of peanuts for just a minute. Being a good sport, Roger did so and was cheered loudly by the fans. He explained that they were on their honeymoon, and they smiled, asking him what they were doing watching a football game.

Probably taking a break.

After the honeymoon, the newlyweds moved in together into an apartment in West Los Angeles. Paul, who was living with Roger until the wedding, decided life would be better for him in the sanctuary of the wooded outskirts of Northern Oregon. No one in his family saw it coming, as Paul simply left to start his life there, growing out his hair and beard, learning to play piano by ear, and finding work wherever he could. He set his mind to becoming a talented, self-taught, piano man. Eventually, over a period of nearly 20 years, he made at least ten CD's, full of rhythmic grooves based on sounds from nature, which sold modestly in small, market squares in Oregon. Roger was baffled by Paul's sudden urge to leave, but no matter the reason, Roger couldn't dwell on it, especially because he now had a new wife and a busy work schedule at the stadium.

Earlier that same month, the Dodgers and the Oakland A's battled it out in the World Series. With Dodger Stadium filled to capacity every game, Roger set a personal record at the stadium for the most bags of peanuts sold in one game when he sold 1,000 bags. The year before, however, at a Los Angeles Rams game played at the Coliseum, Roger set an all-time, personal record when he sold 1,800 bags. But in 1976, Roger would shatter that record, and it wouldn't happen at Dodger Stadium, or even in Los Angeles.

In 1975, Roger received an AFTRA card so he "wouldn't have to work for peanuts." He attracted the attention of a long time fan and Wall Street stock dabbler of 15 years, Mr. Paul Hendison. The opportunistic Hendison saw Roger's potential for taking Roger's story into the financial heights of books and movies. Hendison oversaw the careers of a handful of obscure actors and musicians, and a young and eager Owens accepted Hendison's proposal to be his personal manager. He exacted no commission from Roger but worked to handle the growing load of requests to appear on television. Whether shoe manufacturers attempted to have Roger promote their shoes, or whether Roger was to be cast in small acting roles in made for television movies, Hendison was there to oversee it all.

Even when writer Frank Castellano approached Roger about preparing a script based on his life and selling it to Columbia Pictures,

Hendison was there to step in and handle it. Roger was too busy with appearances and with work, and he was too inexperienced to handle the business side of making movies, so he was more than willing to simply let his "agent" handle it.

Throughout the 1975 season, Roger was featured four more times on television news. On May 5th, he was on the show, *Monday Through Friday*, with hosts Orson Bean & Jaye P. Morgan. News coverage of The Peanut Man continued on July 23rd, with a story presented by Ross Porter of NBC. Incidentally, he was the same Ross Porter who later announced Dodger broadcasts along side the meticulously prepared Vin Scully. Roger's peanut talent was also displayed, on the same day, on NBC's *Time Being* with a youthful host named Paul Moyer. And yet another news reporter, charmed with Roger's down home character and consistent show of charisma, was none other than the gifted and insightful Barbara Walters. She reported on the peanut vendor on the August 5th broadcast of NBC's *Today* show.

With the added exposure, Roger's popularity among the Dodger fans grew at a steady pace. While many fans had been there year after year since the early 60's, there were countless, newer Dodger fans flocking to the stadium to watch their baseball heroes. Such heroes included Wes Parker, Don Sutton, and a promising batch of young players, such as Ron Cey, Reggie Smith, Bill Russell, Dave Lopes, and a rookie third baseman turned first baseman named Steve Garvey. As they sat in their orange fold-down seats, waiting for the Dodgers to take the field, the loge level fans enjoyed Roger's passion and his peanut-tossing theatrics. With every passing game, they amended their list of heroes to include a Dodger pitcher who threw a perfect game every night, and who pleased the crowd with sustained hard work and humor, never once needing a relief pitcher. They admired him for being in the Dodger line up for 13 years, 17 years including the Coliseum days, and they admired him for, quite simply, being the humble showman, Roger the Peanut Man. While other pitchers might have called it a career in the big leagues, he was just getting started.

In fact, the best was yet to come.

Why did the peanut cross the street?
To get to the Shell station.

$\mathcal{C}$ *18*

In the Light of Stars and Lime

The year was 1976, and Roger's career was about to launch with the intensity of ignited fireworks. His popularity would catapult with such a fury that attempting to contain it would have been like trying to put a lid on a box crammed with screaming Piccolo Pete's, dazzling Ground Bloom Flowers, exploding Thunderbomb firecrackers, showering Liberty Fountains, and whistling Moon Traveler Bottle Rockets. If ever there was a man to light this very fuse of success for Roger the Peanut Man, it was the ever-popular, undisputed King of Late Night television.

Mr. Johnny Carson.

As the 1975 regular season neared completion, and as Cincinnati's full throttled, Big Red Machine of Rose, Bench, Griffey, Morgan, and Perez, rumbled through stadium after stadium, instilling fear in the minds of young Dodger players and long time Dodger fans, Steve Brenner, the Director of Public Relations at Dodger Stadium, was busy attracting talent scouts from *The Tonight Show*. With more than a month of Dodger home games yet to be played, Brenner received permission from his boss, Fred Claire, to write a letter to the show, inviting them to come out to the ballpark and watch their prized peanut man put on a show of his own. Brenner had enough fan mail and news coverage about Roger to warrant an invitation for the scouts. He was convinced that excitement generated over Roger would not only help the modest peanut man but would also help shine a brilliant light of Dodger blue in the darkness of a looming Reds shadow.

The scouts showed up, and they loved him.

Roger, who had no idea such arrangements were made by Brenner, worked with enthusiasm, and he sparkled as always. By the end of the game, the talents scouts buzzed with admiration for Roger the Dodger. Brenner had on-going discussions with the booking staff at the show,

189

but they felt that Roger needed something extra special to help solidify their decision to book him with Carson. So Brenner thought it over, and suddenly the idea hit him.

It was opening night at Dodger Stadium, on April 13, 1976, and the capacity filled crowd was bundled up for the frigid evening. They planned to have the ceremony the night before, but the rain was relentless enough to postpone it.

During the pre-game activities, Steve Garvey accepted his second Gold Glove in a row, and third baseman, Ron Cey, also known as "The Penguin" for his waddling, short stride running, received the 1975 Most Valuable Dodger Player Award from the Dodger Booster Club.

Then, suddenly, a booming, deep voice echoed over the public address system, announcing that the ceremonial first pitch was at hand.

"The Dodgers would now like everyone in attendance at tonight's opening game to please direct your attention to the loge level directly above home plate for the ceremonial first pitch. Throwing out tonight's inaugural pitch is long-time Dodger peanut vendor, the Peanut Man, Roger Owens," said the public address announcer. The stadium roared with the thunderous sound of cheering of more than 50,000 people.

All eyes were on Roger.

Roger was unable to hide his boyish exuberance, and before long, his cheeks began to hurt from all the smiling. Had his legs not been in such a strengthened condition, they would have shaken like fettuccini as he stood silently, overlooking home plate from high atop in the loge section. Waiting in anticipation for the signal, Roger stood in concentration, recalling how he had practiced the throw earlier that afternoon. Clutching in his right hand the sacred ball, Roger sensed it becoming heavier, as though he had the world in his hand instead of a brand new, official National League baseball.

Roger the Peanut Man leaned back and let the baseball go. From the section where he made a living bringing life to the stands, Roger threw the baseball high into the night sky. When the white ball reached the pinnacle of its arc, it eclipsed the moon, and for a brief moment, the glowing baseball seemed a natural fit among the stellar cast of shooting stars and orbiting planets. The baseball soared back down to Earth and landed as a perfect strike to Dodger catcher, Steve Yeager, who stood at home plate.

The place went wild.

It was the longest, ceremonial first pitch in baseball history.

Brenner immediately heard the familiar notes of *The Tonight Show* theme song play in his mind, like a cherished sonata. He pictured Johnny walking out from behind the curtain, and before he could imagine a Carson monologue, Steve Brenner sat back and smiled.

Roger cinched the deal.

The next day, Roger called his parents to tell them how exhilarating it was to throw out the first pitch of the season. It was an honor usually reserved for political dignitaries or Hall of Fame baseball players, and Roger couldn't stop talking about it. Neither could the Dodger crowds, who cherished his presence at the ballpark.

"Steve Yeager told me later that he had been shaking, because the ball was camouflaged in the lights and he said, 'If I drop this, the fans will boo me forever,'" Roger said.

Throughout the season, Roger checked in at the commissary at the usual time before game time and, as always, he found time to chat with the people. There were the regulars, and there were new faces, but in any case, Roger saw each person as a potential friend. The atmosphere at Dodger Stadium was almost as cozy as a person's second backyard, a home away from home, and the people were very much considered like family in Roger's eyes.

The stadium filled day after day, night after night, with people dressed in Dodger blue. The ballpark was more than a place to catch "Dodger Fever," it was a haven for the weary citizens of a busy city. It was a refuge for those who sought simplicity and a renewed faith in the warmth of human interaction. It was a stadium to watch honest athletic competition push the limits of physical aptitude. It was a place to gauge humanity through the unlimited depths of kindness shown to children by their parents, whether parents treated them to peanuts and Cracker Jacks, revealed childhood stories to them, removed their own ball caps to place affectionately on their children's much smaller heads, or promised to do it all again sometime very soon. Roger saw these things at every game, and every time he was touched that he could be a part of it. In fact, he also enjoyed the thoughtfulness and playfulness of many fans who approached him, paying him secretly for a handful of bags beforehand, just so they could surprise an unsuspecting friend or group with free peanuts, thrown under the leg or behind the back, courtesy of the Peanut Man.

Following the opening night ceremonies, the Dodger programs, handed out to fans, included a photo of Roger, placed between photos of Garvey and Cey. It was quite a treat for Roger's young fans to see him juxtaposed with their favorite Dodger players.

For Roger, everything seemed to be falling into place. At his sales job that year, Roger was responsible for generating $1.5 million in sales, out of the company's entire revenue of $19 million. But his growing personal and professional happiness was severely threatened, and what had been established for nearly two decades was about to come crashing down in a matter of two seconds.

During an evening game at the stadium in May 1976, an ice cream vendor tried to work in some flair of his own by tossing a frozen, ice cream sandwich to a customer. Throwing frozen, solid objects was strictly forbidden, but the vendor paid little attention and gradually increased the number of tosses since no one seemed to mind. However, this time the throw was out of control, and the flying ice cream bar hit a woman on the forehead. The company in charge of food concessions at the time, Arthur Food Services, found itself in trouble with the offended lady, who actually was more upset than hurt, because the vendor just walked away instead of asking if she was okay. Consequently, the company issued a stunning edict that no food items could ever be thrown to fans again.

A devastated Roger, along with every other vendor, was banned from tossing peanuts.

Soon, fans realized that Roger wasn't throwing the bags anymore, and they sensed something was wrong. As they waited for him to put on a show, the fans were disappointed because he was merely handing the bags to customers. Accustomed to his hypnotic performances, the people found that his forced approach to selling left a residual, bland taste, as stale as uneaten peanuts left carelessly on the gray cement floor.

After just a few games, between 200 and 300 fans asked Roger what had happened, and he did more explaining than selling. As more fans heard the news, they went into an uproar and sent at least a hundred letters to the Dodger front office. Some of the letters even came from city council members. Petitions were circulated on Roger's behalf. One petition alone had 75 signatures.

"I know the Dodgers will listen to the fans. There sure are a lot of people who know me who are taking this thing seriously. I just don't feel right. It's taken the fun out of it for me as well as for the fans," Roger said.

After a month, Roger was back in action. Dodger President Peter O'Malley received so many complaints that he worked out a deal with the owner of the food service company, Tom Arthur. O'Malley confessed, "We got more reaction on Roger than we did on using orange baseballs, or on inter-league play, or on the designated hitter."

"I can't say enough for Mr. O'Malley's helping me so much," Roger admitted.

Happy once again were Roger's fans and customers, which included everyone from working class, every-day people to Hollywood notables such as Hugh O'Brian, Rob Reiner, Foster Brooks, and even singer Rick Nelson. None of the celebrities seemed to be as happy for Roger and as personable toward Roger than straight man Harvey Korman from the lovable and hysterical cast of *The Carol Burnett Show*. Korman had seats for several years in the loge level, and whenever he saw Roger approaching a few aisles away at the stadium, he rushed over to the peanut vendor and greeted him like they were old buddies. Korman charmed his friends on many occasions as he boisterously introduced his friends to Roger.

"Say Roger, have you heard any good jokes lately? I need some new ones," Korman asked often, kidding with Roger.

"Yeah a few, but hey, you're a comedian. Why do *I* always have to find the jokes around here?" Roger replied with a chuckle.

Obviously, the surrounding Dodger fans were thrilled to have some ham to go along with their peanuts.

Just as Roger began to settle in with throwing peanuts again to his delighted customers, Roger received startling news from home.

It was his dad on the phone.

"Hi, Roger. How are you?" Ross asked.

"Hi, Dad. I'm fine. How are you and mom?" Roger replied.

"Well, that's what I called about, Son. We've had some problems lately in the neighborhood. Yesterday, your mother was pushed down by, I don't know, a young, neighbor boy. She's okay, you know your mom. Anyway, they've been setting off firecrackers nearby, and you know how much she hates fireworks. We've had some things stolen from our porch, and we found our lemon trees missing many of the lemons, too," Ross explained.

"All that, and you're just now telling us?" Roger asked, flustered in concern.

"Most of the time, it isn't too bad. Besides, I know the Lord is watching over us," Ross continued.

"Yeah, I know Dad. But you guys are okay, right?" Roger said.

"Yeah, we are. I think it'll be okay. We've been here quite a while anyways," Ross said.

"Well, I don't know. If I told Cindy about it, she'd tell you to move already," Roger added.

"Tell me what, Roger?" Cindy asked as she walked into the room.

"Here, Dad. Talk with Cindy," he said, while handing the phone to his wife.

"Hi Ross. How is everyone?" Cindy asked.

"Hi Cindy. We're doing okay. I was telling Roger about our neighborhood. We've been having problems with some rowdy neighbor kids," Ross said.

He continued to explain to Cindy, but he insisted that perhaps everything would be okay, and that they wouldn't need to move. Mary didn't quite feel like moving either, even with the recent events. Even so, Cindy tried several times to convince them to find a better place. Roger's parents were still quite reluctant, so Cindy and Roger's sister, 15 year-old Grace, talked with them about finding a nice place to live in Cypress, where Cindy's parents lived. After a few phone calls, Ross, now age 66, and Mary, now age 62, found a pleasant mobile home park next to Lincoln Blvd., in Cypress, across from the Forest Lawn Cemetery. The mobile home park had a community pool with an adjacent play area for kids. Located in Orange County, it was the perfect alternative to the threatening streets of inner city Compton. All of Roger's brothers and sisters were happy to hear their parents had finally moved. Now, many of them, including Elizabeth who lived in Cerritos, would be much closer and could visit more often. Ross enjoyed the relaxed Orange County lifestyle, taking in the sights and sounds of splashing pool water and kids running around with ice cream cones in hand or riding on roller skates and skateboards. He enjoyed eating at cozy restaurants in the area, playing horseback in the kitchen and living room with his two youngest grandsons, and loading up on his favorite home-cooked meals, including apple fritters, pecan rolls, coconut cake, meatloaf, mashed potatoes, graham crackers, collard greens, cornbread, baked yams, fried chicken, hominy grits, and anything else as long as it was covered with catsup. Even though he continued working with Immanuel Baptist in Los Angeles, including doing yard work, much of the stress of raising an extremely poor family in Los Angeles had long since disappeared. Yet should there be other reasons to stress about, there were plenty of Dodger games for him to watch on television and yell at the players for dropping a groundball, not turning an easy double play, or missing a fly ball in the sun.

During the week, Mary continued to work as a nurse just a few blocks away at Los Alamitos Medical Center. After work, during the summer, she could make the three-minute trek from her front door to the community pool, smell people's barbecues along the way, and dip her legs into the refreshing water. Her daughters would often visit on the weekends to swim with her and then walk back, planning how to spend a careless afternoon, with the Southern California sun blazing high above outside, and the air conditioner blasting inside. Even Mary's new little dog, a gray and white Pekingese named "Kung Fu," was happy to play in the small patch of grass and flowers growing behind the trailer.

Mary loved their new place. She became more involved with baby-sitting and child evangelism, but in her spare time she read the Bible and read magazines published by the Billy Graham Ministry. She had a small library of books next to the piano. She continued to write poems and sing to the Lord as she played songs like "The Old Rugged Cross." Her piano playing was as jubilant and melodic as ever, a talent she learned when she lived in boarding homes as a young orphan. Other times, she rested on her recliner after putting on an album of her favorite singer of all time, fellow Italian and tenor extraordinaire, Luciano Pavoratti. As she listened to his magnificent voice, tears fell from her eyes as she thought of her mother Josephine, and how her parents left a small town in Italy at the turn of the century to find a new home in America. Then, her thoughts turned to her grandkids, reminding her of the next birthday card to send and which Bible verse to include.

Mary never felt complete unless her grandsons were around. Ruth's three boys, Elizabeth's son, and Priscilla's daughter were each a treasure to Mary and Ross. Of course Roger, who often visited his mom with Cindy, counted himself as a proud uncle ever since March 1964, when Ruth had her first son, Donald. Mary felt blessed to see her two youngest grandsons regularly, since Ruth and Elizabeth were such close sisters, and they looked forward to visiting their mom almost every weekend. Elizabeth's two year-old, little Stephen Lektoi, and Ruth's two year-old, Daniel Scott, spent a lot of time at the swings near the pool, becoming close cousins. They loved running in the living room to take over Grandma Owens' favorite lazy boy recliner as soon as she got up to go to the kitchen.

The 1976 baseball season was almost over, and finally, Roger got the call to come down to the studios in Burbank, for the taping of *The Tonight Show*. During that time, Carson was not always the host. Sometimes, other celebrities or comedians, like George Carlin, were guest hosts of the show. But that evening, on September 7th, parked on the late night throne was the master himself. He was the man behind the "mysticism" of Carnac The Magnificent and his "hermetically sealed envelopes." He was the man behind the nasal voiced salesman who tried to sell every unmarketable product with his "lovely assistant" at his side, and he was the man behind Ed McMahon, or rather *hiding* behind Ed McMahon, as he ran in terror from the likes of monkeys, cheetahs, or lamas that lashed out, hissed, or spat in utter distaste for him, all in the name of a good show.

The talent scouts welcomed Roger and Cindy, his 19 year-old wife. They went over a few things with him, while Carson fans stood outside, waiting to be let inside the studio. Roger was instructed to show his usual energy and be himself. He was told that he would be the first guest, and sure enough, following Johnny's monologue, Roger was introduced by Johnny and was welcomed with a warm reception from the studio audience and a handshake from Johnny and Ed.

Roger took his seat, at the usual place to Johnny's right, where countless stars had shined, seated with crossed legs, wide grins, and cups of coffee at hand.

Johnny asked away, and the whole world began to learn of this theatrical, modest, peanut vendor, a man who knew nothing but poverty as a child, but who grew to be a valuable member of the great Dodger family.

For twenty minutes, Roger and "Mr. Carson," as Roger addressed him, shared a conversation that endeared all who heard the genuine charm and sincerity in Roger's voice. They talked about his trick peanut pitching, his recent honor of tossing out the first pitch of the season, and how he met his wife of two years at the ballpark.

"Yeah, my beautiful wife, Cindy, is here," he said.

"I heard you two actually met one day at the stadium when you sold her a bag of peanuts. Is that true?" Johnny asked.

"Yeah, we did," he answered, smiling and nodding his head in bashfulness. "We had seen each other around but never talked much, until one day she finally asked me for a bag of peanuts. Then after a year or so, we got married."

"Boy, how romantic is that," added Johnny.

At the end of their conversation, Johnny invited Roger to mix it up with the crowd and throw the peanuts the way he did at the stadium. Not to be outdone, Johnny was ready with a Dodger cap pulled down too far by Roger, flattening his ears out at the side. The audience howled in laughter at Johnny's deadpan expression. Before the ball cap was fitted, Johnny was handed his own cardboard, vendor box and was strapped down with a shoulder harness, evidently tightened a bit too much, as he quipped, "Somebody call the governor."

The pair of comedic nuts made their way into the crowd to let Johnny try his hand at trick tossing the peanut bags to the excited audience. His version of the behind-the-back toss was dismally inaccurate, but he kept trying. When he finally gave the under-the-leg toss a try, it was pure, comedic genius. He gave a quick snap from behind, but his hand only managed to hit himself where it counted, and the bag of peanuts failed to go very far. A reeling Carson gathered his composure and uttered a one-liner in response that was so hilarious that the crowd roared for several minutes. Roger stood beside Johnny, laughing so hard it hurt, and with his eyes tearing up, he patted Carson on the back in consolation. The "crushed nuts" segment even made it to the video, *Carson's Comedy Classics*.

Finally, Roger took the helm and threw bags of peanuts left and right, close and far, to those a few seats away and to those all the way in the back rows of the audience. They soared with pinpoint accuracy to the waiting hands of each person, thrilling them with a barrage of uncanny peanut pitching.

The people watching from home, all across the country, were amazed and impressed with the young peanut man. The scouts at *The Tonight Show* encouraged Roger about his performance after the show.

"Roger, you did great," one woman said.

"You think so?" he asked.

"Oh of course, Roger. In fact, we could tell Mr. Carson truly and genuinely liked you, because he didn't mind at all when you patted him on the shoulder. Normally, Mr. Carson doesn't feel comfortable if he's touched during the show, but you were an obvious exception," the lady confessed. She then told Roger to go home and be prepared to be famous. Roger welcomed her optimism, but as he left with his wife, he judged the words to be a bit exaggerated.

She couldn't have been any more right.

To people all over the country, and to Dodger fans everywhere, he was, quite literally overnight, on his way to becoming known officially as Roger Owens, the *Famous* Peanut Man.

DRABBLE Reprinted by permission of
United Feature Syndicate, Inc.

19

Life, Liberty, and the Pursuit of Peanuts

R oger had earned the respect and admiration of everyone who saw him on the show. In fact, winner of 21 games that same season, Dodger pitcher and friend, Don Sutton summed up that respect a month later when he said, "Listen, I would have trouble hitting a wall 15 feet away if I tried to throw a bag of peanuts behind my back. It's definitely easier to throw strikes with a baseball. Man, I saw Roger on the Tonight Show hitting the guy in the polka-dot shirt 35 rows away right on the button." This statement came from a major league hurler who would eventually be tied for 11th place with Nolan Ryan on the all-time wins list with 324 victories, ahead of the likes of Tom Seaver, Lefty Grove, Early Wynn, and Roger Clemens. Sutton would also eventually be inducted into the Baseball Hall of Fame and would be ranked as number seven on the list of all-time strikeout leaders, two places higher than the great Walter Johnson. The Dodger ace knew good pitching when he saw it, even if they were just bags of goobers being thrown by a simple peanut vendor.

Two months after *The Tonight Show*, Roger was flown out to Philadelphia to talk with host Mike Douglas on *The Mike Douglas Show*. Roger's late night appearance with Carson ushered in a flood of television appearances over the next three years.

Only a week after *The Mike Douglas Show*, he was a guest of the ABC show, *AM Los Angeles* with Regis Philbin. A week later, he was featured on a national broadcast of *Newsweek Broadcasting Service*. A month later, on December 31st, he was on with KHJ's *Nine In The Morning* with host Tommy Hawkins, who later became Dodger vice president of communications.

Countless newspaper articles were written about the poor boy turned peanut man who sought to help his struggling, reunited bunch of brothers and sisters and found fame and success through hard work and

199

love of labor. During all of these shows, Roger remained grounded in his character and expressed his overwhelming joy for all the attention he had been receiving.

"Whenever I begin to get a big head, I just take a close look at a bag of peanuts. There are no delusions. That's the real reason I'm here today," Roger admitted. "I see myself as an extension of the Dodger players. I'm as close as many of these fans will ever get to the ballplayers. They can't reach out and touch or get to know personally a Dave Lopes or a Steve Garvey, so I kind of take their place."

For every bag of peanuts tossed behind his back from over fifty feet away, right into the lap of an adoring fan, he received in exchange, both the flip of a 25-cent payment and the toss of that same fan's heart. There was no doubt that Roger was a celebrity among the Dodger fans, but to many of the kids growing up during the 70's, he was larger than life.

"Most of the kids who bring their gloves to the game will never have a chance to catch a foul ball. Catching a bag of peanuts can be the next best thing. So when a kid misses one of my throws, I tell him it was my fault, that the throw was bad, and I ask him to give me another chance. Seeing the face of a little guy being applauded for a good catch by those around him is something…well, something I don't want to give up." Even season ticket holders knew that besides grabbing any one of Roger's trademark pitches, such as the knuckle nut, fast nut, and split nut, Roger himself was quite a catch. They decided not to buy the more enviable field level tickets, because, simply enough, Roger wouldn't be there in that section.

On one occasion, as staff writer Skip Bayless of the *Los Angeles Times* noted, Roger even sent an individual peanut soaring into an open mouth of a fan, landing successfully and amazing the crowd.

He wrote:

> After air mailing a couple of long bomb strikes 15 rows up, a customer yelled that he wanted "one more." With a smile the size of a ballpark hot dog, Owens pilfered one peanut out of the top bag, leaned and fired. The lone peanut soared over the heads of nine rows of fans and—no fooling—landed in the guy's open mouth. The Peanut Man, of course, got a standing ovation.

Even though Roger was busy with televisions shows and news interviews in 1976, he wasn't too busy to take up an invitation to show up as a special guest speaker at El Camino Real High School. Wearing one of his newly made "Roger Owens T-Shirts" that had an action pose of him with the words "Nuts To You," he threw peanuts to excited students in their high school gymnasium. He was warmly greeted with huge posters and even bigger smiles and, as he took the microphone, he challenged them to always work hard and believe in themselves no matter what. He emphasized how "success only comes before work in the dictionary." As a veteran stair climber and peanut hustler for almost twenty years at the ballpark, he encouraged them with another idiom, which he collected over the years to use in motivational speeches, like a kid adding to his prized stack of baseball cards.

"When the elevator to success is out of order, use the stairs."

It was at this high school that a student named Karen Osterheldt penned a short poem on a piece of notebook paper and offered it to Roger. He was so moved with its sentiment and simplicity that he adopted it as his official poem and placed it on the back of his peanut man business cards.

It read:

Roger Owens
Roger Owens is the man
Who throws the peanuts in the stands.
People come from everywhere
Just to see him throw a pair.

So when you see the Dodgers play,
Help Roger Owens make his pay.
Buy your peanuts from him, and you'll see
He's making peanuts go down in history.

During a night game at the stadium, a businessman came up to Roger. The two had a conversation about Roger pitching peanuts to clients of the businessman. The man, Nolan Mills, president of Allied Veneer Company, and his son C.J. Mills, vice president, asked Roger if, before the beginning of the next baseball season, he could send a check to Roger. The check would prepay for a set amount of peanut bags for the entire season. The businessman wanted to drum up business by giving his friends and potential customers free bags of peanuts. He would give Roger information about them that he could work into a comedy routine where Roger could tease or kid around with them until finally admitting that the peanuts were compliments of that particular businessman. Roger loved the idea. Sure enough, by next season in

April 1977, Roger received the prepaid order and when he delivered the peanuts, the customers loved it and loved the businessman. Word spread, and soon Roger had a handful of "season peanut holders."

As if the year wasn't full enough for Roger in '76, by the end of the baseball season Roger's influence on the ballpark caught the eyes of Dallas Cowboys management. In fact, it was Cowboys President Tex Schramm who first saw Roger on *The Tonight Show*.

The Cowboys were "America's Team" in the mid to late 70's, and its All Pro players Roger Staubach, Tony Dorsett, Randy White, and Ed "Too Tall" Jones, were the focus of many *Monday Night Football* broadcasts.

During one particular Monday night in late '76, the Cowboys had planned for its pre-game entertainment to feature vendors and characters from various stadiums and arenas across the nation. Among all the outlandish characters that hollered or danced to fame, Roger stood as a shining example of what L.A.'s Rams and Dodgers offered as the very best in professional service and salesmanship.

Three hours before game time, Roger and the other vendors were allowed to roam the large field, full of reporters and other notables. Roger approached each person with an uncontrollable and infectious grin. He met Tony Dorsett, as well as kidded around with a personable and young Dan Reeves, assistant coach for the formidable Cowboy skipper, Tom Landry. Reeves gave him a tour of the stadium, introduced him to sports broadcasting legends Frank Gifford and Howard Cosell, and even treated him to a steak dinner on the town that evening.

Roger was comfortable around all the big name people, but what really struck him was how far he had come with such a simple job of throwing peanuts and collecting smiles. It blew him away that someone with modest aspirations of helping his own family make ends meet could end up gazing deep into the gold and purple gradient of the vast Texas twilight while standing on the hallowed ground of Texas Stadium's freshly painted 50 yard line.

Before the coin toss and kick off, Roger and the other special guests waited in the tunnel where the players themselves ran out. The signal was given, and the odd cast of vendors and mascots ran out toward the middle of the field. After the special recognition, Roger stepped up on the back of a slow moving, flatbed truck, tossing free peanut bags to fans who were close enough for the salted bags of charity.

The massive gathering of die-hard Cowboy fans counted down the minutes for Roger to gather his peanut inventory and go to work selling the bags of peanuts in the same captivating way in which he had done for hundreds of thousands, if not millions, of Dodger fans over the years. Roger knew it would be a big night for sales, but he didn't realize just how big.

During the third quarter, with another quarter yet to be played, Roger reached for his last box of peanut bags. Aware of his dilemma of running out of peanuts too soon, Roger was nevertheless thrilled that so many peanuts were sold. Yet as he scanned the sea of enthusiastic football fans, still hungry enough to demand peanuts with their cups of beer, he was embarrassed that there was nothing he could do about it. In spite of this, the fans accepted Roger's news that he was "all out" for the night and, in fact, they were proud of him when he announced to them that he had set an all-time personal record for the most bags of peanuts sold in one night.

2,400.

It was a number that meant quite a bit to Roger, in a similar way 1.73 E.R.A. would have meant to Koufax, or 500 victories to Cy Young. In fact, he might have sold a mind blowing 3,000 had he not run out with the entire fourth quarter ahead. Even so, Roger obliterated his previous record with a barrage of momentous, arm-sweeping, wrist-flicking, behind-the-back, double bag, split nut throws and an arsenal of good material from his cache of wise cracks and nutty jokes.

The proceeds from the peanut sales went toward the Boys Club of Dallas, which was much like a YMCA. For 12 consecutive years, from 1976 to 1988, Roger was invited to Dallas to pitch peanuts at a Cowboys football game. Every year, the Cowboys organization gave Roger the first class treatment, arranging hotel accommodations, food, and travel service. In addition, the team also invited him every summer to their training camp at Cal Lutheran College in Thousand Oaks, California. There, Roger mingled with the players, grubbed with them, and planned his schedule for being in Dallas later in the year.

On New Year's Day, 1977, Roger began a whirlwind January by appearing as a guest of ABC's *Good Morning America* with David Hartman.

At this time, Roger's agent, Paul Hendison, was already in contact with the California National Democratic Party about how it would be a treat to have the Peanut Man throw peanuts at the upcoming Inaugural Parties, following the inauguration of President Jimmy Carter, a former peanut farmer from Plains, Georgia. The Democratic Party responded to the idea, stating that they would love for Roger to come, but unfortunately Roger would have to raise his own funds to cover his airfare and hotel expenses. So Hendison wrote letters and made phone calls to the Dodger President Peter O'Malley, Rams President Steve Rosenbloom, and even to Roger's friend, 6 feet 9 inch Bill Ritchie, President of All American Nut Company, located in Cerritos. Hendison asked for donations from the organizations to help send Roger to Washington D.C. to pitch peanuts at Carter's Inaugural Parties. They agreed to the idea and sent enough money for Roger to make the trip.

Towards the end of the month, the day had arrived.

Roger and his agent flew out to Washington D.C. His agent helped show him around and made sure he knew where to go. The ground was covered with snow, and as Roger held his hands together to keep them warm, he blew his warm breath into the air just to see the frost in the cold weather. He walked by trees whose leaves were weighed down by white slush and frozen drops of water, and some of these crystal drops were like miniature waterfalls, frozen in place and unable to drip off the edge of the leaf. Roger noticed how the honey-colored lighting from inside the buildings gave each window an inviting glow and beckoned him to wipe off his shoes, come inside, and take off his coat.

It was nighttime, and following the ceremonial inauguration of the country's 39th President, a number of parties throughout town were beginning. There was plenty of live music and loud people who found any reason to raise a glass and pour one down.

After a couple of parties, Roger made his way to the Hilton Hotel, where he was scheduled to go on stage and throw peanuts before the Fifth Dimension singing group went on. He put on a show, tossing bags of peanuts everywhere to excited politicians, dignitaries, and partygoers in general. The hotel was decorated with an abundance of banners and flags, all of which added to the festive atmosphere.

Loud, energetic, and completely beside himself for being in the nation's capital, Roger was still no match for the exuberance the crowd displayed when President Carter walked in with his entourage of friends and secret servicemen. Everyone loved Carter's huge smile, and when Jimmy and his wife, and First Lady, Rosalynn, lifted their hands in dramatic acknowledgement of their victory, the crowd went crazy.

With more people surrounding Carter, Roger moved in closer, just as excited as everyone else. Poised to call the President's attention to an imminent peanut toss, Roger inched closer. He was within range to throw peanuts toward those standing next to the President. As soon as Carter would acknowledge the famed Peanut Man and hold up his hands to signal his readiness to catch them, Roger would then let them fly behind his back. But more people surrounded the President, and during the entire time, President Carter never saw Roger the Peanut Man in the midst of the chaos. As Roger was about to send a bag of goobers in the direction of the President, his throwing arm was grabbed forcefully.

"Roger, we know who you are and why you're here. You know we can't allow you to throw those unless they have been X rayed first. Have they been X rayed?" the secret serviceman asked.

"Well, no, of course not, sir," Roger replied.

"I'm sorry, Roger, but we cannot allow you to throw a missile toward the President, unless it has been X rayed," the man continued.

"Okay then. I understand," Roger said with slightly deflated spirits.

"Thank you, Roger," the secret serviceman said.

Roger watched as the crowd enveloped President Carter, whisking him away into another lobby, out of the ballroom. He was downhearted at his missed opportunity, but was excited nonetheless to throw peanuts to the people standing around. Finally, he called it a night and went back to his hotel room. He took off his shirt to get comfortable and sat on the edge of the bed.

He stared at the phone.

After a few minutes of staring quietly, he stood up, showered, and went to sleep.

The next morning, Roger cheered up because of an article printed in the *Washington Star*. The writer wrote a catchy line that made Roger smile. He opened up the paper, and he read, "There are two peanut men in town, one who grows 'em and one who throws 'em." Hendison and Roger chuckled, shared their thoughts about being there, and then made plans to leave for home.

A few days after Roger was back in Los Angeles, CBS aired the *Super Night At The Super Bowl*, the night before the Super Bowl. The celebrity-filled television special was taped earlier that same month in the parking lot of the Rose Bowl, and Roger was invited to be a part of it. Roger met John Wayne, Reds catcher Johnny Bench, and country singer Charlie Pride. But the highlight of the evening for Roger was when he was introduced to the audience. He started to throw peanut bags to the crowd, and suddenly the song and dance legend, Sammy Davis, Jr., charmed everyone as he sang a lyrically altered version of his trademark song, substituting the lines from "The Candy Man" with "The Peanut Man." Roger suddenly felt warm from the attention, and he blushed as the entertainer sang the affectionate tribute.

Roger then was asked if he could pitch peanut bags from a pitcher's mound to Cincinatti Red's All-Star catcher, Johnny Bench, who was equipped with a glove and catcher's mask. Roger's nervousness got the best of him and his knuckle bag was off the mark. Instantly, he was re-placed on the mound with a President Jimmy Carter look-a-like, and when the impersonator completed the toss, the people went nuts. After the show, the producers treated everyone on program to dinner at a Hollywood hotspot, Chasen's Restaurant in Beverly Hills.

It was just one of many nights he would always cherish.

As if that particular evening weren't filled enough with special moments, Roger had met a man named Pat Perry in the parking lot of the Rose Bowl. After the show taping, while people drifted back to their cars, Roger saw the man with an adorable Labrador Retriever, and he wanted to find out more about the dog. Perry explained to Roger that he had another one just like it, but it was a puppy. He asked if Roger was interested and, since Roger and Cindy had plans to move in to a large house soon, Roger emphatically told the man he was interested.

"So when would we be able to get the puppy?" Roger asked, while Cindy stood next to him.

"Well, whenever, you get settled in, give me a call, and we'll drop her off. How's that sound?" said Pat.

"Sounds good," Roger replied. "What do you think Cindy? We should have plenty of room for a dog at the house you picked out," Roger said.

"Yeah, it'd be great to have a dog with us. Go for it," his wife an-swered.

The two men shook hands, and Roger now had the man's number.

Little did Roger know at the time that that night formed the begin-ning of his love affair with Labrador Retrievers, spanning the next 25 years and two generations of dogs of the same breed. In fact, so in love Roger would be with this dog that several years later, he would buy an-other one, "Casey," as its backyard buddy, and when those two passed away many years after that, he would buy two more just like them and give them the same names, a sentimental gesture by their loving owner to keep their memories alive.

By the end of January, Roger and his wife were ready to move from their West L.A. apartment into a large, inviting, three-level home. They had visited the house in Torrance, California, just a few months before, and Cindy loved it instantly. It had a spacious back yard, three upstairs rooms, and a lower level den. She convinced Roger that this was the house, and in January they moved in.

In February, Roger and Cindy bought food and water bowls fit for a small puppy. They thought of a few other things a puppy might like, and finally Pat Perry called Roger and asked him if he could bring the "pup" over. Roger said it would be fine, and later that day, the doorbell rang. It was Perry. Roger opened the door. Immediately, a huge, 70-pound Labrador Retriever ran inside the house, wagging its heavy tail around like a slugger swinging around a mighty bat, ready to knock over lamps and whip anyone's legs. Although Roger and Cindy thought the dog was irresistible, they asked where the puppy was.

"Where's the puppy? That *is* the puppy. The Lab is a year old," Perry admitted.

Roger laughed at how big the "pup" was, and so Roger and Cindy had to return all the bowls in exchange for much larger ones. The dog, named "Brande" from a previous owner whose wife changed her mind about keeping it, enjoyed her new home and loved the huge backyard. Roger thought that their new, light-beige Labrador Retriever, with a big brown nose and big brown eyes, needed some company, so they immediately bought another one and named the new dog, "Whiskey."

It was the first time Roger had owned a dog since Bert, who vanished from the Owens home more than ten years earlier. Roger and his siblings were sad to lose Bert, but now, many years later, Roger was overjoyed to have a pair of energetic, obedient, and extremely intelligent dogs.

Not long after the couple moved in, they invited a few friends over. Whether they were salesmen or executives from his day job at the freight company, or his vendor buddies like Jay Bieber, his friends were astounded by the size and comfort of the new house. Jay had just recently quit selling at the stadium so he could dedicate himself full-time to being an accountant. Since then, he has also served as Roger's C.P.A., not charging for his services, except for being treated by Roger to dinner at a nice restaurant.

A few weeks after his trip to Washington D.C., Roger was once again invited to be on the *Tonight Show*. Roger was eager to be on the show a second time. He couldn't believe he would ever be asked to be on it *again*. On this particular taping of the show, however, Johnny Carson had asked comedian George Carlin to fill in as the host for the evening. Carlin asked the famed peanut vendor what it was like to be in Washington, throwing peanuts at the various parties. Roger explained how his opportunity to throw peanuts at President Carter had vanished the moment a secret serviceman ordered him not to toss the peanuts. The two talked for several minutes, and they ended their conversation with Roger throwing peanuts once again to the astounded audience.

During the 1977 baseball season, Roger continued to make friends and amaze the fans. With the Dodgers and Yankees battling it out in the World Series, the Dodger fans were thrilled to watch young Dodger pitcher Bob Welch mow down the Yankee slugger, "Mr. October," Reggie Jackson. The fans in the loge level in Roger's section had a blast watching the games as well as watching the Peanut Man work his magic.

In early June 1977, Roger received an invitation to appear at a special dinner. It was Saint Nicholas Cathedral's annual "Sports Night Father and Son Banquet." Roger was just one of a panel of honored guests. During the dinner and auction, he spoke to the fathers and young boys about "being yourself," about not trying to be like anyone else, and about working hard and enjoying what you do. Roger's peanut pitching and speech made him such a big hit at the charity dinner that he was invited to appear at the church again the next year. In addition, it has become one of the few events that Roger has considered special enough for him to attend annually for 26 years.

In 1978, after spring training ended and the regular season began, Roger was once again ready to throw peanuts to the hungry masses. Roger still couldn't imagine any better place to work than at Dodger Stadium. People asked him to take pictures with them and autograph their bags of peanuts. One fan in particular saw Roger coming toward his seat.

"Hey Roger. I'll take a bag," the man called out.

Roger saw the man and quickly recognized him.

It was Chuck Barris, host of the crazy and popular *Gong Show*.

"Hi Roger. How are ya?" Barris asked.

"Fine thanks. How are you?" Roger replied.

"I'm doing good. I saw you on the Tonight Show, and I couldn't believe how good you are," Barris added.

"Thanks, Mr. Barris," Roger said.

The two talked for a few more minutes, and then Barris handed Roger his card.

"Give me a call at the office, and we'll arrange for you to be a judge on the show. What do you think?" Barris said with a huge grin.

"Sure, I'd love to. Your show needs some peanut power anyway. I'll give you a call tomorrow," Roger answered happily.

Since the program showcased plenty of nuts, there was none more fitting to sit on the panel of judges than the Peanut Man himself.

Within a month, Roger was invited to the taping of *The Gong Show*. Five different shows were all taped in the same day, each of which would be aired many weeks apart. Roger enjoyed the show tapings, but he never had the heart to actually "gong" any of the performers, no matter how deserving they were. Roger's gratitude for his rise to fame as the Peanut Man from his impoverished beginnings were never far from his thoughts.

It was always an honor for Roger to be recognized in this way or to be asked to be a guest on any television show, but there were more intimate moments that touched Roger and made him feel even more special. One such time was when Mayor Bradley called him and invited him to spend the afternoon with him at his office at City Hall.

He arrived, and Mayor Bradley's disarming smile made Roger feel right at home. Roger followed the mayor through large conference rooms until finally they made their way to the secluded, personal office of Mayor Bradley.

"Have a seat, Roger," the mayor said. "It's a nice day outside, don't you think?"

"It sure is, Mr. Bradley," Roger answered.

"Oh, you know you can call me Tom," the mayor insisted.

The two relaxed in their comfortable chairs, with the mayor behind his desk, asking away about Roger and his family. He was charmed by Roger's background, and so the two shared many stories together. They talked about life and how it was growing up as kids. Roger recalled many things, including the times during high school that he let his buddy, Paul Blair, ride on the handle bars of his bike. Blair eventually became an outfielder in the Major Leagues. The two continued to exchange fascinating and humorous stories until Mayor Bradley invited him again, but this time to the Mayor's House, which was a grand house built on a well-maintained piece of real estate in Hancock Park in Los Angeles. When Roger eventually took him up on that offer, Roger showed up at their house and had lunch with a very hospitable Mrs. Bradley.

On the last game of the baseball season, Roger was asked to throw peanuts on Fan Appreciation Day at a San Diego Padres game. He arrived at the game, only to be greeted by a huge crowd and the newly hatched mascot, the San Diego Chicken. The yellow, blue, and red "chicken," which was a crowd favorite, spotted the Peanut Man and started jumping up and down and waving its colorful, fuzzy wings. Roger realized it was taunting him for a bag of peanuts, so he reared back and threw a bag behind his back. It sailed more than twenty feet and landed in the chicken's open beak. The chicken caught it and lifted his wings up in victory. The crowd went crazy.

In addition to these meetings and special appearances, Roger also stayed busy with television shows in '78 and in '79.

Less than a week before Christmas in 1978, he was a guest of Stephanie Edwards and John Bennett Perry on their show *Everyday*. Later, almost two months to the day, on February 20th, Roger the Peanut Man was featured on *All Star Secrets*, with hosts Bob Eubanks and Reggie Jackson. In early March of '79, Roger was a panelist on a game show produced by Chuck Barris, the *$1.98 Beauty Show*, with host Rip Taylor. Roger was on the show again when it aired in August of that same year. On September 4, 1979, Roger was a guest on the *Merv Griffin Show*, and in early November, he was on Bert Convy's *Celebrity Comedy Football Show*.

Merv Griffin's early-evening talk show included Roger tossing out peanuts to thrilled audience members and talking with the media legend Griffin. Griffin, who also created the game show *Jeopardy*, and who worked hard to bring the game's television debut just five years later, admitted he saw Roger at the stadium and found the 36 year-old Peanut Man to be unbelievable.

Griffin asked him if it was profitable working as a peanut vendor.

"Well, I do belong to AFL-CIO union, Local 11, so I don't have to work for peanuts," Roger said with a smile.

Griffin grinned at Roger. Already charmed with Roger's enthusiasm and wit, Griffin then announced, "Okay, enough with the bum stuff. Let's see you work the crowd, Roger." Roger then threw strikes to audience members, left and right, causing enough of a buzz among the crowd, that if harnessed, it could have powered all the electricity needed to broadcast the show.

In 1970, Roger was just beginning to adjust to life after the jeep accident. Now, almost 10 years later, amazingly, he had accomplished so much. He had become so much a part of the

Dodger story, but more importantly, he had become so much a part of why Dodger fans showed up to the ballpark. To his vast number of customers at the stadium, the peanuts somehow tasted that much better when they caught a bag from him.

No matter how the Dodgers might have played on any particular day, the fans sitting in Roger's section were the happiest people in the entire place.

"With a rosy glow, sparkling teeth, cinema blue eyes and close-clipped blond hair, Roger Owens seems to be a living Walt Disney movie. Victim of a broken home. Survived by pitching peanuts with big-league ability. Sprouted into local celebrity."

-by *Los Angeles Times* Staff Writer, Skip Bayless, October 26, 1976

$\mathcal{C}$ *20*

Overture of a Heart

F rom hearing the "Star Spangled Banner" sung before the All-Star Game at Dodger Stadium in July 1980, to seeing that same banner fly high atop the Capitol Building in Washington D.C. in July 1981, Roger went into the 1980's with flying colors professionally, but privately, it couldn't have been any more the opposite.

He was flown to Washington as a special guest of the Division of Performing Arts of the Smithsonian Institution. From July 2nd through the 5th, Roger participated in various events at the world-renowned Smithsonian Institution. That year, the annual 4th of July celebration featured the game of baseball at the National Museum of American History. During that week, officials expected to have 50,000 visitors. Visitors at the museum were treated to meeting and talking with Roger the Peanut Man, as well as with Hall of Famers Monte Irvin, Bob Feller, Johnny Mize, Buck Leonard, Lou Brock, Enos Slaughter, and a few others.

Roger put on a spellbinding show for the fans, as he threw the bags behind his back, under his leg, as long bombs, and as double splitters. If the crowd hadn't been loud enough with all the cheering and clapping over his peanut trick shots, then they would soon send the decibel measurement high into the stratosphere the moment he pulled off a four-at-a-time, behind-the-back pitch. The crowd marveled as the bags sailed into the waiting hands of each member of a family of four. It was a throw especially made for the event, and everyone was simply in awe. As if that weren't impressive enough, Roger showed off his arm strength by hurling a bag of peanuts as fast as he could. The Smithsonian officials inspected the bag to make sure they were indeed full of the salted treats instead of small rocks or anything other than shelled peanuts. They found nothing but peanuts inside, and then, he was told that he would have to throw it three times to make it official. Finally, as soon as Roger was given the word, he let it fly with the might of a Don Drysdale follow-through. The JUGS speed gun clocked the speeding bag at a turbulent, peanut-crunching, 60 miles per hour.

"Concentration is the whole key to this, even more than the arm," Roger said. "It's pure concentration and a flick of the wrist."

According to Joe Reed, spokesman for the Institution's Division of Performing Arts, there "was nothing done at the Celebration which was more popular or entertaining for the visitors than the Famous Peanut Man throwing his wares."

Roger smiled and laughed so much from the great time he had in Washington that his cheeks and his mouth hurt almost as much his heart for having to leave the festive atmosphere.

No matter how great a show Roger put on for the fans in the early 80's, nothing compared to the show he put on to hide the growing depression he faced in his private life. The wide spectrum of emotions he felt left him with a deep sadness regarding his failed relationship with Cindy, his beautiful wife of six years. It was a sadness that ate away at him every day. While the world embraced the Peanut Man, Roger and Cindy's love for one another dwindled, and it hurt both of them immensely.

Cindy, who admitted when they were first married how it "took a lot of planning to capture Roger," was always sentimental regarding Roger, whether it was holding on to her teenage diary, or one of Roger's old peanut vendor hats from the 60's, or the bag of peanuts that they met over that sunny day at the ballpark. Roger himself was an incredibly sentimental creature as well. In fact, ever since his jeep accident and the life-saving brain operations that followed, Roger's emotions were always prone to greater sensitivity. It bothered him tremendously if something hurt others or if it hurt himself. However, it would be difficult to find anything else that the two had in common.

The breakdown of their seemingly fairytale marriage was definitely a gradual process, but just as Ross and his brother Jack were worlds apart in the make up of their characters, so too were Roger and Cindy.

Roger was an outgoing, people person, caught up in the busy world of appearances and his growing success. He wanted Cindy to come along, but much of the time she insisted that she'd rather not. She was much more of an introvert and found it uncomfortable being with him at such events. Roger knew that was there was a lack of communication on his part when he didn't demonstrate enough attention and affection for his young wife. But Roger also felt left out much of the time when, for example, he walked in their bedroom, only to find Cindy on the phone with her mother. It was a sign of a wonderful relationship with her mom but, even so, the two just weren't making enough time for each other to cultivate a stronger relationship. At times, they just seemed to be going through the motions of being married. Even when Roger left for Washington D.C. to throw peanuts at the inaugural parties, there were problems between the two. At home, they lacked teamwork and shared little or no ambitions and dreams, and so it seemed almost pointless to call Cindy from Washington to tell her exciting news when he felt that she wouldn't have cared. In fact, Roger and Cindy had better relationships with Ernie and Beverly than with each other. In short, they had no solid foundation, which would have been vital as fame and success began to pull them apart. The couple found that they were not supporting one another and realized that they were going in two different directions. In late 1979 they separated, and in 1980, despite attempts to make the marriage better, it was official.

Roger and Cindy were divorced.

Divorce was not something Roger believed in, and it hurt both sets of parents and everyone involved. The divorce was emotionally traumatizing for Roger. His sisters felt bad for him, but it hurt him to even talk about it, so he didn't. It took almost two years for the fans at Dodger Stadium to realize he was no longer married. With his wedding ring placed away in a dresser drawer, Roger looked at his hands. It was just a ring, but somehow its absence made his left hand seem so plain, so empty, and so bare.

The couple ended it on friendly terms and had no children together.

With the house seeming so much bigger than ever before, Roger still had his dog, Brande. Cindy went back to live with her parents and kept their dog, Whiskey. Within a year or so, Cindy's parents asked if Roger wanted another dog, one that they couldn't watch anymore since they were going on more vacations. So Roger took in an affectionate, gray Keeshond, which Roger had groomed into looking like a miniature lion, with a shaved body and huge, fluffy mane, and shaved tail with a large ball of hair at the end. Roger now shared his home with Brande and French, who got along together from day one.

Roger found the single life tough once again, but he knew he could get through it by keeping busy, by having a very supportive family and group of friends, and by having his faithful dogs at his side.

The split up wasn't the only one Roger experienced during that time. His brother Philip retired from vending at the stadium in 1979, after working 19 years as a Dodger vendor alongside Roger. They had shared many memories at the ballpark, and Philip had improved upon his own peanut tossing for the crowds. But he decided it was time to give his undivided attention to his beloved students at the middle school in Whittier. It was a job he loved too much. His sister Lois, who proudly graduated from Biola University, also found the rewards of helping eager students to grow and learn too great to pass up.

Within a few months of his divorce, Roger asked his younger sister, 19 year-old Grace, if she would like to move in with him to keep him company. She jumped at the chance, especially because she had wanted to live in a new environment instead of the mobile home in Cypress with her parents. Grace attended Cypress Community College but always found time to help her big brother by cleaning the house and cooking plenty of great meals. However, less than a year after moving in, she met a man in the church she attended, and eventually they married in 1981. After having their first two children, she and her husband Tim Kennedy moved their family to Oregon and became more involved with a Christian community known as the Mennonites, a group similar to the Amish. Throughout the many years ahead, their family grew, and so they moved to Pennsylvania. There they found the simple yet strict lifestyle much to their liking.

Ross and Mary finally had the mobile home to themselves the day Grace moved in with Roger. It was the first time since before Roger was born that they had peace and quiet under their roof. They recalled Ruth's wedding, and Priscilla's wedding as well. They were happy for Priscilla, her husband Jim, and their little girl Wendy, when they left Paramount in '72 to start a church in a small town in Michigan. But they were sad that they had to live so far away. They sat back on their sofa, thinking about how Paul surprised everyone when he moved to Oregon. While Mary petted little Kung Fu, with his scrunched Pekingese face, Ross closed his eyes and thought of all the memories they had as a family. But with all the kids grown up, Ross and Mary now treasured their time together, often going on trips, or just down the street to a restaurant. They continued to grow in their faith in the Lord, and finally, in 1980, Ross' long time dream of traveling to the Holy Land came true.

The trip was put on by a giant Christian media organization, Trinity Broadcasting Network. He flew halfway across the world, and when he eventually toured Israel, he was humbled to think that he walked the same ground as his Savior had walked nearly 2000 years before. He was like a kid when he joined the group of people gathering on the riverbank. TBN President Paul Crouch called them, one by one, so he could baptize them in the Jordan River. It was the same river where, according to the Bible, Jesus himself was baptized. Ross' spirit was calm as he meditated upon God's love and kindness. He also thought how truly privileged a man he was to feel the rush of the murky Jordan flowing up to his chest, chilling his skin but warming his soul. The Baptist preacher was immersed into the cold water, and suddenly was brought up once again. With an unexplainable measure of joy, Ross immediately lifted his hands in praise and came out smiling. The God that had spared his servant's life from the bullet that day in Compton nearly 12 years before now gave him the gift of a dream come true. With his family grown into responsible, loving adults, and with his beautiful wife of almost forty years waiting for him back home, Ross felt a definite completeness. He had been a faithful and giving servant, and the way he raised his children made him worthy of being called a good father. He stared deep into the blue, Middle-Eastern sky, lifted his hands once again, and smiled at the distant heavens while tears poured down the sides of his face and dripped into the river.

"Thank you, Lord. Thank you, Lord," Ross said over and over, his heart melting with gratitude.

$\mathcal{C}$ 21

Vendor and Ambassador

I t was mid-July 1981, and Roger had recently made it back home from the Smithsonian Institution. Roger found out that he was to appear at the Annual Green Derby Award dinner in Los Angeles put on by Kelly Services, a top agency for temporary work placement. This same agency, known for its marketing campaign as the "Kelly Girls," invited Roger to be their award recipient for '81. It was a distinguished award, which was presented to individuals who exemplified the spirit of hard work and pride in one's career. Other notables who had received it were Earvin "Magic" Johnson and Muhammad Ali. In fact, it was Ali who was fitted with the honorary green derby the year before Roger. Roger could hardly believe he could ever be mentioned in the same breath as such athletic legends, let alone be in the same presence.

In mid-August, with the baseball strike of '81 disappointing hard working, paying fans since June 12th, Roger had to supplement his income from Westransco with increased personal appearances at parties, shopping malls, and bar mitzvahs. With Dodger Stadium silent, Roger's group of season peanut holders trusted Roger to hold on to the money they had given him for the prepaid peanut bags. He let them know he would give them free bags of peanuts on opening day of '82 as an interest payment.

"That's just peanuts, so I can afford it," he quipped. But regarding the two month-long strike, he said, "Even with the personal appearances, I've been frustrated. I live and breathe Dodger blue."

By this time, Roger had a new booking agent. He didn't renew Hendison's contract in the late '70s, and so Hendison and Castellano, who was preparing a script on Roger's life to peddle to Disney, drifted away. Disappearing along with them were their attempts at book, television, and movie deals.

Soon, Roger met a man named David Usrey. The man, who had a plumbing business, convinced Roger to let him be his promotional

218

manager. So Usrey prepared some marketing material and, just for Roger's career, the man's business was renamed J.D. Management and Associates instead of J.D. Plumbing. Usrey was a partner with rock and roll promoter, Larry Vallons. Before long, Vallons was allowed to take over the position as Roger's agent.

In just a few months, Ketchum MacLeod & Grove, a New York based advertising agency that represented the Peanut Advisory Board, called Roger at his home. After talking with them, Roger called Larry. Like a slugger called to the plate to be the designated hitter, Vallons went to bat for the peanut pitcher and hit a colossal home run. While dealing with the ad agency, he helped bring Roger one of the most lucrative deals ever for the Peanut Man.

The Peanut Advisory Board, located in Tifton, Georgia, was the official forum for the peanut industry, specifically for the peanut farmers in Georgia, Alabama, and Florida. They had an interest in promoting the healthy, great tasting nut. Due to a severe drought in the South in 1979 and 1980, the entire peanut crop was 42 percent shy of normal. At grocery stores everywhere, this brought higher prices for peanuts and anything related, such as peanut butter. The peanut board was frantic, and they did little advertising. However, the drought had ended, and for the following year they forecast a possible record-setting crop of 1.93 million tons. Excited by the news, the board wanted to spread the word across the nation, covering the country like one, great peanut butter and jelly sandwich.

But they needed a spokesperson.

They wanted someone who could really make an effective pitch for the esteemed peanut snack. While the ad agency thought of who that person could be, they were carefully considering ideas or people related with peanuts. The light clicked on. With the long time association of peanuts and baseball, members of the ad agency immediately thought of the one man who embodied peanuts *and* baseball, the famous peanut vendor from Dodger Stadium.

But the Peanut Advisory Board had to be convinced.

The ad agency had set up a day and time for Roger to go to a film studio. Once there, he was videotaped for a short segment. It was much like an actor's screen test. Roger was not only promoting peanuts, but he was selling himself as being the best, most energetic and enthusiastic peanut promoter.

When the peanut board saw the video, they were won over by the charming and boyish peanut vendor.

Roger Owens was their man.

He was flown to New York, where he met Mr. Tyrone Spearman, the coordinating director for the advisory board. Roger signed a six-month contract, which included a demanding two-week, ten-city tour across the country. He was now the board's goodwill ambassador and was given the name, "America's Premier Peanut Man." In late September 1981, Roger was ready to hit the road as the Peanut Advisory Board's national spokesperson. Provided with chauffeured limousines and first class accommodations during every aspect of his tour, Roger was astonished by the luxurious treatment he received. It was a long way from his childhood days of small houses, hand-me-down clothes and barren refrigerators that cooled the air inside it more often than it preserved food.

His hectic schedule included traveling to major cities like New York, Chicago, Minneapolis, St. Louis, and Atlanta. He also made a stop in Florida. After two weeks, the tour ended in San Diego, California. Throughout the entire time, Roger was accompanied with a representative of the advertising agency, who helped show him around and get him to the places he was supposed to be. Roger gave interviews on television and radio, and he threw peanuts at shopping centers, private functions, and food conferences. Although his presence and his peanut tossing did most of the speaking for him, Roger still had to tell consumers all across America that "peanuts are back, shortages are over and, after the first of the year, prices should come down."

"I really feel good about promoting peanuts. They are the best protein you can buy and contain no cholesterol. They are low in sodium and saturated fats, full of vitamins and minerals, especially B vitamins, and supply eight amino acids," Roger stated.

Every city on the tour was memorable for Roger, and he was tickled at the thought of staying at upscale, ritzy hotels.

In Chicago, he thrilled onlookers with his peanut pitching performance. As taxicabs drove down Michigan Avenue, Roger hurled bags of peanuts to excited taxi drivers who had their windows rolled down, ready to catch the sailing bags.

In St. Louis, a newspaper reporter was waiting to interview Roger at the baseball stadium in town. When he saw Roger arrive in a stretch limousine, he was baffled that a peanut vendor could ever make it so big that he had his own limo. He teased him about it, and Roger just cracked up. He told the reporter that the limo was his just while he was on tour for the Peanut Advisory Board.

One evening, while grabbing the opportunity to get some needed sleep after a busy day of peanut pitching to large crowds and giving interviews to reporters, an exhausted Roger lay sprawled on his hotel bed. He looked up at the ceiling and couldn't help but think how the little peanut, which he believed in so strongly, continued to play such a major role in his life. He thought of what it must have been like for his Uncle Jack to deal with being well known as a singer and songwriter. Roger closed his eyes and remembered the time Uncle Jack called him not long after Roger's first appearance on the *Tonight Show*. He smiled as he recalled their conversation and how Uncle Jack was thoroughly impressed with Roger, admitting that, in all his years performing, he never was so fortunate to be on the show with Johnny Carson. Little did Roger realize that the phone call from Uncle Jack in 1976 was the last time he would ever hear from him again. On January 26, 1982, only a few months after Roger's tour promoting peanuts, Uncle John (Jack) Milton Owens passed away in Phoenix, Arizona at the age of 69. A funeral mass was held for him a few days later at St. Thomas the Apostle Catholic Church, and he was buried at St. Francis Catholic Cemetery. With every swaying of hips and gentle floating of arms in peaceful, rhythmic, hula dancing, the memory of the man who wrote *The Hukilau Song* would always live on, like the distant coastal winds blowing in towards the warm shore of Waikiki.

Roger woke up the next morning in his hotel room, ready for another leg of the tour to begin.

Finally, Roger returned home to Torrance. He was completely worn out from the previous two weeks. He dropped his bags in the living room, sat on the couch, and was affectionately greeted by his two buddies, Brande and French, both of whom were wagging their tails so fast that their whole bodies shook from side to side.

He couldn't believe how much he missed old Branders and Frenchy, his two extremely hairy, four legged "kids."

As the baseball season progressed, more fans learned of his famous feats in the nation's capital, and that gave them just one more reason to be proud of their Peanut Man.

"I always wanted to be a movie star or a baseball player," Roger admitted. "I guess I'm kind of both now." As always, Roger loved being at the stadium. No matter where he traveled, Dodger Stadium was always his home, and it showed.

"I love entertaining. I enjoy people, and Dodger Stadium is my showplace," he said. "I sometimes feel tired and depressed. But once

I'm at the ballpark, I forget my ills and troubles. I'm revitalized by the fans, and I get this tremendous burst of energy. It's my best therapy," confessed Roger.

In May of 1982, the Dodger peanut pitching legend was the subject of a wonderful write-up. The generous, three-page story, written by Tom Hennessy, appeared in the Sports section of the *Long Beach Press Telegram*.

Hennessy, who called Roger the "Cy Young of Peanut Pitching," wrote the following:

> Some pitchers etch their way into the scrapbook of your mind.
>
> A fan who once saw Ewell Blackwell's sidearm or Warren Spahn's perilously high kick can summon up those images in the beckoning of a second.
>
> Roger Owens is that kind of pitcher. See him once and the memory will take up cerebral residence; waiting, like a Gary Cooper film, to be replayed again and again in the theater of your mind's eye.
>
> But don't look for Owens on the all-time roster of major leaguers. Look instead to the left field loge of Dodger Stadium. When Lasorda & Co. are playing at home, you will find Owens in those lofty environs, doing what he does better than anyone else—selling peanuts.

In June, Roger was one of the stars at the World's Fair in Knoxville, Tennessee. Still representing the Peanut Advisory Board, Roger was on hand to promote the peanut industry at the opening ceremonies of the World's Fair International Baseball Tournament. Also present at the ceremonies was Baseball Commissioner Bowie Kuhn. He was presented with a peanut trophy from the Peanut Man himself, on behalf of the advisory board. Roger continued to stir up interest for the unassuming peanuts when he sold them at the Japanese American baseball game, and when he was featured on television shows and news reports in Knoxville.

Roger followed up his trip to the World's Fair in Tennessee with trips to the National Peanut Council Convention in Hot Springs, Virginia, the Blade Food Fair in Toledo, Ohio, and to Disneyland, in California, where he participated in the "Old-Fashioned Easter Parade."

Roger's travels had taken him to all parts of the country. However, in late 1983, Roger the Peanut Man was preparing to go international. With plans to visit Japan's great Yokohama Stadium, the down to earth, simple, and witty peanut vendor Roger Owens was about to become not only a goodwill ambassador for the city of Los Angeles, the Dodgers, and for small, tasty goobers everywhere, but for the United States as well. For almost eight years, Roger had been known as the Famous Peanut Man, but now the man who was never that fond of flying was about to travel over 10 hours to the ancient lands of the Far East, en route to becoming the *World* Famous Peanut Man.

In mid-October 1983, Roger was presented with an honorary County scroll by Los Angeles Supervisor Kenneth Hahn. Hahn's face lit up anytime anyone mentioned Roger the Peanut Man, and for Hahn, to present the scroll to the Dodger vendor and friend was an honor in itself.

"Roger Owens has become an institution, spreading goodwill along with his peanuts at Dodger games and other sporting events," Hahn announced. "He has become internationally famous for his unique peanut throwing abilities and will soon be traveling to Japan to demonstrate his talents at some sporting events. We should all be proud of this goodwill ambassador from our community."

Throughout the early 80's, the famed peanut vendor was featured on more television shows, including *The John Davidson Show*, *Two On The Town*, *Real People*, and *P.M. Magazine*. Now, in January 1984, Roger and a cargo of 7,000 bags of peanuts were on their way to Japan and its frigid, winter climate. Roger was set to begin the year by impressing a stadium full of Japanese fans, who all showed up to watch the 9th Annual Japan Bowl All Star Collegiate Football Game and to enjoy the Peanut Man working the crowds.

"They designed for me a Japanese vendor's costume and are even flying over the same kind of nuts I use here so I won't be thrown off by size and weight differences," Roger said before leaving for Japan.

It was January 16th, and the football game was underway. With America's top college athletes on the field playing a good game and with Roger, high up in the stands, trying to keep his hands warm in the cold weather, the Japanese crowds loved the great time they were having. Roger enjoyed every minute with the gracious sports fans. Each bag sold for 100 Yen, but for Roger it wasn't about the money, it was only about the fun and the experience. In fact, he was thrilled to receive so many letters of appreciation after the trip had ended.

Even after Roger arrived back home, people in Japan continued to show interest in his abilities. Fascinated with his eccentric profession and the accuracy of his peanut throwing, Japanese producers of a popular television program called *The Challenger* asked Roger to be a major part of one particular episode. The overall premise of the show involved a Japanese citizen challenging the skills of an American citizen at their workplace. Living in two different countries, each person had the exact same profession, and the catch was to see who could do it better.

Kengo, a 20 year-old Tokyo Giants food vendor, was allowed to come to Dodger Stadium to try to master Roger's style of selling peanuts in the stands. As a result, the young man would have to learn Roger's array of talented tosses and tricks of the trade, which varied like a heap of assorted nuts poured onto a silver tray for the guests of a black-tie dinner party.

Kengo worked extremely hard, and he trained both on and off the job. Roger and Kengo often went to a nearby park in Torrance so that Kengo could practice throwing into the bleachers. On the way to the park, Kengo always ran up some of the hills of the residential area, all the while smiling as the theme from *Rocky* blared out of a portable boom box. But, even after two weeks, Kengo still could not even be *remotely* considered an equal. Roger loved working with him nonetheless, and the Dodger fans were charmed with the Kengo's personality. Many months later, Roger had the pleasure of meeting the young man again on Roger's second trip to Japan.

With such fond memories of the international scene still fresh in Roger's mind, it was only appropriate that 1984 was the year of the XXIII Olympiad in Los Angeles.

Roger waited each day in anticipation of the Opening Ceremonies of the 1984 Olympics and to begin working the massive Coliseum crowds. Finally the day arrived, but the vendors were not allowed to begin selling in the crowds while the ceremonies were taking place. Some of them, including Roger, snuck in anyway just to catch a glimpse of the grand entrance of the Olympic athletes from all across the globe, parading around the huge track. Roger quietly sat on a step in an aisle, up in some of the highest parts of the packed Coliseum. Roger was thrilled to see first-hand the procession of athletes and the special video displayed on the gigantic video screen. The video clip showed many famous places and faces associated with Los Angeles. The video showed Dodger Stadium, and when it showed Roger Owens, the Peanut Man, as one of the familiar faces, Roger lit up with excitement, as he could hardly believe he was featured in such a way.

Throughout the Olympics, Roger worked the baseball games held at the stadium, as well as all the track and field events at the Coliseum. The Southern California heat soared, causing the skilled athletes to occasionally wipe the pouring sweat off their foreheads. As for the fans, they bought few bags of peanuts, and instead looked for the icy re-freshment of cups of freezing cold water, sold by any of the countless water vendors.

One day at the stadium, Roger was working in the stands. A couple approached him and told him that they remembered seeing him at the Smithsonian a few years before, and that once they had arrived to the Olympics, they wanted to find Roger the Peanut Man, buy some pea-nuts from him, and show him a picture they had taken of him in Washington. Roger was sincerely moved that they had traveled across the country to show him such kindness.

At the end of the Olympics, the Hollywood limelight and the bril-liant glow of distant stars in the Los Angeles night sky all shared the stage with the explosive and colorful bursting of fireworks.

It was indeed a summer to remember.

Why was the peanut afraid to go walking late at night?
He was afraid that he might be as-salt-ed.

$\mathcal{C}$ *22*

Emotions, Like Flowers, Are Gathered

The summer of '84 didn't just bring the world to Southern California. It also brought for Roger a mixed bag of emotions, which ran the entire spectrum from happiness to grief, like a relay race runner covering the entire length of the Coliseum's red, clay track. In early June, Roger, like the rest of his brothers and sisters, had been keeping in touch with Mary to find out how his dad had been doing.

By June of '84, Ross had already been suffering for more than a year. In spite of his increasing heart problems, Mary was vigilant in watching over her husband and taking care of him in every possible way. It took less than two years for Ross' health to steadily decline, and it affected Mary immensely. He became much more irritable and, at best, there remained only faint hues of his once colorful character and little sparkle in his eyes. These remnants, these left over signs of the man he used to be, only seemed to emphasize his present and unmistakably withering frame. The brilliant beacon of light, which once reached into the lives of his growing children and many friends, was now dimmed.

On June 22, 1984, Ross' flame of life was extinguished.

Ross Wheeler Owens, Jr. was buried on his 74th birthday, June 26, 1984.

For Roger and the rest of the family of children and grandchildren, and for Ross and Jack's surviving sister, Evelyn, it was a hard loss to deal with. Ross, whether a father, husband, brother, or community leader, held such a special place in their hearts that it went beyond description. After a memorable service at Forest Lawn, located across the street from the mobile home park where Mary and Ross had lived for eight years, the Owens family, like a vibrant bouquet of flowers, found strength in the sunlight of their mutual support, and found that talking about it in their characteristic ways was the best avenue for healing and acceptance.

As for Mary, it was not so simple.

Mary found the loss of her husband of 42 years to be so emotionally unbearable that it drove her to relapse. For months she experienced a gamut of feelings, including guilt, severe depression, and loneliness. Through good times and bad, she was always Ross' partner, if not his best friend. She was haunted by no longer having him around. She often would say things that made no sense to Roger, either when he visited or talked on the phone. Many times, she heard voices in the trailer home where she still lived. Some nights she was frightened and found it hard to sleep, while other nights she cried herself into sleepiness. It would require a three-month hospital stay and a few months at home afterward for Mary to finally release the sadness and trauma from within and eventually find the goodness of God and the love of her children to support and comfort her during a new era of happiness and joy for a woman forging ahead into her 70's.

Even with the passing of their beloved father, the grown Owens children were fortunate to find 1984 a year of celebration as well. It was that same year that Esther's wedding took center stage, and she became the wife of her best friend, Bruce Fenn. Within just a few months, Lois also tied the knot of holy matrimony with the love of her life, Glenn Hervieux.

Mary was thrilled for her daughters. With each passing day, her elation grew with the thought of more grandchildren on the way.

In January 1985, Roger again traveled to Japan for the Japan Bowl. It was his second consecutive year working at Yokohama Stadium and, in fact, he would go on to throw peanuts to the Japanese crowds each year until 1988.

It was April 1985, and Roger was ready to begin another baseball season at Dodger Stadium. The Dodgers' success had declined during much of the 80's. The Dodger organization gained many fans throughout the 70's, and, by the end of the strike-shortened season of 1981, the Dodgers had miraculously reached the postseason and had defeated the powerful New York Yankees in an amazing World Series. The Blue Crew, which included Cey, Garvey, Lopes, Yeager, and Pedro Guerrero, had faced off against the pummeling players in pinstripe, like Winfield, Randolph, Nettles, and Reggie Jackson. But by '85, many of the Dodger greats of the 70's had reached the twilight of their careers and moved on to other teams. As if the Dodger fans didn't have enough to worry about with dismal, lackluster starting lineups, the baseball strike of '85 only added to their woes. Although the strike ended by August, Dodger fans had one more reason to be upset.

By this time, the Oakland Raiders had moved south and now called Los Angeles their home. With rowdier fans flocking to the football games, it became apparent that the city needed to address the problem of objects being thrown by the tough Raider fans. Their fans took their Raider football seriously and often threw things at fans of the visiting teams. The city had had enough and passed an ordinance that stated that no object or substance, "solid or liquid," could be "intentionally thrown, discharged, launched, or spilled" in any manner, in the public stands of a sporting event. This even applied to Dodger Stadium, but it was intended to apply to rowdy fans, not to service personnel such as peanut vendors.

After the law was passed, the Dodger fans quickly noticed Roger's downbeat demeanor. They found out about the new city ordinance and, just as in '76, fans of the Peanut Man raised their voices on behalf of the unpretentious Dodger legend.

The next day, Roger arrived at the ballpark. Mayor Tom Bradley's wife, Ethel, arrived just before the start of the game and found her seat in the loge level. Within a few minutes, she noticed how Roger was just handing out the peanuts instead of throwing them. There was plenty of "booing" from the fans, obviously venting their frustration for the ban on throwing any items in the stands.

Roger saw Ethel and walked over to her. A puzzled Ethel took Roger by the hand and said, "Come here, Roger. Sit down next to me and tell me what's going on."

Roger explained what happened.

"Okay, Roger, don't you worry about a thing. Tonight, I'll tell my husband about it. We'll get this sorted out, okay?" she said, comforting Roger. Roger, however, didn't quite believe how much or how fast anything would get done about the matter. He knew how busy a man the mayor was, and just took Ethel's words as merely heartfelt sentiment.

The next day, a man approached Roger at the stadium.

"Roger?"

"Yes, sir?"

"Roger, come with me. You're wanted on the field at home plate."

Roger followed the man on to the playing field, where people and members of the media were standing around talking with District Attorney James Hahn, son of the City Supervisor and champion for Los

Angeles, Kenneth Hahn. It was a special ceremony announcing pub-
licly that all peanut throwing vendors, especially Roger, were allowed
to continue.

Despite the city's declaration, the food concession company, Arthur
Food Services, was slow to let Roger and the other vendors get back in
action. Wanting to study the insurance aspects of the new ordinance,
the company kept the ban in place.

The fans were not happy.

Many fans brought friends and customers from out of town just to
marvel at Roger's theatrics. Admitting that half the fun at being at the
stadium and buying peanuts was to have Roger throw them, they found
that with each passing game, the simple, almost necessary, act of buying and eating peanuts was losing its charm. Something had to be done
quickly.

Staff writer Steve Harvey of the *Los Angeles Times* followed the
progress of the ban and the effect it had on Roger. Harvey wrote several persuasive articles in favor of the Dodger peanut hurler. In the
Long Beach Press Telegram, writer Tom Hennessy also colorfully gave
his straightforward opinion about bringing Roger's smile-inducing performances back to the stadium. If that weren't enough, hundreds of fans
were signing petitions on Roger's behalf. In fact, an Orange County
businessman held up a huge banner that read, "Let Roger Throw," and
fans started chanting the phrase as soon as they read it. Finally, the food
concession company woke up and smelled the peanuts.

After two weeks, Roger was back in action, and the fans were delighted.

"It was like a family reunion. I could hear people cheering and saying, 'Hey, he's throwing again!' It brought tears to my eyes," Roger
confessed.

But in just six more years, the Dodger fans would learn that their
freedom to "come from everywhere, just to watch him throw a pair,"
would be challenged once again.

In late October 1985, Roger was invited to entertain and help promote peanuts at the Japanese Baseball World Series. After being
featured on several Japanese television programs, he remained in Japan
for just under a month, endorsing peanuts for the Japan Peanut Advisory Board. Even a national Peanut Day was declared on November
11th. With Roger continuing to work hard both at home and internationally, he debated whether or not he still required the help of a personal
agent. Jim Neuman, who was one of the first band members of the

Beach Boys, met Roger at an event in Orange County in the early 80's, and he soon became Roger's new booking agent. However, after a few years, Roger decided he no longer needed a booking agent and was content with doing the job himself.

By the end of '86, the New York Mets had shocked the world by winning the World Series. Feeling Dodger blue in more ways than one, Dodger fans knew it was just another lousy season to toss away into their mental round files. As for Roger, he kept busy and, oddly enough, he was invited to pitch peanuts at a hockey game.

It was his first time selling the shelled nuts at a hockey game, but it wouldn't be his last. Several years later, he would sell peanuts at semi-professional Ice Dogs games in the L.A. Sports Arena. In addition, Roger didn't just work professional baseball and football games. He had worked college games and professional boxing matches as far back as the 60's. One time, Roger even worked at a Muhammad Ali fight at the L.A. Sports Arena in the early 70's and, since peanuts never sold much once the bell rang, he stopped at ring side to watch the best boxer in the world throw punch after punch, prancing around in calculated steps until his opponent succumbed to a flurry of two steps and one-two combinations. Standing so close to the action, Roger was amazed. He could see every last drop of their sweat, brought on by the rigorous sport.

Even more impressive, Roger began to work every NBA home game of the Clippers, once they moved to Los Angeles and called the L.A. Sports Arena their home. In fact, Roger was on hand for every Clippers game until they picked up their bags and moved on up to the west side to a deluxe arena in the sky, the marvelous Staples Center.

But it was now December '86, and Roger traveled to Buffalo, New York, where he sold peanuts at a Buffalo Sabres game, with the pro-ceeds going to the Buffalo Zoo. Once there, public relations officials warned Roger of the much different atmosphere of a hockey game, not to mention a *New York* hockey game. He was trained how to handle the potential verbal onslaught of any number of hockey fans, who were es-pecially unforgiving if some vendor was in their way of a scored goal. So Roger courageously set out selling his peanuts, putting on a show as always. For the public relations officials, it was like sending a scuba diver into warm waters full of congregating tiger sharks.

Roger continued his energetic performance up and down the merci-lessly steep steps for nearly an hour, all the while accommodating the fans by ducking every so often so he wouldn't block anyone's vision of the rink far below.

Suddenly, a goal was scored, and the place erupted with cheering and the blaring of the goal siren.

"Dammit, you peanut vendor! Thanks to you, I missed that goal!" a man screamed.

Roger was startled. His pulse quickened, and he was abruptly frozen in his tracks.

Calmly recalling what he was instructed to do, in such a situation, Roger sincerely apologized and offered the man a free bag of peanuts.

The tense moment caused more sweat to roll down the sides of Roger's face.

"I don't want a bag of peanuts, I wanted to see that damn goal," the man continued. After a moment of silent awkwardness and another apology from Roger, the hockey fan then finally snatched the salted atonement. After a few minutes, Roger was about to move on to some hungry fans nearby, when the man called Roger over to his seat.

He looked at Roger and smiled.

"Hey, I was just messin' with ya. You really didn't block my view. I saw you throwing those great pitches to those people right over there, and when I was watching you, that's when I missed the goal," he admitting, following it with a subdued chuckle.

Roger eyed the man, and with the smirk of flustered embarrassment felt by anyone who has ever been on the receiving end of a practical joke, Roger nevertheless agreed that the man deserved the free peanuts after such a confession as that.

Roger was so popular with the fans that game that he was invited back for another Sabres game, but it took three years to make the return visit.

Roger returned home and continued to work each day at his sales job.

However, just a few months later, in 1987, Roger learned that it would be his last year working for Westransco.

The freight shipping company went into financial collapse, filed for bankruptcy, and closed its doors. Roger was sad that the company, which had treated him so favorably over the past 21 years, was truly closing down. From before man walked on the moon to the days of MTV's pre-pubescence, Roger had worked there every day, calling on customers, working after hours to prepare his leads, and working up a comedy routine for any potential customers at the ballpark.

One day, while Roger was clearing off his desk amid the somber atmosphere within the building, he quietly recalled the times he shared with the company. There was the time he embarrassed himself at the sales meeting, and the times that everyone showed incredible support for him during his recovery after the jeep accident.

He then stood up and sighed.

He resumed putting more papers into cardboard boxes. Then he thought of the time that he felt he deserved a raise in his salary, and how his request seemed to fall on deaf ears. But the company's resigning president, Ed Downes, approved the well-earned raise as one of his last actions, but he playfully didn't tell Roger. Roger began to notice a substantial increase in his paycheck but thought it was a clerical error. Rather than spend the extra income in case they caught the error and asked for the return of the money, Roger saved it. Still paranoid, he finally received an invitation to Mr. Downes' house for dinner. Mr. Downes was trying to fix Roger up with his daughter, but Roger had a girlfriend at the time.

"Well, Roger, how do you like the food?" Mr. Downes asked at the dinner table.

"It's very good, sir," Roger replied.

"I bet you've noticed by now the size of your paycheck has grown considerably," he added.

"Uhh, yes, sir, I have noticed," Roger answered, hiding his smile behind, the soft, heavy napkin. Finally, a sense of relaxation overcame Roger, and he started to enjoy the dinner. He was now free to spend the money as he pleased.

As Roger continued to pack his things and wipe his bare desk with a cloth, he stared one last time at his workspace. Roger opened up the drawer and found an unopened bag of peanuts.

He smiled.

Roger opened the bag and started to eat a few of the peanuts. As he closely examined one of them, Roger, the consummate salesman, realized that even with Westransco gone, he could always depend on the little, shelled peanuts.

In spite of the closure of Westransco, there were several other shipping companies that wanted him to work as a full time salesman. Within a month, he was working with a rival company, Clipper Exxpress. He confessed that he was only interested in a sales job that was commission-based, and despite their disappointment to not have him full-time, they felt that having him on commission was better than not at all, so Roger was hired. Roger had ceased his full time sales duties at Westransco in '84, when the Olympics took much of his time away.

Since then, his desire to keep a commission based salary carried through to his new job in Carson. Working out of his home, Roger would make sales calls on behalf of Clipper Exxpress for the next 16 years.

Ever since Roger's fame had skyrocketed after the *Tonight Show* appearance, Roger was able to help himself financially by being invited to pitch peanuts at numerous private parties, corporate events, birthday celebrations, and bar mitzvahs, from the San Fernando Valley to the boulevards of Beverly Hills. He gladly accepted opportunities to put on a show at such parties, complete with his trademark tossing and fast wit, which honed in on subject matter provided to him by friends and parents ahead of time. Such events were more than icebreakers. In fact, according to Roger, he was simply helping people "get out of their shells." Roger loved to entertain, but more so, he loved to motivate and inspire young boys and girls. It moved Roger so much that he could be a positive influence on the lives of young people.

"I like to set a good example for the kids," Roger said. "So many come from broken homes, have lived with alcoholism, drugs, or a single parent who must work more than full time. I'm not perfect, but I'll do whatever I can to show them that hard work pays off. In fact, I like to stress to young people that, sometimes, success doesn't always come with a gray suit and a tie."

In March 1988, with NCAA March Madness being all the rage on every college campus, Roger was invited to LSU, Louisiana State University. Playing in the South-Eastern Conference, or SEC, Tournament, LSU was gearing up for a big weekend of fast paced hoops. The Peanut Man, just back from Tokyo less than two months earlier, was also gearing up for what would be the biggest weekend of peanut sales in his life. On Friday, Roger began working the ecstatic crowds, throwing bags of peanuts behind the back and under the leg, impressing everyone from cheerleaders to court side announcers. On Saturday, Roger climbed up and down the stairs in a hurry, marching in his own madness to keep up with the incoming yells for more peanuts. By Sunday, the turbulent weekend brought him to a total of an incredible 5,400 bags sold. Arena officials found out that it was history in the making for the famous Peanut Man, so they passed the word on over the public address system.

"Everybody in today's attendance give a warm LSU congratulations to Roger "The Peanut Man" Owens, for selling 5,400 peanut bags," said the man over the loud speaker. The place went wild with cheering, whistling, and applause. "But wait, he's not done. Buy those peanuts, 'cause we're gonna get to 6,000! How about that everybody?" he added.

The place went nuts.

Completely out of peanuts, Roger was handed boxes full of the arena's own bags of peanuts. The food concession manager placed the boxes on the floor and smiled at Roger.

"Go get 'em, Roger!" yelled the manager. Not thrown off one bit from the size and weight differences of the bags he was accustomed to, an amazing feat in itself, Roger treated the warm, college fans to 600 more bags of peanuts, setting a three-day, all-time personal record of 6,000 bags.

With spent peanut shells covering the stands, the fans roared with excitement as the game became more intense. A sweat-drenched Roger finally sat down, thoroughly sold out and worn out.

"The fans have really accepted me here. It's the first time I've ever thrown peanuts in Louisiana. I've traveled all around the world, but this is my first time here, and they've accepted me well."

After the long weekend, Roger boarded the airplane for his flight back home. Many of the other passengers had been at the game or had heard about him being there, and they immediately gave him a standing ovation for a job well done. Roger had a huge grin, and while walking to his seat, he nodded his head in gratitude, and thanked them for the applause. By the end of that same year, Roger made a return trip to LSU, exciting the football fans during a packed LSU game against Miami.

DRABBLE Reprinted by permission of
United Feature Syndicate, Inc.

$\mathcal{C}$ 23

You're a Good Man, Roger Owens

In April came the arrival of spring, freshly pollinated flowers, morning rain, and a new baseball season. In 1988, the Dodgers had assembled a hodgepodge of talented players, with hustlers like Kirk Gibson, eccentric characters like Mickey Hatcher, and some stellar pitchers like Orel Herschiser. With great Dodger pitching easily outweighing their slugging abilities, the team rode the backs of these same workhorses all the way to the World Series. Despite the record-setting performance of 59 consecutive scoreless innings by Herschiser in the regular season, the Dodgers seemed to be a pathetic choice to fight the Goliath of the American League, the Oakland A's. Towering like two majestic sequoias, young sluggers Mark McGwire and Jose Canseco stood with folded arms, as though insulted that the city of Los Angeles dared to offer such a feeble team.

Yet, in the bottom of the ninth inning of Game 1, with the Dodgers down by one and the best relief pitcher in baseball on the mound for the A's, the Dodgers shocked everyone by calling to the plate their hard working and battered veteran outfielder, Kirk Gibson. With a man on base, two outs, and the count forced to three balls and two strikes, the tense moment erupted into one of the single greatest nights in baseball history. Rejoicing thunderously, the crowds stayed in their seats for at least a half hour after the game had ended, soaking up the electricity of the moment. Their hero had just effortlessly smacked a two-run homer deep into the right field pavilion, stunning every last person on the A's ball club, from batboy to back up bullpen catchers, and from team trainers to big money, all-star veterans. The magical night baffled the A's, and they were never the same. For the rest of the series, they were blown away by great pitching and were haunted by visions of the night Gibson circled the bases in triumph. It was indeed a fairytale World Championship for the Los Angeles Dodgers.

In 1991, 48 year-old Roger embarked on the adventure of a new season. Already one year into the 90's, Roger geared up physically and mentally for his 33rd consecutive year working Los Angeles Dodger games, and his 29th year at Dodger Stadium. Each home game, including many of the football and basketball games played in town, Roger pounded the pavement of rising steps, up and down, dedicating his time to his passion and art of selling. Although his knees began to bother him more every year, he fought off any sense of pain the way a veteran big league catcher would have iced his knees and put the gear back on, or the way a heavyweight boxer would have tended to a wound, and then punched his gloves together with the tenacity and devotion of actually looking forward to the next round.

Roger was driven. He was inspired by the simplicity of sunlight shining upon the faces of playful kids living out their childhood memories in vivid color before Roger's very eyes. He was inspired by the laughter and camaraderie of young teens, and the grown ups who eyed them enviably in fond recollection of their own younger years. Roger found that such moments and such friends drove him to consistency and dedication far more than monetary gain or popularity.

However, with the start of the '91 baseball season at hand, there was trouble in the air, and it smelled nothing like teen spirit.

By early April, younger fans and older fans alike went into an uproar over the new food concession company at the stadium, Marriott Corporation. Their baseball nirvana of tossed peanuts and sweet Cracker Jacks had been rudely interrupted the day Marriott gave all the vendors an exhaustive laundry list of rules, which included the prohibition of throwing peanuts. The vendors were called to a meeting and ordered not to toss any food items. Despite the new edict, there remained plenty of people at the games who knew of no reason why the Peanut Man should be kept from performing his almost thirty year-old tradition.

So fans demonstrated that they had a tradition of their own, supporting Roger by writing hundreds of letters to top Dodger management, including Vice President of Communications Tommy Hawkins, and Dodger President Peter O'Malley. Roger also received copies of such letters, and soon he had large stacks of letters spread out across his dinner table at home. People from all backgrounds and businesses wrote to the Dodger management expressing in no uncertain terms of their desire to have Roger selling peanuts in the manner they had come to love as grown ups and so lovingly recalled as kids themselves throughout the 1970's. They spoke of how Roger has been an institution, and that it simply wouldn't be the same with Roger merely handing out bags of peanuts.

One such letter addressed to Tommy Hawkins and written by fan and friend Eric Shirley, summed it all up when he wrote:

> I have learned recently that the Dodgers sold a portion of the stadium concession rights to the Marriott Corporation. While I happen to like the traditional fare offered at Dodger Stadium, I understand that there are some fans who would prefer a Happy Star to a traditional Dodger Dog, or a Burrito Supreme to your succulent, gooey Nachos.
>
> That's fine. Such is progress…There is, however, a sad twist of fate to this acquisition by Marriott. I have also learned that Roger Owens will no longer be able to throw peanuts to the fans.
>
> This, Mr. Hawkins, is an American tragedy.
>
> I grew up in Venice, and my most fond memories of childhood are my experiences as a Dodger fan and as a patron at Dodger Stadium. The ballpark smells like no other ballpark in the country. It smells fresh, as if Dodger Stadium was the place where baseball was reborn. The grass is real, there is no roof to get in the way, and the employees are always smiling.
>
> Especially Roger Owens.
>
> I can remember being a young boy of no more than four or five years old, and sitting with my father at Dodger Stadium. I would forego buying peanuts until Roger made his way down my aisle. Then I would raise my hand and look him in the eye as he stood at the bottom of the aisle. He would grin, point to me with several bags of peanuts in his hand, and gracefully toss a bag, with the finesse and precision of a Tommy John change up.
>
> And he did it all with a smile.
>
> He is as much a part of my relationship with the Dodgers as Duke Sims, Steve Yeager, Ron Cey, and Von Joshua are. (I know— Von Joshua? I just like his name.) And it makes me ill to think that I will take my children to Dodger Stadium, to give them some of the same memories that are so real and valuable to me, and Roger Owens will not be tossing them a bag of peanuts. He adds to the Dodger enjoyment like no other element.
>
> His enthusiasm for his work and his love of the Dodgers are refreshing and contagious…I have never written a letter to the Dodgers before. The organization is a class act, and I'm proud of the job you do. But I cannot let Roger get squelched without speaking out against it. This is not just another ranting tirade by a frustrated baseball purist. This is a letter written by an average, middle class Southern Californian, who loves baseball and wants to see good things about the game preserved for future generations.

> Roger Owens and others like him are good for the game. They show that baseball is not about salary arbitration, guaranteed contracts, and television revenue. To Roger, and to most of us, baseball is still about a diving catch, a dusty uniform, and a smiling face. I need that reminder. My family and friends need it. And most of all, the game needs it.

In less than a month, Roger's "show within a show" was on tour once again, proudly showing in the amphitheater of the loge level between home plate and left field. Peanuts were sold, but smiles were free. With Disneyland about an hour away, Roger still felt he worked at the happiest place on Earth, and who could blame him with such a supporting cast as his wonderful, peanut-loving, Dodger fans?

In 1994, baseball suffered perhaps its biggest wound in its long, hallowed history. It was a wound that wouldn't heal, even with stitches drawn tightly together like the stitches of a baseball's leather seams. It was a wound that bruised the heart and knocked the wind out of the allegiance of even the most loyal baseball fanatics. It was the year of unsettled differences between filthy rich athletes and even filthier owners.

It was the year of the '94 baseball strike and the cancelled World Series that ensued. Simply mentioning the '94 season brought a definitive callousness, a hardening of hearts, as solid as a Babe Ruth bat, among simple, tax-paying, working class, baseball fans everywhere. Such fans shelled out hard-earned money for expensive tickets to watch over-glorified ball players who would rather fight harder in negotiations and arbitration than for a diving catch near the foul line. The fans weren't asking too much. They simply wanted to put some fun into their spent funds. But the crowds weren't the only ones affected. The vendors, due to the withering ballpark attendance, felt the pinch in their sales, and Roger was no exception. This time, no amount of fan letters could change the problem, because there *weren't* any fans.

"It seems the little person has been hurt the most. This includes not only the food vendors, the people who work in the food stands, and the hawkers like ourselves, but the security guards, the ushers, and the parking attendants. These are people who really count on that extra income every year to keep their families together."

As the strike continued, even delaying the opening day in '95, Roger nevertheless kept the faith in the game of baseball and the happiness it gave him at the stadium. Not all baseball fans were as eager to embrace baseball with the start of the new season. In fact, the game had not only lost about a third of its fans since the strike, but the game itself was in danger of falling off the pedestal of being the national pastime.

Roger and the other stadium vendors first thought the strike would pass quickly. "When it kept going, we just couldn't believe it," Roger said. "I didn't take sides on it. The greed was on both sides." With regard to the sour taste it left with fans, he added, "Even two of my season peanut holders gave up their seats, because they were so bitter." With the big leagues tied up in the strike, Roger was invited to work at minor league games where the action was genuine and hard-fought. At such places as Mavericks Stadium in Adelanto and The Diamond in Lake Elsinore, Roger found the games to be refreshing, especially when younger ones in attendance found it easy to get their baseballs autographed.

During the opening day ceremony in '95, Roger agreed to lead a group of Dodger employees, including vendors, security guards, and ushers, onto the field to be individually recognized. Then, for the second time in his career, Roger warmed up the season by throwing the ceremonial first pitch.

"It was a way of the Dodgers saying to the employees, 'Thank you for coming back,'" Roger said.

In August '97, Roger was scheduled to appear as a featured guest at the Annual Orange County Fair in Costa Mesa. The woman working in marketing and public relations for the fair, Jill Lloyd, was also responsible in part for the fair's theme that year, which was a tropical theme, including fruits, nuts, and fish. Trying hard to make a connection to nuts that would educate and entertain, she finally remembered the Peanut Man whom she had first met the year before.

"Our first conversation was like we were old friends," she said. "That is how he treated me, and that is how, I soon learned, he treated everyone—like a friend."

The two talked about the fair over lunch at Katella Deli in Los Alamitos. After asking numerous questions, she was "extremely touched by the situation he was dealt as a child when his mother had a breakdown and could no longer care for the kids."

"How he weathered that storm and bounced back and kept a positive attitude was inspiring," she added. "The deal breaker was when he kind of chided me to finish everything on my plate, and I couldn't, so he started to eat off my plate. That was so telling about how he felt at home with the world."

At the fair, Roger threw out free bags of peanuts as a warm up to the series of concerts throughout each day. He also participated in activities such as being in a photo with anyone named Hazel, as in hazel nut, in attendance at the fair, and he had a blast officiating a peanut-throwing contest. Roger was a major hit.

"One thing I will always remember about talking with Roger is that no matter what, he never ends a conversation or a visit without telling one of his jokes. He always leaves ya smiling...or laughing. He's like gold. He becomes more valuable as the years roll by. I went through a bout of illness a few years ago and he showed much concern. There are many people that I work with and associate with because of my line of work, but when it gets down to the nitty gritty, there are only a few that openly show their concern, that show you more than just a business side. Roger is the perpetual Peanut Man—part entertainer, part comedian and 100% human," Lloyd added.

During the late 90's, Roger continued to work at the stadium, inspiring generations of fans just as he had throughout his forty years of commitment to the Dodgers and the organization's immaculate grounds on which he felt so privileged to work and to call "home." With more than two and a half million bags of peanuts sold in his unique, crowd pleasing style, Roger managed to turn the simplicity of stadium vending to an art form, worthy of appreciation and remarkable in its winding path of attained success.

Throughout the late 80's and all of the 90's, Roger appeared, even if for brief moments, on several television shows. He made appearances on shows like the *Arsenio Hall Show*, *Dennis Miller Show*, *Pat Sajak Show*, *Rosie O'Donnell Show*, and he also made two different appearances for the audience on the *Tonight Show with Jay Leno* around the time of the '94 strike. That same year, the out of work peanut tossing legend gave an interview for the show *Entertainment Tonight*. In the late 90's, he was one of the three panelists on the game show *To Tell The Truth*. For that episode, he was trying to convince the judges that he was, in fact, the man with the whistling stomach. The character was a man hiding under a huge, black hat, with his bare stomach painted to look like a face, complete with two eyes and a nose. His "mouth" was a ring of red paint around his naval, and it was made to look as though the character was whistling. During that same time, he was also cast on the *Drew Carey Show*, appearing as a peanut vendor tossing bags to mourners at a funeral. In 2001, he was on *To Tell The Truth* again, but this time he was himself, as the famed Peanut Man, while the other two players pretended to be him. In 2003, he had a quick segment on the *Wayne Brady Show* as well. But Roger's largest and most famous Hollywood gig was an appearance more popular with fans than even his part in *The Split* or his brief cameo as a peanut vendor in a courtroom scene of the 70's television film, *Testimony Of Two Men*. It was the bit role he landed in one of the most popular comedies of the mid 90's. Specifically conceived with Roger in mind, it was a quick scene, complete with a spoken line, of the peasant peanut vendor pitching goobers during the archery contest in Mel Brook's film *Robin Hood: Men In Tights*.

While working on the film, Brooks remembered Roger from the old days in the 60's, when Brooks and Carl Reiner had seats in the orange section at the stadium where Roger worked. They admired the peanut peddler and, many years later, Mel Brooks had 20th Century Fox call Roger at home. Brooks also sent him a letter asking if he would be interested in the small role. Without a trace of hesitation, Roger, who had not had a personal agent since the mid 1980's, responded to their offers and agreed to be in the movie. On the set in Santa Clarita, Roger had lunch with one of his comedic idols, Mel Brooks. After a memorable time talking and eating, Roger had a tour of the set and was shown to his own air-conditioned trailer. Not since his days promoting peanuts had so much first class treatment been lavished upon him. For the entire time, he was tickled at the idea of being in a major movie. He didn't care if his part was two minutes or two seconds. Roger was thrilled and, as always, grateful for such an opportunity.

"Once every couple of months, someone will see a rerun on cable, and I'll get people coming up to me saying they saw me. That's always nice," Roger admitted, unable to wipe the huge, boyish smile off his face.

Regardless of the many shows Roger had been on over the years, the Dodger fans would never have guessed that he appeared on even one. He came to the ballpark with the resolve of working hard and pleasing customers. He never had thought of himself as more important than any other vendor, and although separating him from the rest was his talent and the mind-blowing number of events he had worked, which made rookie vendors shudder, he still came to the stadium to serve the customers as diligently as the day he first started as a poverty-stricken, starving fifteen year-old.

But it was his humor that endeared him to his fans almost as much as his peanut artistry and humility. One time, when a fan was trying to throw a dollar bill at Roger for partial payment of a bag of peanuts, the dollar fell dismally to the floor.

"Looks like a dollar doesn't go as far these days," Roger quipped.

"Roger's got a great sense of humor," said long time personal fan of the peanut vendor, Joe Newman. "And he's got the greatest memory for funny stories of anyone I've seen. He's a great asset to the Dodgers," added the 86 year-old world-renowned movie director at MGM. He and his wife, Laurie, for years made it a tradition to treat Roger to the most expensive dinner possible on Fan Appreciation Day, the last home game of each season. Roger and the elderly couple went to Lawry's Prime Rib many times, but one time Roger admitted his peanut tossing was down, and he really only deserved a Big Mac. So Laurie Newman accepted his offer, but insisted they still go to Lawry's. Once there, she told the waiter that Roger was not eating, and she pulled a Big Mac out of her purse and plopped it down in front of Roger. She was kidding, but it nevertheless cracked Roger up. Several years later, now at the age of 93, Joe Newman, along with his wife, still have the same respect and admiration for the Peanut Man.

But there were plenty of people who shared with the Newmans their love of Roger, many of whom he counted on as trustworthy, generous, and special friends.

He met Bill Ritchie, former owner of All American Nut Co., Inc., in the early 70's just after the jeep accident, and since then they had formed a lasting friendship.

"Roger is one of the most honest and friendly people you'll ever meet. He gave me that impression the first time we met and he's still the same. He's the type of person you would want to have working for you or just to be your friend. He's full of hope for the future," said Ritchie.

Another friend, Brian Martin, CEO of Refrigeration Supplies Distributor, saw Roger in the stands in the 60's, but met him professionally in the early 80's when Roger came by selling freight services. Over the years, Roger was invited to Brian's wedding, to his house to relax with the four kids, and also to an Angels game when they played the Dodgers one evening.

"It was fun to watch people see Roger outside Dodger Stadium," said Martin.

A steady visitor at Chavez Ravine for 20 to 30 games a year, Lex Passaris has enjoyed every moment of his friendship with Roger. Before he had known anything about the Peanut Man, he had once taken in a game at the ballpark with his boss.

"When I reached for the peanuts at the concession stand, I was corrected by my boss, 'On this level, you buy your peanuts from Roger.' It didn't take many games to realize what that meant. The Peanut Man was always ready with a smile, a joke, and those fantastic tosses, which sometimes surpassed anything happening on the diamond," Passaris recalled.

"One year, still in the old double-bagger era, I brought a special baseball buddy from Upstate New York to the park and had again set Roger up for the visit. Not only did Roger identify my friend by name, with a few special jokes prepared for the visit, but when I ordered the four bags of peanuts, one for each member of our group, Roger went halfway down the aisle and threw all four bags at once, behind his back, fanning out perfectly to each of us," Passaris added.

In the summer of 2002, Passaris, a Hollywood director and producer known for directing the popular sitcom, *The Golden Girls*, in the 1980's, decided to give something back to his friend, Roger. He hosted a barbecue in his honor at Passaris' house.

"It was such a huge success, and so many of my friends were upset because they couldn't make it. We had two more, each just as successful and fun," he said. On the invitations, Lex played off the popular Mastercard commercials.

He wrote:

2 Loge seats to Dodger Game: $58.00
12 oz. Beer: $6.00
Big Foam Finger: $5.00
Hanging Out at a BBQ with Roger Owens after the game: PRICELESS

Eric Shirley, who had been to more than a hundred Dodger games since he was four watching Roger sling the peanuts, was like so many other young fans. From childhood into adulthood, his admiration of Roger grew steadily. Eric Shirley even invited Roger to his wedding to pitch peanuts in late 1991. Twelve years later, and still a friend of Roger's, he said, "I've never been there for Roger, but like millions of people, I would if he needed it. He's been there for us. Like Vin Scully, the blue roof in the bleachers, the sunshine on the hill at game time, the crisp, white uniforms, he is Dodger baseball—constant, fun, classy, the best." And, he admitted that the Peanut Man of the 70's is the "same as today, cheerful, friendly, and accurate."

Already in his 50's, Roger showed an enthusiasm that few vendors half his age could display. He began taking medicine for high blood pressure, and he began to stop running up and down the steps, helping to protect his joints. In the late 80's, he had a severe, week-long bout with bursitis in his hips. Reduced to literally dragging his legs up and down the stairs, he was ordered to rest. With rest and medication, he was over it.

Over the years, Roger was not just thankful for work at the ballpark and the many friends, but he was thankful for the care he received from his personal doctors and optometrists, who sometimes insisted that they simply be paid with bags of peanuts for their services. Whether it was Roger's physician, John Gebhard, or his first optometrist, Dr. Louis Galasso, who fitted Roger with glasses for the first time in 1989, Roger was always touched by their warmth and generosity.

The day they had first met in the office, the Italian eye specialist looked at Roger and said, "I hope you know what you're doing here today, because I don't. After all, I'm not an optometrist, I'm an optimist."

It made him laugh and feel at ease. Over the next few years, Roger was invited to his house for dinner and was given discounts on his eyeglasses. Even on Super Bowl Sunday, when his office was normally closed, Dr. Galasso insisted that Roger could pick out glasses because he needed a pair quickly.

Another optometrist, Dr. Robert "Skip" Brill, became Roger's new eye doctor when Galasso retired. They met at the stadium and, since then, the two have been special buddies, with Skip always taking peanuts as payment.

One day at the ballpark, Skip, who knew Roger from the stadium for over 20 years, went to a souvenir stand and bought a baseball. He had seen a Hispanic couple, with their little boy sitting right behind him. The boy was amazed at the energy Roger displayed. Skip walked over to Roger, now four aisles away, and asked him to autograph it, because he was about to hand it to the boy as a gift. Roger smiled at his friend and signed it. The doctor walked back to his seat and gave the baseball to the kid. With a smile as wide as the entire loge level, the boy accepted the ball, careful not to rub his chubby fingers over the freshly penned signature.

When Skip brought his eight month-old son, Darren Brill, who now has plans to enter college and one day become a major league prospect, to the ballpark for the first time, Skip sensed that Roger was more like another family member enjoying the game with them than a distant peanut vendor trying to make a living. From that first day he saw little Darren, to the day he pitched peanuts at Darren's bar mitzvah, to the day he pitched peanuts at Darren's high school graduation, Roger displayed an admirable consistency of showing special attention to his friends and their children, even if it meant sacrificing personal time to visit them if problems arose in their families.

One such time was when Roger's friend, Stu Cahn, called him one weekend because his youngest son was hurt in a baseball accident.

Stu had previously met Roger at Legends Sports Bar in Redondo Beach in 1991.

"I struck up a conversation with Roger at the event, and we exchanged telephone numbers. I was booking bands part-time, and felt that Roger, with his talent, could possibly get some business at corporate parties or weddings," said Cahn.

Stu called Roger and explained that his 6 year-old, Ben, had just been hit with a baseball while playing at park with his older brothers. The ball had been hit from home plate and had struck him squarely in the eye while he stood at the pitcher's mound.

"He had to have surgery to repair his eye and was in lots of pain. A six year-old boy does not understand why it is necessary to be hospitalized with needles and so on. I called Roger and told him about what had happened. I asked if he could call Ben to cheer him up. He said that he would rather just come out to the house and surprise him, and he did just that. He showed up in full regalia, bringing along bags of peanuts for Ben as well. He had Ben come out into the front yard, bandaged eye and all, and threw bags for Ben to catch. Before long, many of the neighborhood children came out of the woodwork to see the show," Cahn stated.

But Cahn's admiration, as well as stories, of Roger didn't end there.

"Then there was the night of Cub Scouts, and again Roger came to the rescue," Cahn added. "Our oldest son, Sam, was a Cub Scout, and we needed a guest speaker at the annual Cub Scout dinner. Naturally, since Michelle Pfeiffer wasn't available, I called Roger. He only asked what meal the dinner would be. Roger came by our house first, and met our new dog, a yellow Lab named Boomer. We had been having big problems with Boomer doing things to our house when we would leave him alone. Roger fixed our problem with one word. Television. Roger informed us that Boomer was merely lonely, and when we left, he would find things to keep himself occupied," Cahn said.

Whether their dog had chewed up part of their new oak staircase, had eaten a mini-blind slat, or had ripped up the mailbox slot that fed into the house, and had torn into their oak front door, the Cahn family had had just about enough and almost returned Boomer to his previous owner.

"Roger said to leave the television on whenever we left the house, and that would solve the problem. We did what he suggested, and it worked that very night. When we arrived home after the Cub Scout dinner, Boomer was lying in front of the television, with nothing out of place in our previously destroyed home," Cahn said.

On another occasion, Stu decided to have a fundraiser for the NYPD and FDNY shortly after September 11, 2001.

"I asked some friends in a very popular Long Beach band to play for the event, and called Roger as well. Roger never batted an eye, showing up on November 11th, two months to the day after, and threw peanuts to the crowd. Two television news crews came by, and there was coverage by the local Long Beach paper," Cahn added.

One night at Stu's house, Roger was speaking with Stu's mother. After their lengthy discussion, Roger later told Stu about a well-known saying that was brought up that evening.

"Roger told me what my mother had said. She told him, 'Do you know why they call today the present? Because yesterday is in the past, tomorrow is in the future. Today is a gift. That is why it is called the *present*,'" Cahn said. "Roger loved that," he added.

In 1990, after many years of pitching peanuts annually at a golf tournament fundraiser for the Alisa Ann Burn Foundation, Roger was asked again to make an appearance there. He agreed. However, some of the people who were involved with the fundraiser were also roofing contactors. Ken Hewett, Rob, Rick, and all of Roger's friends with the Roofing Contractors Association surprised Roger by offering to give him a new roof as a gift for his many years of generosity and time for the organization. They knew his wood shingle roof was a fire hazard, so the association chipped in funds to subsidize the entire cost of a new, cement, shake tile roof. Roger was in awe at such a gesture. While they worked hard to install the roof in one day, Roger was taking orders at the barbecue grill to feed the large group of kindhearted roofers.

As they packed up their trucks around sundown, done for the day, Roger walked outside to the front, examining the roof.

"Hey guys, what about the warranty?" he joked.

"Well, Roger, when the rain comes in, the warranty runs out," Ken responded, getting a laugh from all the workers. Roger laughed, too, but everyone there knew that the minute they left, Roger would be beaming with pride at having such a wonderful new roof on his house.

Yet another friend, Ernie Montano, recalled meeting Roger to do business with him for the first time.

"As Roger pulled out a note pad to write down name of my customer I wanted him to entertain, I noticed a name of a dear friend of mine, C.J. Mills of Allied Veneer, was listed, and I told him of the coincidence that I had golfed with C.J. a couple days earlier," Montano said. "Roger then told me that C.J.'s father, Nolan Mills, was Roger's first customer ever at Dodger Stadium for servicing company customers by throwing peanuts to them, and by entertaining them by telling them jokes. From that day on, Roger has entertained hundreds of my customers, friends, and relatives at the stadium."

When preparing to entertain such customers, Roger would always find out as much as possible about them. According to Montano, "He would ask me for a list of names of attendees and for a short biography of the people going to the game, and with very little information Roger prepared, and still does today, a very excellent and funny monologue. That really shocks people, as a complete stranger would come up to them and start talking to them about their lives, and I must say with the caliber of comedy you see on Comedy Central."

Roger not only entertained Montano's customers at the stadium, but he also made regular visits to his company office, throwing peanuts and joking with the staff. For Ernie's son's fifth birthday, Roger visited his kindergarten classroom to entertain the kids. He gave them a small peanut-throwing show as well as a motivational talk regarding doing one's best in life by working hard to achieve one's goals.

"Once, Roger entertained ten of my family members who all sat together at Dodger Stadium, and Roger was able to put on a show personalized for each and everyone there," Montano stated. "Another time, Roger handed over his 3-inch stack of bills to my brother's wife, telling her that she deserved this money for putting up with my brother for so many years. He even entertained over 300 people at a golf fundraiser for my children's school by throwing peanuts to the crowd. Then he spoke on the podium and encouraged everyone to help by donating to a good cause," he said.

"Roger is who he is, and I don't see any changes in him over the past 13 years." Montano added.

But Roger wasn't the only one to act with such generosity. In fact, two other individuals worked with the Peanut Man to bring happiness at ball games. In the same spirit of Dr. Skip Brill's purchasing of the baseball to give to the young boy, Roger's friend Bill Cook had already been making such gestures of kindness at the stadium for nearly 30 years. Each year, during more than half of all Dodger home games, Bill Cook got up from his seat in aisle 107 and approached Roger.

"Hey, Roger, I just spotted a family that looks like they could use some peanuts. Here's the money for five bags okay?" Cook said.

"Okay, Bill," he replied with a smile. "Just point them out as usual." Immediately, Roger found them and explained to the family, or in other cases small children, that they were about to receive free bags of peanuts. The seemingly needy family sat up in their seats and grabbed the bags out of the air, thankful for such a display of talent and benevolence.

However, even the Coliseum had its Bill Cook. For almost 30 years, George Fry bought $20 worth of peanuts from Roger to be thrown to those who seemed to be the most needy at almost every USC football game.

Over the years, Roger had made a countless number of friends. Each one was valuable to him for different reasons. Their relationships with him added color to his life in a way unmatched even by the brilliant hues of the red, blue, yellow, and orange seats at the stadium on a Sunday afternoon game.

He had met every-day people and celebrities alike, hard-working parents and prosperous CEO's. One such CEO, Steven Nichols of K-Swiss Athletic Footwear, has enjoyed being Roger's buddy since 1989. One day, the two met and Nichols asked him what his shoe size was. From that day, K-Swiss began providing the Peanut Man with several pairs of shoes each year. Because of such generosity, the two had begun an enduring and special friendship. Often, Nichols went to the Coliseum to attend USC football games with friends. On each occasion, he hid under a large coat or hat so Roger would not recognize him. He sent his friend to pay for $15 worth of peanuts and to give a substantial tip. Nichols admitted to Roger many years later that he had been buying peanuts from him all that time without him knowing it. He explained that he had been hiding so Roger wouldn't insist on not charging him for the peanuts, especially because of the free shoes each year.

Like so many fans and friends, Nichols realized how important it was to show the Peanut Man just how much he had meant to them.

In a sea of fans at the Coliseum – 1973

Roger Owens handing bags of peanuts to his fiancé Cindy Brazil – 1974

Enjoying time together, Roger and Cindy –
1970's

Honored by Los Angeles City Council,
the day before the wedding – 1974

Roger and Cindy on their
wedding day – 1974

Cindy's parents, Ernie and Beverly, Cindy, Roger, and Roger's parents

At the reception with Mayor Tom Bradley, his wife, to Roger's right...
...and with Dodger pitcher Don Sutton and his wife, to Roger's left – 1974

Roger at the Coliseum – 1975

Photo by Nick Gleis

Almost looks like Elvis singing into a microphone –
Roger at the Coliseum – 1975

Photo by Nick Gleis

Hustling to make the people happy at the Coliseum – 1975

Photo by Nick Gleis

At the Coliseum – 1975

Photo by Nick Gleis

Too much style for the Coliseum to hold - 1975

Photo by Nick Gleis

Roger enjoying a sunny day at the ballpark – 1973

The Peanut Man scarfing down a Dodger Dog?

Good thing no one's around – 1980's

Roger's trademark under-the-leg toss at Dodger Stadium –
1976

JEANS

21416 Chase St. Canoga Park, Ca. 91304 (213) 998-8961

June 10, 1976

Mr. Art Roche, Vice President
c/o Westransco Freight Co.
P. O. Box 54810
Los Angeles, Calif. 90054

Dear Mr. Roche:

I want to take this opportunity to write you a long over due letter.
The subject of this letter is Roger Owens, your Sales Representative,
who represents you in dealings with Luv-It Jeans.

I would like you to know quite frankly that you probably wouldn't have
gotten any of our business if it wasn't for Roger Owens. We would
probably have given it to Western Carloading or some other company.
But, because of Roger's persistance and strong follow up several times, I was
convinced by him to give you our business.

I have found through the years that if a company is to do a large amount
of business and have continued strong growth, they should reward those
employees substantially. Unfortunately, in society, today, incentives
are taken away from people to produce the maximum effort possible. When
I, personally, find an individual in my organization who out performs
most people, I reward them substantially. I think you should realize just
how powerful an influence Roger Owens has on our business and several other
companies which I am very familiar with.

I ordinarily do not get involved in things like this, and I want to make it
very clear that this letter is completely unsolicited on Rogers part. I
am so strongly motivated by the fact that his service to us has been so
great that I must write this letter.

It has been my experience in the past, that companies tend to overlook top
performing employees. Many times they lump performances of all employees
together without realizing whom in their organization consistently out
performs others.

Thank you very much.

Sincerely,

Tony Kouffman
Executive Vice President

TK:mj

*Roger leaning back to throw out the ceremonial first pitch at
Dodger Stadium from the loge level – 1976*

Photo by Mark Malone

*Throwing out the ceremonial first pitch from the loge level
to home plate – 1976*

Photo by Mark Malone

Roger's career-launching appearance with the king of late night, Johnny Carson on The Tonight Show – 1976

Entertaining students at El Camino Real HS – 1976

Cartoon of Roger, used for self-promotion – 1970's

In Dallas, before a Cowboys game, Roger being honored on the field – 1976

With Cowboys legendary running back, Tony Dorsett

THE DALLAS COWBOYS

NEW ADDRESS:
DALLAS COWBOYS FOOTBALL CLUB
Cowboys Center
One Cowboys Parkway
Irving, Texas 75063-4727

NEW PHONE NUMBERS:
Executive Offices 214/556-9900
Information Line 214/869-3322
Ticket Office 214/556-2500
Travel Agency 214/556-2800
Dance Academy 214/556-9999

TEXAS E. SCHRAMM
President

November 11, 1986

TO WHOM IT MAY CONCERN:

Roger Owens, America's famous "Peanut Man", is one of the true
sports personalities of our time. His fame has not been achieved
as a result of any athletic prowess on the field, nor by any
skills as a master coach. He has come to be known and loved by
fans throughout the world because of the service he provides in a
unique and cheerful manner.

Roger has donated his time and special talent to charity annually
at Texas Stadium, home of of the Dallas Cowboys, since 1976. His
amazing technique and genial wit make him a big hit with the fans.

There's nothing more American than peanuts, and consequently,
there's nothing more American than Roger Owens.

Sincerely,

Texas E. Schramm
President & General Manager

TES/cm

With Mom and Dad – 1976

Roger and Cindy at the stadium – 1976

*Roger and Cindy cuddling together in his mom's
favorite chair – 1976*

Ruth, and three sons, Daniel, Randy, and Donald – Ross "Grandpa Owens" in disguise as Santa Claus at a department store – 1978

Randy, Roger, Daniel, and Donald at Ruth's house – 1977

Here it comes, Roger's famous behind-the-back throw
at Dodger Stadium – 1978

CITY HALL
LOS ANGELES, CALIFORNIA 90012
(213) 485-3311

OFFICE OF THE MAYOR

TOM BRADLEY
MAYOR

July 1, 1980

TO WHOM IT MAY CONCERN:

I have known and carefully observed Roger Owens, affectionately known
by his fans as "The Peanut Man," for twenty-two years as he has worked
at the Los Angeles Coliseum and The Los Angeles Dodgers stadium serving
and entertaining the fans through his intriguing technique of tossing
his bags of peanuts to them and then catching their money in return
with uncanny accuracy. But it was more than the technique that captures
the fancy of the spectators and makes him as much of a celebrity and
attraction in the stands as any athlete on the playing field.

Roger has a warm and captivating personality which sets him apart
as a super star. He is a great salesman for the peanuts he sells
as he is a great image personality for the City of Los Angeles.

I am proud to know him as a personal friend and proud of the manner
in which he serves as a Goodwill Ambassador for the City of Los Angeles.

Sincerely,

TOM BRADLEY
Mayor

TB:ku

July 13, 1981

Mr. Peter O'Malley, President
THE LOS ANGELES DODGERS
1000 Elysian Park Avenue
Dodger Stadium
Los Angeles, California 90012

Dear Mr. O'Malley:

For the 4th of July Celebration at the Smithsonian, which this
year featured baseball, it was a great pleasure to have Roger Owens participate in
the events.

He is a fine ambassador for the Dodgers and a great crowd pleaser.
Of all the participants, he was photographed more and televised more than anyone
else. He made many friends for the Dodgers during his stay, and, of course, the
many Dodger fans here with the new administration were delighted to have this
connection with their hometown team.

Enclosed is a program from the Celebration, a news release,
an article that appeared in The Sporting News before the event, and an article
which appeared after the event, for your information. Among other feats, Roger
threw a bag of peanuts over 60 miles per hour against the JuGS Speed Gun while
here and threw bags of peanuts at one time to each member of a family of four.

We only had the pleasure of his work at the Smithsonian for
three days, so we are aware of how valuable he must be in his work at Dodger
Stadium.

Members of your staff were helpful in making it possible for
Roger to be at the Smithsonian. Thank you.

Yours sincerely

Joe Reed
Division of Performing Arts

BUSINESS

Los Angeles Times

), 194 Sunday   **Friday, September 25, 1981**   MF / 140 pages / Copyright

Dodger Peanut Man to Deliver Industry Pitch

BEN OLENDER / Los Angeles Times
Peanut vendor Roger Owens

By NANCY YOSHIHARA, *Times Staff Writer*

Someone will be conspicuously absent at the next Dodger home game.

For the first time in 12 years, the Peanut Man, also known as Roger Owens, won't be pitching peanuts to Dodger fans here next week. Instead, he will be on the road as the spokesman for the Peanut Advisory Board of Tifton, Ga., pitching the selling of goobers to consumers at large.

The peanut vendor begins his first road trip on Monday, when he sets out on a two-week, 10-city tour to promote peanuts through personal appearances and interviews on radio and television stations and newspapers.

"The message they want me to tell the public," Owens said in a telephone interview Thursday, "is that peanuts are back, shortages are over, and after the first of the year, prices should come down."

Owens, who has gained a national reputation for his colorful and skillful peanut pitches (he tossed them during the 1977 Presidential inauguration of Jimmy Carter), was hired by New York-based Ketchum MacLeod & Grove, the advertising and public relations firm for the Peanut Advisory Board.

Last year, the board did little or no advertising or promotion because a severe drought in the South cut the 1980 peanut crop to 1.15 million tons, 42% short of normal. This led to higher prices and a dip in consumption. This year, the Agriculture Department is forecasting a near-record crop of 1.93 million tons. So the board is sending Owens out to stump for peanuts.

He has signed a six-month contract but won't disclose how much he will earn, saying only, "As far as monetary value goes, it's the most lucrative yet. Right now there are no commercials." Mitch Head at Ketchum MacLeod says, "We discussed it (advertising) but nothing is planned right now."

Story by Nancy Yoshihara – Photo by Ben Olender
Copyright 1981, Los Angeles Times.
Reprinted with permission.

At the Green Derby Award Banquet – 1981

No chumps here, just a couple of champs –
Roger with "The Greatest," Muhammad Ali

Roger with another champion, Los Angeles City Supervisor,
Kenneth Hahn – 1983

COUNTY OF LOS ANGELES

ROGER OWENS
THE·PEANUT·MAN

whereas, ROGER OWENS, THE PEANUT MAN, HAS EXHIBITED RARE DEDICATION AND TALENT WHICH HAS MADE HIM THE MOST CELEBRATED PEANUT VENDOR OF ALL TIMES, AND

whereas, HE HAS BECOME AN OUTSTANDING REPRESENTATIVE OF LOS ANGELES TO THOUSANDS OF PEOPLE ACROSS THE COUNTY WITH HIS AMAZING DISPLAY OF PITCHES WITH WHICH HE HAS DELIVERED WELL OVER ONE AND A HALF MILLION BAGS OF PEANUTS, AND

whereas, HE HAS "PITCHED" WITH THE LOS ANGELES DODGERS SINCE 1958, WORKED THE RAMS, USC, AND UCLA FOOTBALL GAMES AT THE COLISEUM AND HAS ALSO APPEARED ON DALLAS, HAWAII, SAN DIEGO AND WASHINGTON, D.C., AND

whereas, HE THREW OUT THE OPENING BALL OF THE 1976 BASEBALL SEASON, IS THE OFFICIAL SPOKESMAN FOR THE PEANUT ADVISORY BOARD, AND HAS APPEARED ON MANY RADIO AND TELEVISION PROGRAMS

Now, therefore, be it resolved BY THE BOARD OF SUPERVISORS OF THE COUNTY OF LOS ANGELES THAT ROGER OWENS IS HEREBY HIGHLY COMMENDED FOR HIS GREAT TALENT AND DEDICATION WHICH HAVE MADE HIM A WIDELY RECOGNIZED UNOFFICIAL AMBASSADOR FOR LOS ANGELES AND OUR TEAMS; AND HE IS EXTENDED SINCERE BEST WISHES FOR CONTINUED SUCCESS IN ALL OF HIS ENDEAVORS.

ADOPTED BY ORDER OF THE BOARD OF SUPERVISORS OF THE COUNTY OF LOS ANGELES
STATE OF CALIFORNIA

OCTOBER 18, 1983

Mary and Ross celebrating their
40th wedding anniversary – 1982

In Japan for the first time – 1984

Working a USC football game – 1993

In Japan selling peanuts at Yokohama Stadium – 1986

*Roger's beloved pooches, French, the first Brande, and
the first Casey, always wagging their tails in excitement
and doing tricks*

*Even Clark Kent had a day job – Roger visiting at his mom's
house after a day's work as a salesman – 1990*

Roger and Philip at Elizabeth's house – 1987

Mom and Roger at Esther's house for Christmas – 1989

Paul and Lois at Esther's house for Christmas – 1989

Paul playing piano in Oregon outdoor markets – 1990's

*Relaxing with sisters Ruth and Elizabeth at
Mom's house – 1987*

*Elizabeth, Grace, Mary, Roger, Esther, and Ruth
at Mary's house – 1994*

At home with the first Brande – 1987

Roger with his kids, the first Casey and the second Brande
1992

With his adoring mother – 1992

Roger, Esther, Priscilla, Mom, Ruth, Elizabeth, and Philip at Mom's house – 1996

Philip and Roger – 1992

Charcoal drawing of Roger by
Daniel S. Green – 1993

Copyright 1993, Daniel S. Green,
DSG Design

With his little buddy Matthew,
the son of Roger's friend Brian Martin – 1998

Autographing bags of peanuts for his admiring fans – 1997

With Steve Garvey – 1989

Roger and buddies, Ron Cey and Steve Garvey – 1999

Standing with the man himself, former Dodger President
Peter O'Malley – 1989

With Vin Scully and his wife – 1989

With Tommy Lasorda – 1990

Clowning around with Jay Leno – 1990

With Mel Brooks on the set of Robin Hood: Men In Tights – 1992

With the one and only Whoopi Goldberg – 1995

*Backstage with Jay Leno, on The Tonight Show, for
the fourth time – 1995*

With long time friend Don Sutton – 1992

With Dodger player, Todd Zeile – 1997

Working the party at CSU, Fullerton – 1999

*At Dodger Stadium, posing with a fan's baby and
celebrating a new life...*

...and celebrating a new season – opening day 2002

In sunny Santa Barbara – 2003

*Roger and Sharon enjoying some vacation time
together – 2003*

$\mathcal{C}$ 24

Ordeals of the Body, Healing for the Spirit

In 1996, the Dodger organization donated Dodger Dogs and peanuts for the workers helping out in the housing program, Habitat For Humanity, created and assisted by President Jimmy Carter. The program helped low-income families build their own homes, and it sent a message about how people could make a difference in reshaping their very own communities, even in troubled areas like Watts.

One day, Roger saw President Carter and approached him. The President, wearing casual work clothes and a leather utility belt full of carpentry tools around his waist, signaled to his secret serviceman that it was okay. Roger introduced himself to Carter. Roger explained how, during one inaugural party in 1977, he tried to throw him a bag of peanuts.

"Well I never got a bag," Carter said.

"I know, sir. One of your secret servicemen ordered me not to throw it your way, so I didn't," Roger replied.

"Okay then, stand back young man and throw me a bag," Carter insisted.

As everyone sitting at the park benches eating their lunches stopped to look at the throw Roger was about to make, Roger felt the sudden pressure to complete the longest throw of his career. From the time the throw was attempted to the time it was completed with a behind-the-back toss, 18 years and five months had passed. The people clapped for Roger as soon as Carter caught the bag.

By the end of the 1990's and into a new millennium, Roger surpassed even his own expectations of longevity with regard to selling peanuts at Dodger Stadium. During his career, he has thrown over two and a half million bags of peanuts, and has worked at every major event at the Coliseum except the 1932 Olympics. He has worked two Major League All Star games, one in Los Angeles, and the other, just recently, in Pittsburgh, Pennsylvania. He has also amazed the fans at all Los Angeles Dodger World Series games since 1959, six Rose Bowl games during the 70's, one Olympics in '84, and four Super Bowls, two of which were held at the Rose Bowl and two at the Coliseum. He has even worked every home game for the Los Angeles Clippers until they left for the Staples Center.

In late February and in early March 2002, at age 59, Roger began to experience unexplained dizziness at his Torrance home. Each day, the severity of the dizziness continued. He had just worked an event where there was loud noises and music, and he had been walking the entire day. In fact, he was so dizzy that he could hardly drive home. Now, Roger's stiffening knee joints were quickly becoming the least of his problems.

One Friday night, on March 29, 2002, Good Friday in fact, during a preseason exhibition game between the Dodgers and the Cleveland Indians, Roger noticed the entire stadium was spinning. Holding his head, the noise, colors, and lights swirled into a blur of undistinguishable shapes and hues, like the colors of an abstract painting. Lacking any sense of balance, he stumbled and fell, hitting his knee on a chair. Thoroughly embarrassed, Roger tried to gather his composure, but after two more steps, he had to reach for the back of a seat for support.

Fans asked if he was okay.

"Yeah, I'm fine, really," insisted Roger.

He fell again.

"Roger? You aren't okay," one fan said.

Immediately, Roger was helped to the food commissary. Employees called for a wheelchair and for him to be taken to first aid.

"No wheelchair. No, I don't want a wheelchair," Roger said. "Just have someone on both sides of me walk me over." So they agreed and went up the escalator to first aid at the stadium. Trying to assure the stadium physician that he was okay, Roger stood up, took one step toward the door, and he fell down again. He lay down, and the physician noted that Roger's blood pressure was very high. The doctor gave him Meclizine, which helped prevent dizziness. An ambulance was called, and an embarrassed Roger was taken to the Good Samaritan Hospital, where he was diagnosed with vertigo.

By morning, he was back home. It was Saturday, and Roger wanted to see his regular doctor. He was out, but his assistant was in. Roger was ordered to miss the game that night and then come back to see his regular doctor on Monday, April 1st.

Roger did as instructed. Although the dizziness lingered, it had subsided quite a bit with extra rest. He saw his doctor, but he insisted that he be allowed to be present at the stadium for opening day on Tuesday, April 2nd, the very next day. He was scheduled to be one of a handful being honored at home plate for 40 years of Dodger history in Los Angeles. In fact, Peter O'Malley, who had already sold the team many years before, was set to throw out the ceremonial first pitch. The doctor reluctantly agreed to allow Roger back at work, but he ordered that he only work the flat, concourse area and could not walk on the stairs under any circumstances for at least six days. Somewhat lightheaded and off balance, Roger managed to pull it off at home plate on opening day. It was especially memorable for Roger when Vin Scully's voice could be heard over the public address system, a rare event itself, since the broadcasting legend only spoke on the radio.

"His behind-the-back throws are as famous as the Dodger Dog. Please give a round of applause for Roger "The Peanut Man" Owens," Scully announced. The fans in Roger's section of the ballpark went wild, giving him a standing ovation.

At home plate, Roger leaned over to O'Malley.

"Hey, can you believe that? Those fans are cheering for me," Roger said.

"Yes, Roger, I know," he said smiling at him.

Many of the fans were unaware of Roger's recent bout with dizziness. Just like writer Steve Harvey of the *Los Angeles Times* and his featured column, "Only In L.A.", fellow journalist Tom Hennessy was one of the long-time supporters of Roger's career. Hennessy was in the crowd that day in Roger's section and asked him why he wasn't in the stands as usual. After he explained to the veteran writer, a story appeared on April 11th in the *Long Beach Press Telegram*. In it, Hennessy explained Roger's recent ordeal with vertigo. Hennessy, who was also putting on a poetry reading night for Community Awareness Week at a Long Beach Barnes and Noble bookstore, asked Roger if he would like to attend and read the classic, *Casey At The Bat*. Roger wholeheartedly accepted the invitation to appear on the 15th at the bookstore.

A few days after opening day, Roger visited a neurologist at UCLA. The doctor was a specialist in vertigo. A MRI was performed on Roger, and it revealed scar tissue in his inner left ear. It was a result of the army jeep accident nearly 33 years before. He was diagnosed with Meniere's syndrome. As endolymphatic fluid built up in his ear each day, it created increased pressure and caused a noticeable imbalance in Roger's equilibrium. People who have the syndrome, for which there is no cure, have a one out of three chance of developing permanent hearing loss in both ears. Roger was immediately restricted to a low sodium diet and was given a water pill to help reduce overall body fluid, thus decreasing fluid build up in his inner ear. With dedication and persistence, Roger maintained a strict diet, often meticulously counting the amount of sodium in his food.

During his first six days at the stadium, Roger occasionally snuck into the aisles to hand peanuts to some of his season peanut holders, but they quickly chastised him and told him to return to the concourse for his own safety. He became a bit bolder with his attempts, nevertheless, and soon, the food concessions heard he was in the aisles where he shouldn't have been. They strictly forbade him from selling in the steep aisles until he had medical authorization to return. He apologized and reluctantly sold only in the concourse area until his doctor finally agreed it was okay. The enthusiastic kid in him obviously didn't want to stop doing what came so naturally to him, pleasing the fans. After more than 40 years, it was a habit much too hard to break.

By May 2002, Roger became increasingly depressed, and he had lost quite a bit of weight due to his disciplined diet. Feeling weak and unhappy, Roger was not himself, and his friends knew it. One of his closest friends for 25 years was Steve Hall, a bank branch manager who later became one of America's top Steinway pianists. He called Roger and told him that a relaxing vacation was in order. Hall and his wife, Robyn, had planned to take a week-long, Alaskan cruise and, being such good friends, they invited Roger to come along. They were aware of how therapeutic the trip would be for the workaholic peanut vendor, who hadn't taken a vacation in 15 years. Roger, however, kept declining their invitation to go on the cruise, thinking that the altitude of the flight would cause him problems, and the rocking of the boat would cause him seasickness.

"Roger, it's not a boat, it's a ship. You won't get seasick," Hall said.

Finally, Roger was talked into it.

A few days later, Steve called Roger back.

"Hey, Roger. It's Steve here. Listen, about the cruise. My son just got into some trouble in class, and my wife and I can't go now. But before you say anything, I want you to know that we still want you to go by yourself."

Steve again had to convince him to go on the cruise, even though Roger would be going without his friends.

Persuaded to go, Roger packed his things, and by July 1st, he was on the huge cruise ship in Alaska.

During the cruise, Roger could see the vast expanse of Alaskan wilderness. As the mountains rose up into the cloudy mists of the lowered, overcast sky, the dense forest of firs seemed like thousands of Christmas trees decorated not with lights and shiny frills and ornaments, but adorned with the majesty of their grand scale, standing in the midst of open space and refreshing air. Numerous bald eagles sat perched in the trees, making the trees appear from a distance to be sprinkled with snow. As Roger stood on deck watching these things in quietness of spirit, he reflected on how untouched and how beautiful these lands were. Seeing the Alaskan wilderness this close was like standing less than a foot away from an Impressionist painting, with its heavy, tangible brush strokes. While the oil paint was scraped into thick smears of brilliant colors up close, a step back revealed the intended scene. Such was this land, the artistry of flying eagles, brown bears standing at land's edge, and huge humpback whales arching their backs above the pristine, cold ocean, forming deep blue, frothy waves, finally making their way from the tropical waters of Hawaii. It was as though this land was the Creator's studio where, each morning of the cruise, He was just finishing His latest painting, entitled *Alaskan Sunrise*.

Roger couldn't imagine anything more breathtaking.

He closed his eyes, unable to smell the clean air, but listened closely to the sounds of the birds, and the water spouts rushing up from the air holes of the mighty whales. It was indeed a healing, if not spiritual, experience.

But the immense landscape wasn't the only factor in Roger's recovery.

The ship was full of friendly people.

The first thing Roger noticed was the amount of food available. Roger treated himself to the huge buffets several times a day. His sodium counting went on a vacation, and he ate with the gusto of a whale swallowing a mouth full of plankton. There was such a wide variety of food, from seafood to barbeque to chicken to dreamy desserts. While Roger stood in line for the buffet one afternoon, he noticed a sign that read, "You arrive as a passenger. You'll leave as cargo." He laughed at how true that was, considering how much food they had been stuffing themselves with. Suddenly, he felt a tugging on his sleeve. Teasingly, he told the elderly gentleman that he wasn't allowed to cut in line.

"No, I just wanted to ask you a question," said the 80 year-old. "Are you the Peanut Man at Dodger Stadium? My wife wanted to know."

Roger had a large smile on his face.

"Yeah, that's me," Roger answered.

"Okay thanks. You know, between you and me, that's the first time she's ever been right in her life. She'll be happy to know. I'll go tell her," the man replied.

Roger patted the man on the shoulder and laughed at the elderly man's comment.

When Roger got to his assigned table, half the people sitting with him already knew him as the famed peanut vendor. A Korean couple eating at the table had not heard of him, and so they were introduced to him. Everyone at the table was having a great time. While sharing stories and preparing for seconds at the buffet line, one of them mentioned the short, Filipino man working at the buffet. The outgoing, crew member loved to talk with the people standing in line as he served them, but what they noticed more than his smile and heavy accent was his name tag. His name was Muhammad Ali.

The man quickly heard them talking about him and rushed over to the table. He leaned over with a smile and loudly said, "Yeah, the boxa stole muh name." Everyone started laughing, including Roger.

While Roger walked around to find what else the cruise ship offered, he noticed there were seminars to attend, spas, a workout room, and even live, stand-up comedy. Roger quickly found a seat and began laughing at the funny comedian. Finally, on July 8th, the cruise ended, but Roger couldn't have envisioned anything more helpful for his mental and physical well-being. It was the best vacation he had ever had, and it healed him in ways he never realized.

Famous Peanut Man Song

-words by Geary Chansley

Take me to the ball game. There's a man I'd like to see.
He's a favorite of the crowd, a big celebrity.
Make sure we sit in his part of the stands.
I want to see him throw peanuts to his fans.
I want to see the famous peanut man…oh yeah

Watch him do his stuff as he runs up and down the aisles.
He never gets enough of seeing all the children's smiles.
We all want to see the twinkle in his eye.
He's a very special kind of guy.
We want to see the famous peanut man…oh yeah

He can take a peanut snack, throw a strike behind his back.
He's the Peanut Man! Yeah!

Take me to the ball game. If we lose I won't be sad.
We still had fun with the peanut man.
Make sure we sit in his part of the stands
I want to see him do all he can.
I'll be rooting for the famous Peanut Man.

Hey…throw me some. Hey two bags…ha ha. No, make it three!
Famous, famous, famous Peanut Man…yeah yeah. (repeat line)

$\mathcal{C}$ *25*

Under the Sky So Bright and Blue

R oger made it back home, sat on the couch, and greeted his loving canines. He was thankful for such a trip, for two great dogs, and for his loving and supportive family.

In Pomona, March 2003, some of Roger's personal memorabilia was displayed at the Baseball Reliquary exhibit, put on by Terry Cannon. In addition, the event included a celebrity-filled night of comedy at the Ice House in Pasadena, with scheduled appearances from the likes of Kevin Nealon, George Wendt, and Don Knotts, just to name a few. On the program to keep up with the heavy-hitting humor of such comic greats, and to dish out a few bags of peanuts as well, was Roger the Peanut Man, who found himself at ease around the comedians.

In May 2003, at his home, Roger was interviewed for a show produced by a Japanese television network to air in Japan. They were doing a story about people who have eccentric jobs and are considered the best in their field. They also heard about a book coming out on his life story, so they also interviewed the author, Roger's nephew Daniel. The show was set to air on a Saturday evening in June 2003. Roger was thrilled to have more coverage about him and for the book, which excited him each day since he was first told about it. Nearly a year before at the poetry reading put on by writer Tom Hennessy at the Long Beach bookstore, his nephew approached him about writing a biography based on the famed Peanut Man's life. A surprised Roger asked him how he knew he would be in town for the poetry reading, and he told him it was because of the Hennessy article about vertigo. At least four other writers had wanted to write the book about Roger's fabled career, but it had never came to fruition until now. From 2002 through 2003, Roger had been telling friends of the book on his life, and they had expressed their excitement each time.

None seemed happier for him than his own mother, Mary.

After a couple of years living in a nursing home in Anaheim, she finally moved to Pennsylvania. At 87, she was living with her youngest daughter Grace, and her husband and children, in Pennsylvania. She flew back to California to visit everyone for Christmas, 2002. Mentally alert and still an avid book reader, she asked when she could read the book about her son. When told it would be out sometime in 2003, she smiled at the thought of reading it.

However, on June 12, 2003, with little warning, Mary Nicoleta Owens passed away from pneumonia, a few hours after arriving at the emergency room at a local Pennsylvania hospital. She died six months before her 89th birthday and was buried on June 17th at Forest Lawn in Cypress. She was finally reunited with her loving husband, Ross, almost twenty years after his passing. Although she was closing in on her 90's, it was nevertheless a heart-wrenching day for her brother Joe DiRisio, her nine children, 17 grandchildren, and three great-grandchildren.

Mary Owens was a selfless woman who fought desperate times to raise a family in poverty, but she became a warrior in the Faith in her later years, becoming one of the Godliest women ever to be shaped by the Master Potter's hands. She often attended Grace Bible Church on Compton Blvd. when the family lived in Paramount. During part of the 80's and much of the 90's, she attended Grace Community Church in Long Beach, where she was always the first to volunteer if they needed a pianist. She often went with church members to play piano for the Long Beach Rescue Mission, and the people just loved her. She gave her time to the Cubbies of the Iwana Kids Group, a group of toddlers who learned about the Bible at her local church. Too embarrassed to recite their memorized verses to just anyone, they always warmed up enough to tell their verses to Mary. She loved her family, whether it was her own grandchildren or the many children she helped in the community.

She enjoyed reading books throughout her life, especially during the long, winter afternoons in Pennsylvania spent with her small grand-daughters. She quietly read books about missionaries, like the story of John and Betty Stam, martyrs of China. She enjoyed *Keep A Quiet Heart* by Elizabeth Elliot, the story of the life of Oswald Chambers, and another book, about missionaries in the Philippines. She was also fascinated with the memoirs of Barbara Bush, Sandra Day O'Connor, and the lives of each U.S. President from Harry Truman to George W.

Bush. She always started her day with a daily devotional book that was given to her as a Christmas gift. One particular chapter, entitled "Healthy at One Hundred," was one she read and reread. It had mentioned that the mother of the Queen of England had turned 100 years old in 2000. The devotional pointed to Jeremiah 33:6, and it was just one more verse on which this loving, aged woman pondered. The Saturday following Mary's passing, Grace found her mother's devotional book. The bookmark was left in that same chapter.

As the one woman who had meant so much to Roger had now departed for an existence filled with all the extravagance heaven could afford, another woman had entered into Roger's life.

For several years, Roger longed for more than his fatherly and friendly relationship with his affectionate dogs, Brande II and Casey II. These two were the second generation of Brande and Casey, the dogs Roger had loved for many years before. In fact, the day the first Brande had died at the ripe old age of 14, Roger found her hanging on to life. The canine had loved Roger so much that she waited until Roger got home from work before passing. According to the vet, she could have left at any time that day. Despite his countless memories and endless love for his dogs, he still missed the love of a woman in his life and the completeness that it offered him. After having resorted to many misguided adventures of romance in the 90's through personal ads in the local paper, Roger almost had enough of it.

One day, in fact, the day after his birthday, he decided to call the service for one last try. His patience had been worn, like a candle's wick burned into shriveled, charred blackness, not from romantic escapades but from solitary vigilance.

He had a new message.

He never had a message; a computer "match" yes, but never a message.

Intrigued that a woman had left a message for him, Roger quickly left a response. The woman, named Sharon, had recently lost her husband. Soon after, she wanted anything but to be alone in life. Like Roger, she had enough of the dating scene and the lousy personal ads. She checked with the service one more time and found that she too had a message.

It was Roger's response.

The two finally talked on the phone on several occasions. They planned a night of hot chocolate and talking at a Carrow's restaurant in

Chatsworth. After a few minutes of awkwardness, Roger finally felt at ease with Sharon. From Tracy, Minnesota, a small town of 2,000 people and, like Roger, the eldest of nine children, she was everything he had been looking for, a vision of womanhood and intelligence, humorous and inviting. A woman in her 50's, Sharon appeared to Roger as a graceful, golden-haired treasure whom he looked forward to seeing more often.

The two hit it off, going out together as often as their schedules allowed.

At first, Roger was an admitted motor mouth on the phone, and he even offered to pay her phone bill since he never let her get a word in. Troubled at the thought of him being a talkative, non-listener, she quickly realized that he simply was over excited.

Charmed with his easy-going manner, humor, and affection, Sharon admitted finally to Roger that their growing feelings were indeed mutual. She told him that she "felt very comfortable with him from the day they first met." She also confessed that she was attracted to him even during the 1980's, when she had seen him at the ballpark while taking her son to the game a couple of times a year.

Upon hearing her true feelings, Roger couldn't have been any happier. Like a kid who saved his quarters to catch a bag of peanuts from the Peanut Man in the stands, Roger felt a surge of happiness. It was a love forged in maturity, but it was a joy formed in youthful sincerity.

At last.

After 45 years, Roger still called Dodger Stadium his home. Working there, in spite of physical setbacks, always proved to be his daily dose of therapy. Whether tossing peanuts at the ballpark or at private parties, Roger still enjoyed each day as though it was his first day on the job.

Every year, he would find more sayings, mottos, and poems to pass along as inspiration at such parties.

One favorite poem read:

Success
You can use most any measure,
When you're speaking of success.
You can measure it in a fancy home,
An expensive car or dress.
But, the measure of your real success,
Is one you cannot spend.
It's the way your kids describe you,
When they're talking to a friend.

But there were plenty of times in which he was on the receiving end of short quips and wisdom-filled lines, even from children. He always got a kick out of the fans, especially the kids, just as much as they got a kick out of him.

One day at the ballpark, a four year-old boy was trying to get Roger's attention. After a few attempts failed, the toddler yelled, "Hey Peanut Boy!" Thinking it was a vendor's wisecrack, he turned around, only to find that the little boy had enough bravado to call the veteran peanut man a peanut "boy." It cracked Roger up.

Another time, Roger was handed a large bill by a five year-old to pay for the peanuts. When ready to receive his change, the boy looked at Roger and said, "No, you keep it. You work hard for it." Roger, again, was blown away at the words spoken by such little ones. But four and five year-old kids weren't the only ones to impress Roger.

During one evening game, a gentleman reached into his wallet, pulled out some large bills, and stuffed them into Roger's vending box. A gracious Roger said, "Thank you, sir, but you didn't have to do that."

"No, no, Roger. That's just for being consistent," the man said, smiling up at him.

Such kindheartedness meant so much to Roger, not for the money itself, but for the fact the people loved his dedication and cared about him as a dear friend, a brother, or a son. One elderly couple, Mort and Sadye Tooredman, had even bought a hand-made sweater during their vacation in China in the early 1980's and gave it to him at the ballpark.

On one occasion, season-peanut holder, businessman, and avid golfer, Ian MacLeod, had given him a large tip at the ballpark.

"Oh, come on Ian, you didn't have to do that," Roger said playfully.

"I know," Ian replied, smiling innocently.

Other times, his friends Ted Shaw, Bruce Moses, and Cathy Mendenhall, partners at Shaw, Moses, Mendenhall and Associates insurance firm, had treated him for lunch at the San Antonio Winery in Los Angeles. Infamous for his bottomless pit that he calls an appetite, Roger unashamedly has considered dessert as his favorite part of the meal. Ted didn't have to ask twice what Roger wanted when he saw him eye the menu, look up, and smile. He knew what he wanted.

Chocolate-lemon cake.

"Man can he eat," Shaw said.

One warm afternoon at the stadium, Roger noticed an elderly gentleman in his 80's having a hard time climbing some stairs to reach the men's restroom. Roger quickly recognized him. It was his old friend,

Sherman Margolis. He was once a businessman who gave Roger business for his work at Westransco during the 60's. He was also one of Roger's season peanut holders for many years.

"Hey, Sherm, let me give you a hand there," he said, affectionately helping him up the stairs.

The man caught his breath and looked at him.

"You give me a hand now, Roger, but do you remember the time I gave you a hand when you were in that accident?" Sherm replied.

He remained quiet.

"You might not remember, but when you were lying in bed recovering, I took up a collection for you in the stands. I told everyone how we should help you out, and we raised $1,000 for you. I gave it to your brother, Philip, to give to you," the gracious man said, his eyes gleaming in the soft light coming into the concourse area.

"I remember now," Roger said quietly, smiling as tears filled his eyes.

This was Roger's world. It was his job, selling peanuts at the ballpark. But somehow, it was much more than that. It was a way of making a living off the income of people's warmth, finding the value of a hug, applause, and a bright smile worth far more than all the quarters and dollar bills he collected over the past four decades. With the cracking of baseball bats echoing on the field below in harmony with the cracking of peanut shells in the stands, Roger once again looked up into the blue heavens, only a few shades lighter than the beloved Dodger blue encompassing him. He then smiled his biggest smile for his parents, who no doubt were taking in the sunny ballgame from high above.

With each passing season, he was asked more often about retiring, and every time, he interrupted the question in mid-sentence.

"Never. Never. It's such a part of my life. Dodger Stadium is like my health spa, and I'm getting paid for working out. It's the family atmosphere. I live and breathe this place," Roger said. "My life is so complete when I'm here entertaining. I almost feel like that song from Cheers—you go someplace where everybody knows your name."

The everyday people, who have paid to come to watch the Dodgers play and enjoy the peanut trickery going on in the loge level on the third base side, weren't the only ones to admire the tradition of peanut tossing by Roger. Long-time favorite Ron Cey said that Roger's "unique style of delivering peanuts has always been a welcomed addition." Another Dodger hero of the 70's, Steve Garvey, said, "Quite simply, Roger is still the greatest pitchman in Dodger history."

In addition to fans and Dodger players, even broadcasters and Dodger management have been just as proud of Roger as they have been of the majestic stadium itself, and the volumes of history that could be told by the stadium's symmetrical, blue, outfield walls.

Dodger broadcasting commentator Ross Porter said, "Roger is an icon at Dodger Stadium. His rapport with the fans is something to watch, as I have done from the broadcast booth. It's not just the behind the back tosses of the peanut bags and the accuracy at long distances that are memorable. Roger's hearty laugh while doing his tricks makes everyone around him happy. The fans love him for his cheerfulness and for making them feel good about being at Dodger Stadium. Ballparks need more people like Roger Owens."

A letter from Team Historian and Publications Editor, Mark Langill acknowledged Roger's contributions.

In part, it read:

> During my 30 years of attending Dodger ballgames, I have discovered there is more to baseball than collecting autographs, trading cards or even measuring the wins and losses from each season. A trip to the ballpark means a chance to visit with people, whether relatives or strangers, who have a common bond in their appreciation for the stadium atmosphere and competition on the field.
>
> Even as a youngster, I always knew Roger Owens held a special place at Dodger Stadium in terms of his popularity and enthusiasm. He was "The Peanut Man," someone with an obvious love of his job whose attitude sparkled on a daily basis. Even when the fans aren't watching, his "hustle" and hard work behind the scenes is a tribute to his character.

Even one of the top officials in the organization, Senior Vice President of Communications Derrick Hall, said, "Roger Owens is an institution. His name is synonymous with his trade...not just a peanut vendor, the best there ever was. Roger has been as much a part of the Dodger Stadium experience as looking up and seeing Vin Scully in the press box, enjoying a grilled Dodger Dog in the seats, and taking in the breathtaking views of downtown and the San Gabriel Mountains. He is a master and a pioneer, with tremendous charm, charisma, and customer appeal."

With characteristic energy and passion at 60 years old, Roger has continued to thrill fans as he sails a flying bag of peanuts to each hungry customer. During one afternoon game, he raised his strong arms and, with hands lifted high, held up the five-dollar bags of peanuts to sell. The warm sunlight beat down upon his shiny event badge, highlighting the number printed upon it, *3,897*. It was the unfathomable number of games he had worked at the stadium since it opened more than 40 years before. It included the 81 home games each year, some, but not all, of the Dodger games at the Coliseum, and even the Angel home games when the Anaheim Angels were an infant, expansion team playing in Los Angeles in the early 60's.

Like the Gehrigs and Ripkens and all the iron horses of the playing fields of yesterday's summers, Roger's endless work ethic has placed him among the elite of larger than life legends of baseball as well as on the esteemed roster of everyday heroes, the fathers and mothers who have tirelessly showed up to work, providing for their families so self-lessly. And through it all, Roger was no stranger to obstacles. Any day that sidelined him with an ailment was a day that only reinforced his belief that the DL did not stand for disabled list, but rather, for deep languish.

"It's a labor of love for me, just knowing how much those fans appreciate me and what I do, and how much I enjoy the self satisfaction I get in just putting on a show for the people. I guess I was just born to be an entertainer. And Dodger Stadium is my stage," Roger said. With multi-million dollar athletes, the almost "untouchables" in today's society, playing on the field below, the Peanut Man has remained as approachable as a Dodger Dog to a child's wide-eyed face.

"Somehow, when I get to the ballpark, and I start going up and down those stairs, I forget about all my cares," he acknowledged.

It was former Dallas Cowboys General Manager and President, Tex Schramm, who best summed up the talent and offerings of the Peanut Man. He said, "Roger Owens, America's famous "Peanut Man," is one of the true sports personalities of our time. His fame has not been achieved as a result of any athletic prowess on the field, nor by any skills as a master coach. He has come to be known and loved by fans throughout the world because of the service he provides in a unique and cheerful manner."

Roger inhaled deeply, squinted his eyes from the bright sun, and surveyed the large crowds, full of admiring fans dressed in Dodger blue and waving their huge, "number one" foam hands. With teenage-like enthusiasm, ready to sell and eager to please, he straightened his posture and announced joyously, "Peanuts here! Peanuts! Get your peanuts here."

And bought them they did, from Roger Owens, the famous Peanut Man.

$$\mathcal{C}^{A}$$

Acknowledgements

Personal Thanks-

To my Lord, God – for loving perfectly an imperfect person. To say I owe You so much is *the* understatement of the century. To say the very least, thank You for an amazing family and for Your strength.

Samantha (K.S.P.) – for your love and patience and for putting up with me during the writing of this book. Take a close look at the Table of Contents.

Roger Owens – for your time, your homemade chicken, newspaper articles, personal photos, and your many thoughts in helping make this book possible.

Ruth Green – for your contributions, fact proofing, and tons of personal photos. I know that if Yankee Stadium is the House that Ruth Built, then Kodak Film is the Empire that This Ruth Built.

Dr. David Hood, Ph.D., California State University, Long Beach – for your meticulous editing of the book, your generosity, and your invaluable friendship, which is unexplainable with mere words.

To Family and Friends of Roger – for your contributions of stories and personal thoughts. They have added so much to the book.

Steve Harvey of the *L.A. Times* – for showing your support of Roger and following his career over the many years.

Tom Hennessy of the *L.B. Press-Telegram* – for showing your support of Roger and following his career over the many years. Also, thank you for the article about Roger's vertigo. If you hadn't written it, and David Hood hadn't saved the article for me to read, I don't think I would have put "two and two" together and written this book.

To my Friends at work – for your friendship and support every day.

To my best friend and mentor all through college, Steve Weik – Even in the midst of the many struggles of your bone marrow transplant, your constant faith in God has always made me stand in awe. At this time, I'd like you to know how much you and everything you have stood for means to me. Should the Lord decide to take you home, your wife, two kids, countless friends, and I would miss you beyond description. This book is for you, too, Steve.

Last, but certainly not least, to Dr. Victor Schorn – for your incredible skills in the medical field, your staff of helpful doctors, your compassion, and your guided hands and steady mind in saving Roger's life and giving the world a wonderful man and a great story.

Sources-

Bayless, Skip. "It's In The Bag For The Peanut Man," *Los Angeles Times*, Sports Section, October 26, 1976.

Chaplin, Richard. "Nuts About Those Peanuts," *The Press-Enterprise*. Section C-1, July, 1996.

Doolittle, John. *Don McNeill and His Breakfast Club*. University of Notre Dame Press. Notre Dame, Indiana. Copyright 2001.

Hennessy, Tom. "He's The Cy Young Of Peanut Pitching," *Long Beach Press Telegram*, Sports Section, May 5, 1982.

Hillinger, Charles. "Religious Tracts Stop Bullet Fired At Minister In Holdup," *Los Angeles Times*, Metro/Local City Section, November 18, 1968.

Report from the Medical Board, Naval Hospital, September 29, 1969.

Soto, Onell. "Baseball Strike Kills Many Jobs," *Long Beach Press Telegram*, Local News, September 19, 1994.

"Vaunted Vendor Plays Shell Game," *The Sporting News*. July 4, 1981.

Watts, Leslie. "Peanut Man Pitches His Way To Fame," *Houston Chronicle*, November 5, 1981.

Westchester Journal, October 27, 1983.

Yoshihara, Nancy. "Dodger Peanut Man To Deliver Industry Pitch*,* " *Los Angeles Times*, Business Section, September 25, 1981.

Printed in the United States
34573LVS00004B/157-255

9 781932 560299